TYPING
FIRST COURSE
Fifth Edition

Archie Drummond

Anne Coles-Mogford
Oxford and County Secretarial College

McGRAW-HILL BOOK COMPANY

London · New York · St Louis · San Francisco · Auckland · Bogotá · Guatemala
Hamburg· Lisbon · Madrid · Mexico · Montreal · New Delhi · Panama· Paris
San Juan · São Paulo · Singapore · Sydney · Tokyo · Toronto

Published by McGRAW-HILL Book Company (UK) Limited
MAIDENHEAD · BERKSHIRE · ENGLAND

British Library Cataloguing in Publication Data

Drummond, A. M. (Archibald Manson)
   Typing: first course.—5th ed.
   1. Typewriting—Examinations, questions,
   etc.
   I. Title   II. Coles-Mogford, Anne
   652.3'0076   Z49.2

   ISBN 0-07-707035-6

Library of Congress Cataloging-in-Publication Data

Drummond, Archie.
   Typing: first course/Archie Drummond, Anne Coles-Mogford.
      p.   cm.
   Includes index.
   ISBN 0-07-707035-6   :
   1. Typewriting.I. Coles-Mogford, Anne.   II. Title.   III. Title:
Typing, 1st course.
Z49.D8 1988
652.3—dc 19   87-18448

3 4 5 NI 90

Typeset by Eta Services (Typesetters) Ltd, Beccles, Suffolk

Printed and bound by New Interlitho, Milan, Italy

INDEX

PREFACE

In March 1988 it will be 25 years since the first edition of *Typing First Course* was published, and during those years millions of people have used this textbook to acquire the basic skills and knowledge of current business practices necessary for employment.

Since its invention in the 1870s, the typewriter has been at the core of the communication of information and, today, the QWERTY keyboard is an integral part of many machines and is the basic means for rapid communication of data: the family at home use the personal computer keyboard to play electronic games, to estimate their income tax liability, to find answers to problems; in business it is used to type an immense variety of correspondence, to input and retrieve information, to compute, to transmit and receive electronic communications locally, nationally and internationally; in schools and colleges it is used to teach the keyboard, to train typists, to calculate, to take tests and examinations, etc.

Typing First Course, Fifth Edition, offers a keyboard course that has been tried, tested and used to train an inestimable number of typists. In addition, this text includes the best features from four prior editions and, at the same time, it introduces significant new features that will help students to become more efficient typists.

The student who completes the course, and executes the directions as instructed will be:
(a) A competent copy typist.
(b) Capable of passing an elementary typewriting examination.
(c) A suitable trainee for a word processor operator.

The purpose of *Typing First Course* is to help students:
(a) Acquire smooth and correct finger movement.
(b) Operate the nonprinting parts of the typewriter efficiently.
(c) Raise the level and broaden the foundation of the skills and techniques practised in (a) and (b).
(d) Apply the skills and techniques to practical work.
(e) Acquire an insight into modern business terminology.
(f) Apply basic language arts principles correctly.

Instructional design

UNITS 1-50 In all blocked exercises with open punctuation, consistency of style has been followed because we felt it was unfair to expect students, in the learning stage, to change from one style to another and thus become confused. The simplicity of the presentation will help learners eliminate errors because doubts about correct display have been removed and, therefore, the student can concentrate on accurate typing, speed and efficient manipulation of the machine.

UNITS 51-56 These give continued emphasis on the points presented in the previous units, with exercises in open and full punctuation, blocked and centred styles.

Keyboard coverage

UNITS 1-22 Because it has proved very successful and popular, the keyboard approach used in the third and fourth editions has been retained with minor adjustments. To cover the needs of all learners, we have:
(a) introduced only two alphabet keys in each unit, and after the introduction of the home keys, only one new key is presented at a time;
(b) included only two lines of drills on each new key, followed by a further two lines of Word family drills on these keys;
(c) at the beginning of each keyboard unit, included three lines of Review the keys you know and at the end of these units, three lines of Apply the keys you know;
(d) for students who prefer to spend a little more time on the alphabet keys, offered three improvement practice units—8, 12 and 18—each with two pages of drills on the keys introduced prior to the particular unit;
(e) prepared special drills on:
(i) homophones;
(ii) words often misspelt.

UNITS 23-28 Figures and symbols follow on immediately after the alphabet keys and because of the lack of standardization in the placement of symbols on keyboards used with electronic typewriters and word processing machines, the figures have been presented as a group and the symbols introduced separately. In these six units there is a sequence of:

(a) Alphabet reviews that provide ample keyboard revision and practice.
(b) Intensive drills on figures/symbols.
(c) Skill measurement practice.
(d) Record your progress practice.

SKILL BUILDING AND PRODUCTION DEVELOPMENT From Unit 29 onwards, Skill measurement, new work and production work are developed in a carefully balanced sequence of activities:
(a) Skill building:
  (i) Keyboard techniques;
  (ii) Language arts drills (spelling, apostrophe, subject and verb agreement);
  (iii) Skill measurement;
  (iv) Record your progress;
(b) Production development — introducing new work in small and easy specific steps.
(c) Consolidation and Integrated production typing projects.

New features of fifth edition

Features especially designed to develop and refine the important skills, knowledge, terminology and techniques, that the changing office environment demands, have been built into the course.

SKILL MEASUREMENT As only the student and/or the teacher will know whether, at any given time, the student should be practising for speed or accuracy, we have called the speed/accuracy material Skill measurement, and a choice must be made as to whether the practice should aim at increasing speed or working for greater accuracy. There is a special Skill measurement chart in the *Handbook and Solutions Manual*.

PERSONALIZED AND REMEDIAL DRILLS As each individual has different weaknesses when using the keyboard, the drills on pages 173–177 have been specially prepared for corrective practice on keystroking errors made when typing the Record your progress exercises. On examining these drills, it will be seen that each drill gives intensive practice in typing a particular letter in combination with other letters. There is a Personalized remedial drill sheet in the *Handbook and Solutions Manual* on which students can record errors, and watch their progress in mastering the reaches that initially caused difficulty.

RECORD YOUR PROGRESS In this edition, each Record your progress exercise contains every letter of the alphabet. The usual Record your progress chart is in the *Handbook and Solutions Manual*.

SYLLABIC INTENSITY This means the average number of syllables in the words of a passage. Thus, in Skill measurement SM14, on page 38, SI 1.11 means that there is an average of 1.11 syllables per word. As in previous editions, we have used a controlled but random and unselected vocabulary for Skill measurement and Record your progress, as we feel this is the most effective way of building accuracy and speed. In this edition, the syllabic intensity of most exercises is slightly higher than in previous editions.

BUSINESS VOCABULARY There is a multiplicity of new words used in the text, eg, formatting, proofreaders' marks, 12-pitch printwheel, electronic mail/machines, text-editing electronic typewriters, keyboarding, function keys, etc, and it is hoped that the inclusion of word processing and data processing terminology throughout the text will enable students to prepare more fully for the electronic office. In addition, wherever we considered it appropriate, we have mentioned **word processing concepts and applications** that would apply to the operations being practised.

INTEGRATED PRODUCTION TYPING PROJECTS Our objective here is to simulate typical office typing, and the project is prefaced by a Typist's log sheet which gives the name of the organization, the originator's name and department, additional directions for operators using word processors, text-editing electronic typewriters and correction only electronic typewriters. Each document has a Target time and the typist has to calculate a timing for the whole project. As the course progresses, fewer and fewer instructions are given, and students must make their own decisions and establish work priorities. Further, it is hoped that the thematic project approach will develop the student's ability to follow through a project under simulated office conditions.

PROOFREADING Because proofreading is such an important part of the typist's training, we give greater emphasis and a greater variety of proofreading exercises on pages 178–180.

PERSONAL LETTERS As some learners may not wish to have a great deal of formal tuition beyond the keyboard stage, we have presented **display** and **personal letters** immediately after the symbol keys.

KEYBOARD AND PRODUCTION DEVELOPMENT SCHEDULE A copy of this schedule will be found in the *Handbook and Solutions Manual* and we suggest that copies should be duplicated so that each member of a class will be able to keep a record of her/his progress.

In addition to *Typing First Course*, there are two complementary books that will be found helpful; they are:

Practical Typing Exercises—Book One. This book contains further examples of exercises introduced in *Typing First Course*. Many of these exercises give the exact layout of typed documents and, therefore, are very easy to follow. At the bottom of the pages in *Typing First Course* reference is made to the relevant pages in *Practical Typing Exercises*.

Keyboarding disk

The purpose of this disk is to train the individual to operate the keyboard by touch in the shortest possible time. It is based on (and follows the same sequence and drills as) *Typing First Course, Fifth Edition*, and quickly and easily develops keyboarding skills for the alphabet keys, punctuation, figures and symbols. By the end of this short course, the learner should be able to type 25 words a minute for three minutes with not more than three errors.

Handbook and Solutions Manual

Part I contains:

(a) A brief explanation of how *Typing First Course* was planned so that it incorporates a complete and systematic skill-building plan—there are also hints on how to use the textbook.

(b) A brief but concise review of the basic principles of how typing skill is acquired and developed.

(c) Syllabuses and schemes of work for full- and part-time courses, and helpful suggestions on how to plan a lesson.

(d) Ideas on the presentation of a lesson.

(e) Recommendations for classroom management.

(f) Pointers on profiling.

Part II contains:

(a) A review of each unit of *Typing First Course* and suggestions for lesson presentation.

(b) All exercises not set out in the main text are displayed as they should look when typed. These examples give margins and tab stops together with calculations for horizontal and vertical display.

(c) As the book is loose-leaf, students' records sheets (Technique check list, Record your progress chart, etc) and printed letterheads, invoice forms, form letters, etc, may be copied and duplicated.

Acknowledgments

The contents of this textbook reflects the comments, suggestions and recommendations made to us by teachers who have used previous editions, and we attach a great deal of value to their contributions which, over the years, have helped enormously in the effectiveness and popularity of our typing publications.

We also wish to thank our colleagues for their helpful advice and assistance given in copying the manuscript exercises.

NOTE References in this book to the *Handbook and Solutions Manual* are to the fifth edition, and to *Practical Typing Exercises, Book One*, to the third edition, both of which are published at the same time as this, the fifth edition of *Typing First Course*.

We sincerely hope that students and teachers enjoy working through *Typing First Course* and the supplementary books and aids, and that they will also find pleasure and reward from using the second series, details of which are given on the back cover of this text.

The authors wish to thank Eidersoft Software Limited and British Olivetti Limited for permission to reproduce the photographs on page 3.

Archie Drummond
Anne Coles—Mogford

Essential Machine Parts

A Typebar Machine

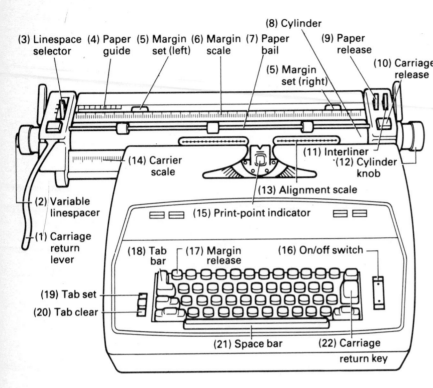

(3) Linespace selector
(4) Paper guide
(5) Margin set (left)
(6) Margin scale
(7) Paper bail
(8) Cylinder
(9) Paper release
(10) Carriage release
(5) Margin set (right)
(14) Carrier scale
(11) Interliner
(12) Cylinder knob
(13) Alignment scale
(2) Variable linespacer
(1) Carriage return lever
(15) Print-point indicator
(18) Tab bar
(17) Margin release
(16) On/off switch
(19) Tab set
(20) Tab clear
(21) Space bar
(22) Carriage return key

An Element Machine

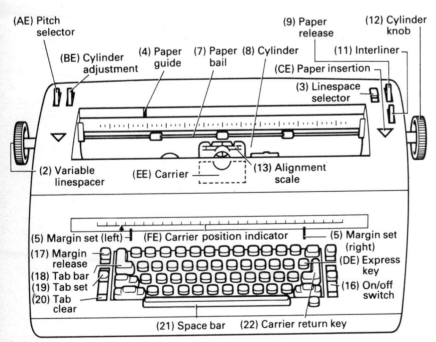

(AE) Pitch selector
(BE) Cylinder adjustment
(4) Paper guide
(7) Paper bail
(8) Cylinder
(9) Paper release
(12) Cylinder knob
(11) Interliner
(CE) Paper insertion
(3) Linespace selector
(2) Variable linespacer
(EE) Carrier
(13) Alignment scale
(5) Margin set (left)
(FE) Carrier position indicator
(5) Margin set (right)
(17) Margin release
(18) Tab bar
(19) Tab set
(20) Tab clear
(DE) Express key
(16) On/off switch
(21) Space bar
(22) Carrier return key

ALPHABETIC LIST

In the alphabetic list, the figures refer to both machines, the capital letters to element machines only.

Alignment scale (13): indicates base of typing line.

Carriage release (manual – 10): moves carriage to left or right.

Carriage/carrier return key (22): moves carriage/carrier to left margin and advances paper.

Carriage return lever (manual – 1): moves the carriage back to the left margin and advances the paper.

Carriage scale (manual – 14): numbers show through at print-point indicator.

Carrier (electric – EE): moves the element across the paper.

Carrier position indicator (electric – FE) shows at what space the machine is ready to print and is a guide when setting margins.

Cylinder (8): holds and moves paper in and out of the machine.

Cylinder adjustment (electric – BE): multiple copy control.

Cylinder knob (12): enables you to turn the cylinder.

Express key (electric – DE): moves carriage rapidly to left without turning up paper.

Interliner (11): frees cylinder and temporarily changes line of typing.

Linespace selector (3): controls spacing between lines of typing.

Margin scale (manual – 6): a guide when setting margin stops.

Margin sets (5): controls points where carriage/carrier will stop.

Margin release (17): temporarily unlocks margins.

On/off switch (16): controls power to motor.

Paper bail (7): holds paper against the cylinder.

Paper guide (4): movable upright which guides paper when it is inserted.

Paper insertion (electric – CE): draws paper round the cylinder.

Paper release lever (9): loosens the paper for straightening or removing.

Pitch selector (electric – AE): choice of pitch.

Print-point indicator (manual – 15): shows scale point at which machine will print.

Space bar (21): moves the carriage/carrier a space at a time or, if held down on an electric machine, will give continuous spacing.

Tab bar (key) (18): moves carriage/carrier to set tab stop.

Tab clear (20): clears tab stop(s).

Tab set (19): sets tab stop(s).

Variable linespacer (2): can be used to permanently change line of typing.

Spelling skill — words misspelt

Page 42 — until, separate, accommodation
Page 51 — necessary, truly, stationery
Page 62 — privileges, committees, advertisement
Page 72 — sheriffs, guaranteed, committees
Page 78 — admissible, withhold, cheque
Page 94 — knowledge, inaccessible, incompetent
Page 101 — arguments, possesses, underrate

Page 47 — believe, cancel, temporary
Page 55 — cursor, develop, liaison
Page 69 — benefited, Wednesday, manufacturer's
Page 75 — inconvenience, unnecessarily, believe
Page 88 — parallel, miscellaneous, discretion
Page 98 — occasion, guardian, familiar
Page 113 — ensuing, eighths, arrogance

Language arts — apostrophe

Page 117 — lines 6 and 8   Singular (one only) nouns not ending in **s**, add an apostrophe **s**
           lines 7 and 9   Plural nouns ending in **s**, add an apostrophe
Page 122 — lines 10 and 12   Singular nouns not ending in **s**, add an apostrophe **s**
           lines 11 and 13   Plural nouns not ending in **s**, add apostrophe **s**
Page 132 — line 10   Singular noun (Mary) not ending in **s**, add an apostrophe **s**
              Plural noun (weeks) ending in **s**, add an apostrophe
           line 11   The contraction **it's** needs the apostrophe before the **s** to show the omission of the letter **i**. The pronoun **its** (The dog chased its tail.) does not require an apostrophe.
           line 12   To avoid confusion, the apostrophe is used for the plural of single letters and numbers (2 **c's** and **2 m's**).
           line 13   Single quotes (the apostrophe) is sometimes used in place of quotation marks to indicate the exact words of a speaker or writer.

Language arts — agreement of subject and verb

Page 137 — line 6   **Keyboarding** (singular noun) requires singular verb **is**.
           line 7   **keys** (plural noun) requires plural verb **are**.
           line 8   A plural verb is always necessary after **you**.
           line 9   Although **s** or **es** added to a noun indicates the plural, **s** or **es** added to a verb indicates the third person singular.
Page 141 — line 2   The subject is **box** (singular); therefore, the singular verb **is** should be used.
           line 3   Singular subjects (**report** and **letter**) joined by **and** require a plural verb (**are**).
           line 4   Two subjects (**name** and **address**) preceded by, or joined by, **every** (**each, neither, one, another**)
           line 5   require a singular verb.
Page 151 — line 2   When singular subjects are joined by **nor** the verb should be singular; however, if one of the subjects is plural (**students**) the verb should agree with the subject immediately preceding it (**students are**).
           line 3   Parenthetic expressions such as, **including, together with, as well as**, do not affect the number of the verb and should be ignored.
           line 4   **None** means **not one**; therefore, singular verb **is** should be used.
           line 5   Use singular verb after a phrase beginning **one of**, or **one of the**.
Page 155 — line 2   Words like, **works, news, means**, etc, take singular verbs.
           line 3   You would say: My shoes are missing; but you require a singular verb after **pair**. Plural words such as **wages, valuables, headquarters**, etc, take a singular verb when they are singular in meaning.
           line 4   Collective nouns (**committee**) take a singular verb when the nouns apply to a group or unit, and a plural verb when the members of the group are thought of as acting separately.
Page 158 — line 2   **Set** is singular and, therefore, requires a singular verb (**has**).
           line 3   Subject consists of two singular nouns (**friend** and **neighbour**) joined by **and**, but both nouns denote the same person, therefore, the verb is singular.
           line 4   **Neither** always takes a singular verb.

Electronic keyboard

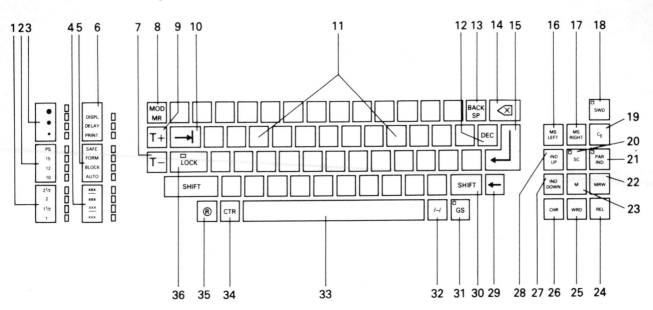

1. Linespace selector.
2. Pitch selector – PS = proportional spacing; 15 = 15 characters to the inch; 12 = 12 characters to the inch; 10 = 10 characters to the inch.
3. Impression control – heavy, medium, light.
4. Four print variations – normal, bold, underscore, bold/underscore.
5. Four typing modes – auto: typed matter stored in working memory; block: justified right margin; form: preparing formats to be used with forms; safe: storing text in the phrase memories.
6. Operating modes.
7. Tab clear.
8. Margin release.
9. Tab set.
10. Tabulator – moves carrier to tab stops.
11. Keyboard.
12. Decimal tabulator – automatically aligns decimal points at tab stop.
13. Backspace key.
14. Correction key.
15. Carrier return.
16. Margin set – left.
17. Margin set – right.
18. Searchword – a method of finding a particular word(s) in a document.
19. Clear entry – clearing text and memory.
20. Stopcode – to stop the printout at a particular point.
21. Paragraph indent.
22. Memory rewind – returns to beginning of working memory.
23. Memory – used to store and recall text.
24. Release/relocate – to print a page of text; to find last print position.
25. Word – print or delete a word.
26. Character – print or delete a character.
27. Index down – moves the paper down.
28. Index up – moves the paper up.
29. Express return – returns carrier to left without turning up.
30. Shift keys.
31. Graduated spacing – less than half spacing: moves paper about 1/60th of an inch.
32. Conditional hyphen – used when finished text is justified.
33. Space bar.
34. Centre key – centres automatically.
35. Repeat key – repeats all characters.
36. Shift lock.

Keys to proofreading exercises

Page 178 (a): line 1—program; line 2—visual; line 3—100; line 4—a daisy-wheel printer; line 5—stock; line 6—Spreadsheet.

Page 178 (b): line 1—your; line 2—top and bottom; line 3—interrupt; line 4—dictation.; line 5—omit the word 'the'; line 6—omit comma after 'pencil'.

Page 178 (c): line 1—GARDENING; line 2—month; line 3—or; line 4—lettuces; line 5—spring-flowering; line 6—line not at left margin; line 7—omit the word 'ANY'.

Page 179 (d): line 1—definite; line 2—two spaces after full stop; line 3—handling; line 4—index cards; line 5—loose-leaf; line 6—omit 'they may'.

Page 179 (e): line 1—retrieval; line 2—accessed; line 3—insert 'an' before annual; line 4—varied,; line 5—retrieve; line 6—a telephone line; line 7—adapted; line 8—insert full stop after 'use'.

Page 180 (f): line 1—disks; microcomputers; line 2—disk,; line 3—two spaces after full stop; 800; line 4—3½"; line 6—disks,; line 7—Winchester; line 8—computer,; line 9—large; space before and after dash; megabytes.

Page 180 (g): line 1—two spaces after 'advantages'; line 3—roll; 3,000; to; line 4—10 m; 10.5 cm; line 5—500; cheap; line 6—made,; line 7—handle; line 8—35 mm; line 9—insert 'not' before deteriorate.

Word processor operator—Text-editing instructions

UNIT 44—Page 109, Document 1
Change prices of 2′ × 2′ × 1½″ smooth paving slabs to £1.30 and £1.50. Change FAST DELIVERY SERVICE to FAST AND FREE DELIVERY SERVICE. Proofread soft copy and, if necessary, correct. Print out original only in 12 pitch.

UNIT 44—Page 111, Document 3
First paragraph—after 'dealing with correspondence' add 'attending informal meetings'. Change 'Reasonable GCE 'O' levels' to 'At least 4 GCE 'O' levels. Last paragraph—insert 'have an enthusiastic and willing approach,' after 'The successful applicant should'. Proofread soft copy and, if necessary, correct. Print out an original and one copy in 12 pitch.

UNIT 48—Page 128, Document 1
Third paragraph—insert ', The Daily News,' after 'local paper'. Last paragraph—change 'at your earliest convenience' to 'by next Friday at the latest.' Proofread soft copy and, if necessary, correct. Print out an original and one copy in 10 pitch.

UNIT 48—Page 131, Document 5
First paragraph—insert ', or tenants,' after the word 'tenant'. Transpose paragraphs one and two. Proofread soft copy and, if necessary, correct. Print out original only in 15 pitch.

UNIT 48—Page 131, Document 6
Change 'detached' to 'semi-detached'. Insert a separate line above 'Garage . . .' 'Would suit 3 to 5 adults, sharing.' Proofread soft copy and, if necessary, correct. Print out original only in 12 pitch.

UNIT 52—Page 147, Document 1
Insert a subject heading: PART-TIME APPOINTMENT First paragraph—delete the word 'permanent'. Change the hours on Thursday to 0900–1130. Fourth paragraph—change 'one full term's notice' to 'two months' notice'. Proofread soft copy and, if necessary, correct. Print out an original and one copy in 12 pitch.

UNIT 52—Page 150, Document 5
Transpose the paragraph dealing with Attendance with the second paragraph dealing with Students' Property. Third paragraph—delete 'in full'. Last paragraph—change 'General Certificate of Education' to 'GCE'. Proofread soft copy and, if necessary, correct. Print out original only in 12 pitch.

UNIT 52—Page 150, Document 6
First paragraph—change 'teacher' to 'tutor'. Transpose 'Examining Body concerned' with 'Group taking examination'. Inset all the items eight spaces. Proofread soft copy and, if necessary, correct. Print out an original and one copy in 12 pitch.

This is a symbol that we will use to draw your attention to information and instructions for **electronic typewriters** and **word processors**. In business today, it is important that you understand how these machines may be employed to format more easily a great variety of documents.

If you are typing on an electronic typewriter or a word processor, study the manufacturer's handbook that accompanies your machine, and practise the functions, movements and settings. You will probably find that there are a number of automatic operations — these will vary greatly from one machine to another — and we suggest that you apply the automatic function keys only when they are referred to in the textbook or on the advice of your teacher. As it is essential for you to know the types of errors you make and how to overcome errors, **do not** employ the correction key during the keyboard-learning stage or when typing from Skill measurement, Record your progress or any skill building page.

Margins

Some electronic typewriters and word processors have pre-set margins which will need changing from time to time. When the pre-set margins are not suitable for any of the exercises, change the setting by following the instructions given in the manufacturer's handbook.

Pitch

When only manual typewriters were marketed, the two typefaces available were 10 pitch (pica) **or** 12 pitch (elite). Then the golf ball electric typewriter brought dual pitch and a choice of 10 or 12 **on any one** typewriter. Most electronic typewriters and word processors now offer 10, 12 and 15 pitch; however, on the more sophisticated machines there is a wider selection including proportional spacing (PS). The instructions and exercises in this edition of *Typing First Course* are based on 10 or 12 pitch, and we use the word **pitch** when referring to margin settings — not pica and elite as in previous editions.

Single-element typewriters

There are now many electric and electronic typewriters with single-element heads. These typewriters have no movable carriage, and there are no type bars. Instead, they have a printing head attached to a carrier that moves across the page from left to right, stroke by stroke. When you wish to return the carrier to the left margin, you press the return key as you would with the electric typewriter. On most electronic keyboards, the automatic carrier return is employed.

The printing element may be a golf ball head which whirls and tilts to make an impression on the paper, or it may be a daisywheel which is a rapidly spinning disk with flexible arms. On the tip of each arm there is a typeface character. The required character stops at the printing point and is struck by a small hammer which imprints the image on the paper.

The following two exercises contain 12 errors each. Read each passage carefully, and compare with the correct copy typed below. When you have found and noted the errors, type the corrected passage using margins of 12 pitch 22–82, 10 pitch 12–72. Use blocked paragraphs. Do not type the figures down the left side.

Line number

(f) Exercise to be corrected

1 There are 3 main types of discs used for micro computers. The most
2 common is the 5¼" floppy disk which is permanently protected by a
3 plastic sleeve. This disk holds between 100 and 8000 kilobytes.
4 Then there is the 3¼" disk which is built into a rigid plastic box
5 with a cover which slides back when you put the disk into the
6 machine. These disks have a similar capacity to the 5¼" disk,
7 ie, between 100 and 800 kilobytes. The winchester disk is a hard
8 disk which is permanently built into the Computer, and has a very
9 big capacity-several megabites.

Correct copy

1 There are 3 main types of disks used for microcomputers. The most
2 common is the 5¼" floppy disk, which is permanently protected by a
3 plastic sleeve. This disk holds between 100 and 800 kilobytes.
4 Then there is the 3½" disk which is built into a rigid plastic box
5 with a cover which slides back when you put the disk into the
6 machine. These disks have a similar capacity to the 5¼" disks,
7 ie, between 100 and 800 kilobytes. The Winchester disk is a hard
8 disk which is permanently built into the computer, and has a very
9 large capacity - several megabytes.

(g) Exercise to be corrected

1 There are various advantages of using a microfilm system of filing.
2 Obviously expensive filing space is saved, viz, a microfilm jacket
3 holds up to 70 documents, role film holds from 3 000 - 20,000
4 documents per 10 mm, and microfiche 15 cm x 10.6 cm holds from 98
5 to 5000 images. The film is cheep to send through the post,
6 duplicates can be easily made storage costs are less and the
7 system is easy to handel and control. Documents are filmed on
8 16 mm or 35 cm roll film, which means that originals are not
9 constantly handled and do deteriorate or become torn.

Correct copy

1 There are various advantages of using a microfilm system of filing.
2 Obviously expensive filing space is saved, viz, a microfilm jacket
3 holds up to 70 documents, roll film holds from 3,000 to 20,000
4 documents per 10 m, and microfiche 15 cm x 10.5 cm holds from 98
5 to 500 images. The film is cheap to send through the post,
6 duplicates can be easily made, storage costs are less and the
7 system is easy to handle and control. Documents are filmed on
8 16 mm or 35 mm roll film, which means that originals are not
9 constantly handled and do not deteriorate or become torn.

Manual and electric machines
(For electronic machines, see manufacturer's instruction manual)

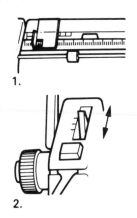

1.

2.

1   Paper guide

One of the marks on the paper rest shows where to set the paper guide so that the left edge of the paper will be at '0' on the paper guide scale. Check that the paper guide is set at that mark.

2   Linespace selector

The linespace selector has a *1*, a *2* and in some cases a *3* printed on or beside it. Adjust the selector so that it is in the desired position. In addition, many machines are now fitted with half-line spacing to give 1½ and 2½ linespaces. Examine your machine and check the linespacing.

3   Margins

3.1   On some machines you can see the margin stops on the front of the carriage or behind the paper rest. On such machines: (1) press the button on top of the stop, (2) slide the stop to the point you wish and (3) then release the button.

3.2   On other machines you cannot see the margin stops. You must use a margin-set key. You may have a separate margin-set key at each end of the carriage, or you may have one key on the keyboard for use with both stops. On such machines: (1) move the carriage to the present setting of the stop, (2) press the margin-set key while you move the carriage to the point where you want the margin and (3) then release the set key.

3.3   In the keyboard learning stage (pages 7–38) only the left margin need be set. From page 40 onwards set margins at scale-points given.

3.4   As you progress through the textbook, you will find instructions such as 'Use suitable margins'—in such cases you must decide what margins to use. What is important is that, in the majority of exercises other than display and tabulation, your left margin should be wider than your right margin, eg, 12 pitch 22–82 (there are 21 clear spaces on the left and 19 clear spaces on the right).

In other cases you may be given measurements for your margins, eg, 25 mm (one inch) on the left and 13 mm (half an inch) on the right. This would mean that, when using A4 paper, you would have margins of 12 pitch 13–94, 10 pitch 11–77. With 12 pitch type there are 12 spaces to 25 mm and with 10 pitch type there are 10 spaces to 25 mm.

4.

4   Paper bail

Before inserting the paper, pull the paper bail forward or up, temporarily away from the cylinder, so that you may insert paper without its bumping into the paper bail.

5.1

5   Inserting paper

5.1   Hold the sheet in your left hand. Place the paper behind the cylinder, against the raised edge of the paper guide. Turn the right cylinder knob to draw the paper into the machine.

To prevent damage to the cylinder of the typewriter, use a backing sheet such as is usually supplied in boxes of carbon paper, or use a sheet of stout paper.

5.2   **Check that the paper is straight**
Push the top of the paper back. If the left side of the paper, at both top and bottom, fits evenly against the paper guide, your paper is straight. If it is not straight, loosen the paper (use the paper release), straighten it, and return the paper release to its normal position.

5.2

5.3   **Place the paper bail against the paper**
Slide the rubber rollers on the bail to the right or left to divide the paper into thirds. Then, set the bail back against the paper.

5.4   **Adjust the paper for the top margin**
5.4.1   When typing drills (keyboard learning stage and first part of skill building pages), turn the paper back, using the right cylinder knob, until only a small portion of paper shows above the paper bail.

5.4.2   When typing production exercises (apart from display and tabulation), the majority of exercises typed on plain paper start on the seventh single-line space from the top edge of the paper, which means you leave six spaces (25 mm or one inch) clear. To do this proceed as follows:
5.4.2.1   Insert paper.
5.4.2.2   Check to see that paper is straight. (See 5.2 above.)
5.4.2.3   Turn paper back so that top edge is level with top edge of alignment guide.
5.4.2.4   Turn up seven single-line spaces.

5.4.1

Read each passage carefully and compare with the correct copy typed below. Each line in the incorrect copy contains an error that may be spelling, spacing, hyphenation, omission of apostrophe, etc. When you have found and noted the errors, type the corrected passage using margins of 12 pitch 22–82, 10 pitch 12–72. Use blocked paragraphs. Do not type the figures down the left side.

Line number

(d) Exercise to be corrected

1 Visible indexing systems have the definate advantages of easy access

2 and clear labelling or indexing. The information can be seen at once

3 with very little or no handeling. Also cards can be inserted or removed

4 without disturbing others in the container. Visible card indexes may

5 be held flat in trays, in loose leaf binders, or they may hang from

6 walls, or they may be free-standing on table tops or desks.

Correct copy

1 Visible indexing systems have the definite advantages of easy access

2 and clear labelling or indexing. The information can be seen at once

3 with very little or no handling. Also cards can be inserted or removed

4 without disturbing others in the container. Visible index cards may

5 be held flat in trays, in loose-leaf binders, or they may hang from

6 walls, or be free-standing on table tops or desks.

(e) Exercise to be corrected

1 Prestel is a public database Retrieval service operated by British
2 Telecom. The data is stored on computers and accesed via telephone
3 lines. Various agencies subscribe to input information for annual
4 fee. The information is very varied: eg, household hints, sports
5 results. In order to retreive information a Prestel user can call
6 the computer centre on telephone lines, using a keypad. The informa-
7 tion will be shown on his television screen, which can be adopted for
8 Prestel use

Correct copy

1 Prestel is a public database retrieval service operated by British
2 Telecom. The data is stored on computers and accessed via telephone
3 lines. Various agencies subscribe to input information for an annual
4 fee. The information is very varied, eg, household hints, sports
5 results. In order to retrieve information a Prestel user can call
6 the computer centre on a telephone line, using a keypad. The informa-
7 tion will be shown on his television screen, which can be adapted for
8 Prestel use.

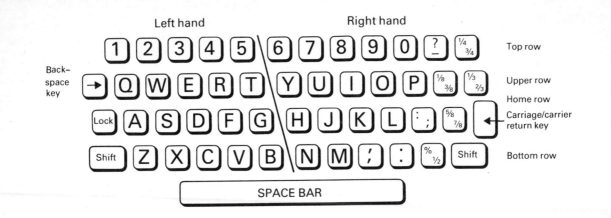

Left hand   Right hand

Top row — 1 2 3 4 5 6 7 8 9 0 ? _ ¼ ¾

Back-space key — → Q W E R T Y U I O P ⅛ ⅜ ⅓ ⅔ — Upper row

Home row

Lock A S D F G H J K L ; : ⅝ ⅞ ← — Carriage/carrier return key

Shift Z X C V B N M , . % ½ Shift — Bottom row

SPACE BAR

Preliminary practice

1 Place your book on the right-hand side of your machine, or as indicated by your teacher.
2 Place your finger tips on the home keys. Left finger tips on **A S D F** and right finger tips on **J K L ;** Check that you place them correctly.
3 Keep your left thumb close to your left first finger.
4 Extend your right thumb so that it is slightly above the centre of the space bar.
5 Now check your **posture**.
  Your head—hold it erect, facing the book.
  Your shoulders—hold them back and relaxed.
  Your body—centre yourself opposite the J key a hand-span away from the machine.
  Your back—straight, with your body sloping slightly forward from the hips.

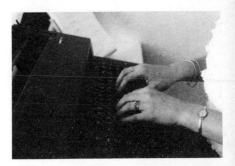

  Arms and elbows—let them hang loosely.
  Wrists—keep them low, barely clearing the machine.
  Hands—close together, low, flat across the backs.
  Fingers—curved as though to grasp a handle bar.
  Waist—sit back in the chair.
  Feet—on floor one foot slightly in front of the other.

A *Finger movement drill*

1 Without typing, practise the finger movement for the exercise you are about to type. During this preliminary practice, you may look at your fingers. You will find it helpful to say the letters to yourself. Continue the preliminary practice until your fingers 'know' where to move from the home key. Always return finger to its home key.
2 When you are confident that your fingers have acquired the correct movement, repeat this practice **without looking at your fingers**. Keep your eyes on the copy in your book and do not strike the keys. If you hesitate in making the finger movement, go back and repeat step 1.
3 Practise the finger movement for each new key until your finger moves confidently and crisply to that key.

Proofreading target for each exercise: 2 minutes
Typing target for each exercise: 3 minutes

In the exercises below, the sentences in COLUMN ONE have been repeated in COLUMN TWO. Those in column one are correct, but in each sentence in column two there is a typing error. Compare the sentences and see how quickly you can spot the errors. Then type the sentences correctly.

(a) *Column one*   *Column two*

1 A program for a computer is recorded   1 A programme for a computer is recorded
   on a disk.   on a disk.
2 The visual display unit looks like a   2 The vizual display unit looks like a
   TV screen.   TV screen.
3 A disk can hold 100 kilobytes or more.   3 A disk can hold 101 kilobytes or more.
4 A matrix printer is faster than a   4 A matrix printer is faster than
   daisy-wheel printer.   daisy-wheel printer.
5 Bar codes may be used in stock   5 Bar codes may be used in Stock
   control.   control.
6 Spreadsheet programs may be used   6 Spread sheet programs may be used
   for management accounting.   for management accounting.

(b) *Column one*   *Column two*

1 Keep your shorthand notebook handy.   1 Keep you shorthand notebook handy.
2 Date each page at top and bottom.   2 Date each page at bottom and top.
3 Do not interrupt the dictator.   3 Do not interrupt the dictator.
4 Raise any queries at the end of   4 Raise any queries at the end of
   dictation.   dictation
5 Rule a left margin for reminders.   5 Rule a left margin for the reminders.
6 Keep a pen or pencil by your   6 Keep a pen or pencil, by your
   notebook.   notebook.

(c) *Column one*   *Column two*

G A R D E N I N G - October   G A R D N I N G - October

Tasks for the month   Tasks for the Month

Plant fruit trees or soft fruit canes   Plant fruit trees of soft fruit canes

Transplant cabbages, and lettuces   Transplant cabbages, and lettuce

Plant hardy, spring-flowering plants   Plant hardy, spring flowering plants

Mark out boundaries of new borders   Mark out boundaries of new borders

SWEEP UP DEAD LEAVES   SWEEP UP ANY DEAD LEAVES

B Practise carriage/carrier return

1 MANUAL MACHINES
   (a) Preliminary practice *without returning the carriage*. Look at the carriage
        return lever and raise your *left hand* and put the first finger and next finger
        or two against the lever. Practise the movement from the HOME KEYS to
        carriage return lever and back to HOME KEYS
   (b) Right- and left-hand fingers on HOME KEYS
   (c) Right-hand fingers remain on JKL ;
   (d) With eyes on textbook
        (i) raise left hand and return carriage
        (ii) return left hand to ASDF

2 ELECTRIC MACHINES
   (a) Preliminary practice *without returning the carriage/carrier*. Look at the
        carriage/carrier return key (on the right-hand side of the keyboard) and
        make the reach with your right-hand little finger from the semicolon to the
        return key and back to semicolon
   (b) All fingers remain just slightly above their HOME KEY except right-hand
        little finger
   (c) With eyes on textbook
        (i) raise the little finger of the right hand and lightly press the return key
        (ii) return little finger to semicolon key immediately

3 ELECTRONIC MACHINES
With electronic keyboards you can, by depressing a function key, use automatic carrier return. You will notice that
the carrier returns automatically at the set right margin when the line is full. Follow the instructions given in the
machine handbook or ask your teacher for advice.

Striking the keys

Manual machines—strike keys firmly and sharply
Electric/electronic machines—stroke keys

Prepare to type

In order to prepare yourself and your machine for typing, take the following action:

1   Electric machines—insert plug in socket and switch on machine
2   Place book on right-hand side of machine or as instructed by your teacher
3   Place blank typing paper on left-hand side of machine or as instructed by your teacher
4   Set left margin at 12 pitch 30, 10 pitch 22
5   Set linespace selector on '1'
6   Set paper guide on '0'
7   Move paper bail out of the way
8   Insert sheet of A4 paper
9   If necessary, straighten paper
10 Return paper bail to normal position
11 Turn the paper back, using right cylinder knob, until only a small portion of paper shows above paper bail
12 Place front of machine level with edge of desk so that the J key is opposite the centre of your body
13 If necessary, adjust chair height so that your forearms are on the same slope as the keyboard
14 Place chair so that you are about a hand-span away from edge of desk
15 Feet apart and firmly on floor
16 See that carriage/carrier is at left margin

 Computers, word processors and electronic typewriters can be programmed to provide whatever top margin
you consistently require.

W
```
wages weary which widow write Wyatt drawl awoke
dwell ewers Gwent kiwis Elwin owner swing twist
byway Wales fewer Irwin swims dwarf crews awful
```

Berwyn Dewhurst lived in Cwmbran, Gwent, Wales, and
never wearied in winding his way through the byways
and highways of that wonderful land. I always find
that waterway awkward but worthwhile for our visit.

X
```
axiom excel oxide exact mixed pyxie exert exits
expel extra exude Xiang Xebec Xenon X-ray oxbow
proxy maxim toxin Xerox Oxfam annex affix mixer
```

We will examine the text of the excellent tax guide
which Maxine bought. Sixty days ago Max Wilcox saw
the quixotic and exquisite film EXULTANT XYLOPHONE.
Rex offered no excuse for losing the toxic mixture.

Y
```
yacht yearn yield Ypres yucca Ayers bylaw cynic
Dyfed eyrie gypsy hymns lunch myths nymph pygmy
Ryder synod tyres vying crazy wryly unify syrup
```

Sydney sent sympathy to Sally who cycled home after
they lost a typing test. You were ruled by tyranny
and an arbitrary bully. In the dusty, shady area I
saw a gypsy help a very tiny, bonny baby to safety.

Z
```
Zaire zebra zippy azure czars ozone zonal zooms
adzes maize Franz graze pizza dizzy aztec oozes
waltz Czech gauze dozes zeros zloty zones Zulus
```

Puzzled but zealous Zelda won both my quizzes about
zebras living in zoos in New Zealand. The owner of
the dozen sheep grazing in the field won an amazing
prize of a gazelle. This sizzling sun is a hazard.

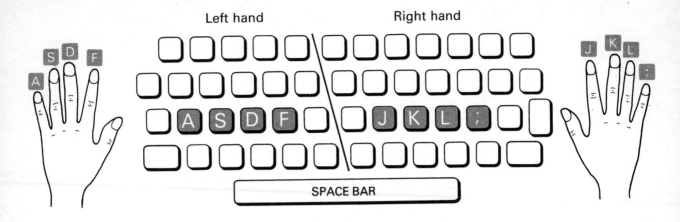

Introduction to home keys

Type the following drills.

Exercise 1

(a) Curve fingers as though to grasp a handle bar
(b) Look at keyboard and place fingers on HOME KEYS
   —left hand **A S D F**, right hand **J K L ;**
(c) Type the two lines exactly as they are—**do not look at the keyboard**

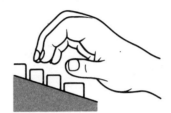

fffjjjfffjjjfffjjjfffjjjfffjjjfffjjjfff   return carriage/carrier
fffjjjfffjjjfffjjjfffjjjfffjjjfffjjjfff   return carriage/carrier
                                                       twice

(d) Sit back, relax and look at what you have typed

Exercise 2 – operating the space bar

A clear space is left between each group of letters or words. This is done by striking the space bar with the right thumb. Keep your other fingers on the HOME KEYS as you bounce the thumb off the space bar. Practise striking space bar and returning carriage/carrier.

See that carriage/carrier is at left margin.

Cursor

If you are using a machine with a visual display unit, or a window display, you will notice that this is a movable dot (hyphen) which indicates the typing point at which the next typed character will appear.

Exercise 3

(a) Curve fingers as though to grasp a handle bar
(b) Look at the keyboard and place your left-hand fingers on **A S D F** and right-hand fingers on **J K L ;**
(c) Type the three lines exactly as they are—**do not look at the keyboard**

fff jjj fff jjj fjf jfj fff jjj fff fjfj   return carriage/carrier
fff jjj fff jjj fjf jfj fff jjj fff fjfj   return carriage/carrier
fff jjj fff jjj fjf jfj fff jjj fff fjfj   return carriage/carrier
                                                       twice

(d) Sit back, relax and look at what you have typed

Exercise 4

Repeat exercises 1, 2 and 3.

Q   quote quail quart queen query quest quiet quite
     quail quote quick queue equal equip pique quack
     squad quake quilt quits quirk query quart quick

I questioned the value of the unique aquarium which
Quinton Asquith had acquired. A subsequent enquiry
queried an odd bequest of quartz glass to the quis-
ling. I had an adequate quantity of new equipment.

R   rapid reach rhyme round rules arise brand cream
     drive error fruit group irate kraft order print
     trade urges write yards birch scarf shrub arson

That thrill of securing rare turquoise curtains and
carpet was truly appreciated. The corvette carried
one tier of crude guns which were fired when on the
practice trials. Carmel saw the lark near a barge.

S   saves scale serve short sight skirt sleep small
     snowy solid squad asset stuck suits sweet sylph
     aside goods issue essay calls osmic users bombs

Sally Tompson stayed on for a course in Spanish for
summer visitors. I disbelieve that the mischievous
lad tried to bring disgrace to a distressed family.
The shrewd businessman should buy that system soon.

T   talks tease those tired today trend rests myths
     tulip tweed typed atlas ether width doubt rifts
     night items kilts boots optic start utter extol

She substituted battle tactics to settle the terri-
torial dispute. The partition of Vietnam started a
quarrel that had devastating results. The title of
Tom's textbook is certainly ecstatic and traumatic.

U   ulcer umbra union upper upset urban usage utile
     uvula Uzbek audit build cured ducks funny guide
     hurry jumbo lungs muddy nurse pulse quick rural

On a sunny day the ubiquitous uncle wore a tunic of
unusual blue when he queued for his supper. Truth-
fully, the manufacturer pursued an unequalled and a
unique course to further our aims for extra output.

V   valid verbs vigil vocal avoid event civil elves
     envoy overt ivory delve vivid verve every solve
     valve vogue haves ovens overs saves vocal Olive

Vivian provided a vivid picture of Valery Vowles on
a visit to prevail upon her sister. He was invited
to play the provocative villain. Very soon Vanessa
will involve Vi in a vicious and vituperative book.

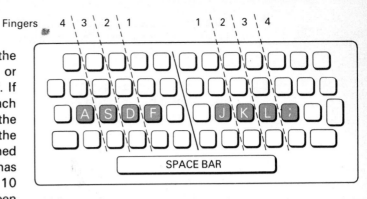

Follow the routine suggested on page 6 under the heading **Prepare to Type**, then type each line or sentence three times, saying the letters to yourself. If time permits, complete your practice by typing each group of lines as it appears. Keep your eyes on the copy while you type and also when returning the carriage/carrier. The carriage/carrier must be returned **immediately** after the last character in the line has been typed. Set left margin stop at 12 pitch 30, 10 pitch 22, and use single spacing with double between exercises.

A Practise **F** *and* **J** *keys—First fingers*

Keep other fingers on home keys

1 fff jjj fjf jfj fjf jfj fff jjj fff fjfj

Always turn up TWICE between exercises

B Practise **D** *and* **K** *keys—Second fingers*

Raise first fingers slightly. Keep little fingers on home keys

2 ddd kkk dkd kdk dkd kdk ddd kkk dkd dkdk

3 fff jjj ddd kkk fkf kfk jdj djd fjk fdjk

Use an even stroke for space bar

C Practise **S** *and* **L** *keys—Third fingers*

Raise little fingers over home keys. Keep first fingers on home keys

4 sss lll sls lsl sls lsl sss lll sls slsl

5 fff jjj ddd kkk sss lll fds jkl fds jklj

Feet firmly on floor

D Practise **A** *and* **;** *keys—Little fingers*

Keep first fingers on home keys

6 aaa ;;; a;a ;a; a;a ;a; aaa ;;; ;a; a;a;

7 f;f jaj d;d kak a;s lal aaa ;;; a;a a;a;

E Word-building

8 aaa lll all lll aaa ddd lad ddd aaa dad;

9 fff aaa ddd fad sss aaa ddd sad fad lad;

F Apply the keys you know

10 dad fad sad lad ask all dad fad sad lad;

11 lass fall lads fads lass fall dads fads;

12 all sad lads; a sad lass; a lad asks dad

13 all sad lads ask a dad; a sad lass falls

14 as a lass falls dad falls; all lads fall

One space after semi-colon

K   Katie kebab kicks knock Korea krona eking bulky
      lurks flack works seeks black kilns picks skews
      Akron khaki knelt quake Kevin fluke locks junky

Karen and Jack had bulky packages which they bought
in the market from a gawky crook. The lucky worker
lunched with a well-known cricketer who spoke in an
unkind, husky voice. Take the bricks to the truck.

L   label legal Lloyd lodge lunch alike bluff claim
      elegy flour glove Klein older place slang ultra
      Allen idled ankle madly pylon altar allow ankle

Lily Lyles delivered an excellent table to my uncle
living at Blind Alley Bay. Walters was not able to
collect the lion and alligator from Lulworth. Call
on Liz Bolton when you are in Ballinluig next July.

M   makes merge Miami mount mufti myrrh amuse emend
      imply omega small combs dogma tramp calms McNee
      Amman charm pigmy films dummy remit admit human

Mrs Mimms was empowered to promote Marjory McMaster
to Games Mistress. Mary may have committed herself
to take command of the mission to Mexico. In a moment a memorandum will be mailed to my new Manager.

N   names needs night nouns nudge ankle enjoy index
      onion under meant thing spend prawn tongs tense
      scent lynch thank penny fungi ankle fence sneak

Nancy announced that she cannot attend the national
plant exhibition until next Monday when another man
from Tanner and Company's Personnel Department will
be absent. The ninety-ninth meeting was mentioned.

O   oasis obese ocean odour offer Ogden olive Omagh
      onion opera orbit Oscar other ought ovens owner
      oxide ozone borne count doves forms goats homes

This forenoon another of our followers will hope to
visit the zoological forest. Young Jon Morley rode
south through many towns in my well-worn Zodiac car
and Nora Porters located a hotel in Colwyn for him.

P   paper Peter photo piano plans ports press pulls
      Pyrex apart empty input opens space upper warps
      expel gipsy helps optic alpha apply pupil quips

Philip put his computer on display so as to explain
the preparation of proper programmes. Please put a
copy of the opposition's campaign pictures in Peter
Philpott's post before he opens the people's parks.

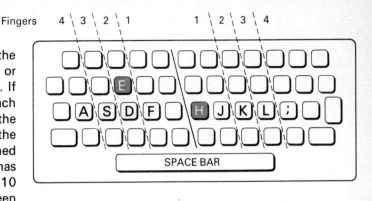

Follow the routine suggested on page 6 under the heading **Prepare to type**, then type each line or sentence three times, saying the letters to yourself. If time permits, complete your practice by typing each group of lines as it appears. Keep your eyes on the copy while you type and also when returning the carriage/carrier. The carriage/carrier must be returned **immediately** after the last character in the line has been typed. Set left margin stop at 12 pitch 30, 10 pitch 22, and use single spacing with double between exercises.

A Review the keys you know

1 aaa ;;; sss lll ddd kkk fff jjj asd jkl;

2 ask a lad; ask all lads; ask a sad lass;

3 all lads fall; dad falls; dad asks a lad

Return carriage/carrier without looking up

Turn up TWICE between exercises

B Practise E key—D finger

Practise D to E back to D. Keep other fingers on home keys

4 ddd eee ded ded see ded lee ded fee ded;

5 ded sea ded lea ded led ded fed ded eke;

C Practise H key—J finger

Practise J to H back to J. Keep other fingers on home keys

6 jjj hhh jhj jhj has jhj had jhj she jhj;

7 jhj has jhj had jhj she jhj ash jhj dash

D Practise word-building

8 hhh eee lll ddd held jjj aaa fff jaffas;

9 sss hhh aaa lll shall fff eee ddd feeds;

E Apply the keys you know

10 see lee fee sea lea led fed eke see lee;

11 ash dash fash sash hash lash; heel shed;

12 a lass has had a salad; dad sees a lake;

13 a jaffa salad; she held a sale; he shall

14 she feeds a lad; dad has a hall; a shed;

Use right thumb and even stroke for space bar

eaten edges eerie Egypt eject elder embed entry
          epics equal erase estop evade duvet cells Derby
          feign heavy keeps merge peeks weary years blaze

The messengers had to proceed to the exit gates and
collect the receipts from the referees. It will be
expedient not to reject the guarantee given for the
new temperature gauges you received only yesterday.

F   fatal fewer fifty flame focus frank fully cliff
          turfs often after refer lifts cleft elfin offer
          infer wharf staff affix edify forms tufts feign

After Frank referred to Faith's offer of a fabulous
car as a gift to the fighting fund, they found that
an unfriendly thief had faked the accounts. Father
fought to safeguard the foolish and fretful fellow.

G   gains germs cough given glare gnome going grand
          guard Gwent gypsy again Egypt aggro igloo Ogden
          argue sugar Edgar bulge muggy edged guard Gregg

Gideon, who played the guitar, gained good marks at
college for giving regular concerts. The great and
gracious Grace giggled as she guided the genial guy
through the aged and lengthy thoroughfares to town.

H   hands heard hired hoard human ahead chase photo
          shout there rough south night harsh laugh thugs
          honey ghost teach phone aloha ghoul rhino abhor

Their teacher showed them how to centre headings in
a horizontal fashion. We went ahead throughout the
harsh, dark night and reached the hallowed halls at
a late hour. Hugh and Homer hailed Hal and Hellen.

I   Ibiza icing ideal igloo image index ionic irate
          issue items ivory aisle birth cigar diary first
          girls hired kinds light miles ninth piece right

Visibility was very poor and we did not participate
in the official visit to that island. It is surely
not permissible for pensioners to give publicity to
their objective. The privilege had been withdrawn.

J   Japan jetty joker judge jolly joins enjoy major
          Bejam fjord banjo jazzy jaded jaunt jewel jerky
          Fijis juror jinks jumps jolly jeans jeers jelly

Judith and John listened to Junior's disjointed and
jumbled speech. My prejudices were justified and I
rejected the joyful joker whose jacket is jade. He
jumped and jeered at the jockeys injured yesterday.

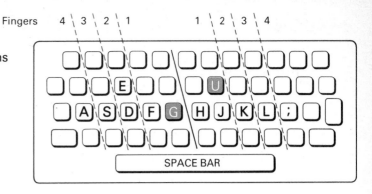

Follow **Prepare to Type** on page 6 and instructions
given at top of page 9.

Margins: 12 pitch 30, 10 pitch 22.
Spacing: single, with double between exercises.

A   Review the keys you know

Wrists and arms
straight

1   asd ;lk ded jhj def khj fed has lee had;

2   add salads; a sea lake; lads feed seals;

3   add leeks; she had leeks; he has a hall;

Turn up TWICE between exercises

B   Practise G *key — F finger*

Practise F to G back
to F. Keep other
fingers on home
keys

4   fff ggg fgf fgf fag fgf lag fgf sag fgf;

5   fgf jag fgf gag fgf hag fgf keg fgf leg;

C   Practise U *key — J finger*

Practise J to U back
to J. Keep little
fingers on home
keys

6   jjj uuu juj juj due juj sue juj hue juj;

7   juj sug juj jug juj dug juj hug juj lug;

D   Practise word-building

8   uuu sss eee ddd use uses used useful us;

9   jjj uuu ddd ggg eee judge judges judged;

E   Apply the keys you know

Feet firmly on floor

10   fag sag lag jag gag hag keg leg egg keg;

11   dues hues jugs hugs lugs suds eggs legs;

12   he had a dull glass; a judge has a flag;

13   see she has a full jug; she used jaffas;

14   dad had a full keg; he shall guess; use;

UNIT 4   Keys: G and U   **10**

Individual letter drills

As each individual has different weaknesses when using the keyboard, you will require individual remedial practice based on your needs; therefore, we have prepared the following drills for corrective practice on keyboarding errors made during **Record your progress** practice. Of course, there is no reason why you should not use the drills for remedial practice on any alphabetic keystroking errors.

When you examine the drills that follow, you will see that each letter drill gives practice in typing a particular letter in combination with other letters. For example, in drill **A** below, the first word begins with Aa, the second word with ba, the third word with ca and so on to the last word which begins with Za. It is not necessary for the purpose of the drill that the letters within any one drill are presented in any particular order.

Type each line of words at least twice, and each paragraph at least once. Use a left margin of 12 pitch 30, 10 pitch 25.

If you type the first exercise once, you will have typed the letter **A** 65 times (in 45 different combinations); the letter **E** 34 times; the letters **R** and **T** 20 times; and the letter **S** 15 times.

A
```
Aaron baled cares dazed eager gains major ahead
trial kayak aorta axles naked oasis paced Qatar
radio saved table aquae vague aware exact Zaire
```

I am rather glad that these facts were available at the hearing last May. Aunt May was not afraid when I travelled on Arabian Airways, and she appreciated the caviar, bread and tomato sandwiches, and cakes.

B
```
badly begin bible black board brick build byway
about ebony Ibsen obese ember unbar blurb rugby
cubic oxbow Bobby elbow maybe doubt abhor abide
```

Her absence seemed abnormal but she was subdued and bright when Barbara Babbacombe bought a brown ball. Betty Gibson sat by Bobby Dobson at the back of the bright blue mobile bus bound for beautiful Babylon.

C
```
cable check cedar claim McGee civil cover cocoa
black crack cupid cycle Czech acted icing birch
uncut ulcer eclat incur octet occur scion excel
```

The committee met in Cwmbran in October. The cool, practical mechanic accepted the challenges and completed the service on the bicycle. That clock they acquired is scratched, and they are much concerned.

D
```
daily defer dhobi dials dodge draft dunce dwell
dying hands admit edict ideas odour oddly badge
older order fudge Floyd fluid idiom crowd outdo
```

They decided to double the dividend and to readjust and adapt the oddments. Edwin sold the cuddly bear and my rowdy admirers said he was a dutiful dodger. David had daffodils in his garden beyond the dykes.

Follow **Prepare to Type** on page 6 and instructions given at top of page 9.

Margins: 12 pitch 30, 10 pitch 22.
Spacing: single, with double between exercises.

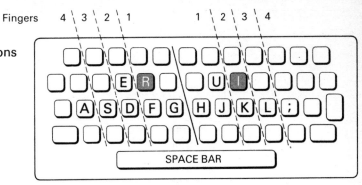

A   Review the keys you know

```
1  fds jkl ded juj fgf jhj hag jug dug leg;
2  a lass uses a flask; all lads had a jug;
3  sell us a full keg; see she has a glass;
```
Eyes on copy always

B   Practise **R** *key—F finger*

Practise F to R back to F. Keep other fingers on home keys
```
4  fff rrr frf frf jar frf far frf rag frf;
5  frf are frf ark frf red frf fur frf rug;
```

C   Practise **I** *key—K finger*

Practise K to I back to K. Keep other fingers on home keys
```
6  kkk iii kik kik kid kik lid kik did kik;
7  kik dig kik fig kik rig kik jig kik gig;
```

D   Practise word families

```
8  fill hill rill drill grill skill frills;
9  ark lark dark hark; air fair hair lairs;
```

E   Apply the keys you know

```
10  fill his flask; he is here; he had a rug
11  her red dress is here; she has fair hair
12  she likes a fair judge; he has dark hair
13  his lad fills a jug; she has rare skills
14  she is sure; ask her here; he likes figs
```
Sharp, brisk strokes

TO   C I Knight Esq
1 ~~Chestnut~~ Chestnut Square
LEAMINGTON   SPA
Warwickshire
CV32   9HJ

Preparing Income Tax Return
for 1987/88 relating to
income received for the yr.
ended 5 April 1988.

Submitting this Return, after
signature, to H M Inspector of
Taxes, together w. supporting
schedules & information .

Checking Notices of Assessment,
etc .

Generally dealing w. yr. taxation
affairs for the period to date .   300·00

Plus VAT   15%   45·00

                                                45·00

Please calculate
& insert total

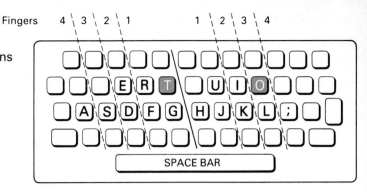

Follow **Prepare to Type** on page 6 and instructions given at top of page 9.

Margins: 12 pitch 30, 10 pitch 22.
Spacing: single, with double between exercises.

A Review the keys you know

1 fgf jhj frf juj ded kik aid did her rug;
2 his full fees; she likes a dark red rug;
3 his girl is here; he is glad she is sure

Practise F to T back to F. Keep other fingers on home keys

B Practise T key—F finger

4 fff ttt ftf ftf fit ftf kit ftf lit ftf;   Check your posture
5 ftf sit ftf hit ftf sat ftf hat ftf fat;

Practise L to O back to L. Keep other fingers on home keys

C Practise O key—L finger

6 lll ooo lol lol lot lol got lol hot lol;
7 lol rot lol dot lol jot lol tot lol sot;

D Practise word families

8 old hold sold gold; look rook hook took;
9 let set jet get ret; rate late hate date

Homophones

These are words that are similar in sound but spelt differently and have different meanings. It is often difficult to decide which of a pair is the correct one to use in particular circumstances; therefore, use your dictionary to check the meaning of any word you are not sure about. **Always** check on the meaning and spelling if you are in doubt.

E Homophones   Use your dictionary to check the meaning

10 sea see; here hear; tide tied; aid aide;
11 ail ale; right rite; tare tear; fir fur;

F Apply the keys you know

12 get her a set; he took a full jar to her   Back straight
13 he had sold the gold; at this late date;
14 that old dress looks just right for her;

MEMO – Please type
an envelope

From C R Formby   CRF/DA

To   Mrs G Wedgewood

NEW PERSONAL COMPUTER PRINTER [COLLEAGUE]

~~The~~ a colleague~~off~~ ~~a~~ (business) has recom. a new
printer wh. is said to be almost silent !
[The attached sheet ~~looks~~ gives a few details, & I wd ✓
like you to arrange for a demon.]

[You wl no doubt remember th. I am not
available on & Tuesdays.

[I like the idea th. it does not require special
paper & the fact th. one can switch typefaces
w'out interrupting printing.

(Please use A5 headed paper. Take a carbon copy)

Our Ref CRF/LJ/DA

C I Knight Esq,
etc – see Task 6
Dear Mr ——
As usual at this time of yr., I encl. my firm's
charges for dealing w. yr. current Tax Return
& generally looking ~~for~~ after yr. tax
affairs. [I also encl. the Consolidated
Statement for A — C — PLC. You wl
remember th. you asked me last week
for a copy of this.
Yrs sincerely

Follow **Prepare to Type** on page 6 and instructions given at top of page 9.

Margins: 12 pitch 30, 10 pitch 22.
Spacing: single, with double between exercises.

Fingers 4 \ 3 \ 2 \ 1   1 \ 2 \ 3 \ 4

SPACE BAR

A Review the keys you know

1 ftf lol frf juj ded kik tot out rot dot;

2 this is a red jet; the lad took the gold

3 he asked a just fee; the old folk agree;

Return carriage/carrier without looking up

Practise S to W back to S. Keep F finger on home key

B Practise **W** key—S finger

4 sss www sws sws low sws sow sws row sws;

5 sws hew sws few sws dew sws sew sws tew;

Practise J to N back to J. Keep little finger on home key

C Practise **N** key—J finger

6 jjj nnn jnj jnj fan jnj ran jnj tan jnj;

7 jnj sin jnj kin jnj din jnj lin jnj tin;

D Practise word families

8 end send lend tend fend rend wend trend;

9 low sow how row tow saw law daw jaw raw;

E Homophones *Use your dictionary to check the meaning*

10 sew sow; weak week; wear ware, fair fare

11 oar ore; new knew; knead need; not knot;

F Apply the keys you know

12 we saw her look at the new gate; we knew

13 he sent us a gift of red jeans last week

14 we had left a jade silk gown and the rug

Wrist and arms straight, fingers curved

UNIT 7 Keys: W and N   13

Use A4 paper. Leave 2 clear spaces wherever this mark (X) appears. Please align the decimal points underneath each other and insert leader dots.

ALBERT COHEN PLC

Consolidated Statement – 31 Dec. 1987

	1986 £m	1987 £m
Operating profit	5.9	44.2
Interest	31.4	13.7
(X)		
Profit before taxation	25.5	30.5
Taxation	9.9	11.3
(X)		
Profit after taxation	15.6	19.2
l.c. Minority Interests	1.1	0.1
(X)		
Profit before extraordinary profit	14.5	19.1
(X) Profit assignable to shareholders	14.5	39.3
(X)		
(X)		

1 The 1986 figures are from the group a/cs wh. were filed w. the Registrar of Companies.

2 The extraordinary profit arose on the disposal of business operations & is net of taxation.

l.c. Retained Profit – – – – – – 4.3   24.5

CRF/DA

6 Dec. 1988

Improvement practice

Set left margin stop at 12 pitch 30, 10 pitch 22.

A Improve control of carriage return

1 Type the following lines exactly as shown. Repeat the exercise twice.

```
as a lass
as a lass falls
as a lass falls dad falls
```

Return carriage/carrier without looking up

In the following exercises type each line three times, saying the letters to yourself.

B Improve control of T and H keys

```
2 the then than that this thus these there
3 she thus feels that this is rather good;
4 these lads are there for the third week;
```

C Improve control of space bar

```
5 a s d f j k l ; g h w e r t u i o a s d;
6 at it we he go to as are not for did ask
7 we are sure he did not ask us for these;
```

Use right thumb and even stroke

D Improve control of R and O keys

```
8 our for road work word offer order other
9 she works near our road; the other word;
10 he wrote the order; sort out our offers;
```

E Improve control of paper insertion

By means of the paper release, take out the sheet of paper you are using. Put it back quickly in the machine, so that the left edge is at 0 on the carriage-position scale, and see that the paper is straight. Repeat this drill several times daily.

Please retype. Use double or 1½ spacing & correct the words th. I hv. circled.

THE SILENT PRINTER

<u>A High-quality Machine</u>

This machine shows a dramatic change in technology from any other printer that has (preceeded) it. This printer does not punch the letters on to a page; it electronically forms characters and (transfer) them to paper using a unique thermal method - heat releases the ink from a special typewriter ribbon so that the characters are 'painted' on the paper.

Other points to note are:

l.c.

l.c.

.c.

i   It does not require special paper and can even print on transparencies.

ii There (is) 10 different typefaces available, including several European languages.*

iii Two typefaces can be stored in the machine at any one time, and you can transfer from one to the other without (interupt-ing) printing.

There are 2 models and Model 'B' (handels) both text and graphics with equal silence.

Both models are available with an optional automatic paper feed unit.

---

* There is also a wide range of typefaces with mathematical and scientific symbols.

F *Improve control of* **E** *and* **N** *keys*

11 en end tend new keen then when need near;
12 then she went; he knew the news was sent
13 we need the new jugs; near here; the end

Feet firmly on floor

G *Improve control of* **W** *and* **I** *keys*

14 win wish wife with will wait writ while;
15 his wife will wait with us; the wise lad
16 we will wish to write while we are there

H *Improve control of* **U** *key*

17 our hour sour dull lull full hull gulls;
18 all our dull hours; he ruled for a week;
19 use our usual rules; let us rush out now

I *Improve control of* **G** *key*

20 go got good goods sigh sight light right
21 urge her to get a rug; the girl is right
22 go on the green light; the night is long

J *Improve control of suffix ING*

23 ing going taking selling dealing heating
24 he is going; we are selling; owing to us
25 ask if she is dealing with that heating;

K *Apply the keys you know*

26 now that joke is not good; our old safe;
27 for fun ask if the jars she got were old
28 do join us; walk to that green fir tree;

Shoulders back and relaxed

Notes

Your centre number is 7566/R23.
Calculators and English dictionaries may be used in this examination.
Type your name and centre number at the top of each page that you type.
Use headed paper where appropriate.
Put your completed work in task number order.
Put a pencil mark through any work which you do not wish the examiner to mark.

Task 1

Our Ref CRF/DA

PERSONAL

(Please address a suitable envelope)

Mrs Désirée Moore
Moore's Staffing Agency
WARWICK   CV35 8NA

Dear Mrs _____

SECRETARIAL VACANCIES

As a result of the redistribution of duties + an increase in business commitments, I am now resp. for the engagement of sec. + clerical staff and, therefore, I write to introduce myself to you. During the next few weeks I wl hv the following vacancies:

(a) Two shorthand-typists - min. shorthand speed 100 wpm.

(b) One copy-typist - min. qualification: Stage II typing.

(c) One audio-typist - min qualification: Stage II audio transcription.

In addition, we do like our office staff to hv suitable ~~industrial~~ qualifications in English language.

As you know, ~~we do like~~ ~~our~~ office ~~staff~~ our salaries are not high by industrial standards, but the work is interesting to young persons (+ shd appeal to) who are not attracted by work in an industrial concern. I encl. 12 copies of our application form + a leaflet showing conditions of service.

Yrs sincerely

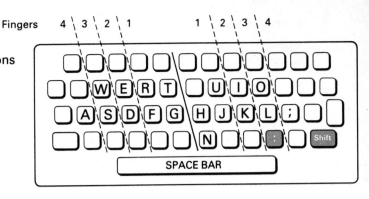

Follow **Prepare to Type** on page 6 and instructions given at top of page 9.

Margins: 12 pitch 30, 10 pitch 22.
Spacing: single, with double between exercises.

A Review the keys you know

Eyes on copy

1 sws jnj ftf lol frf jhj won win new now;

2 we do not like those jars she got for us

3 the red dogs will go for a walk just now

B Practise right shift key

To make capitals for letters typed by the left hand:
(a) With right-hand little finger depress and hold right shift key well down.
(b) Strike left-hand capital letter.
(c) Remove finger from shift key and return all fingers to home keys.

4 fF; dD; sS; aA; Ada; Sad; Dad; Fad; Wade

5 Gee; Reg; Ted; Sue; Flo; Ede; Dora; West

C Practise full stop key ⬛ —L finger

Practise L to .
back to L. Keep
first finger on
home key

6 lll ... l.l f.l j.l Good. Dear. Ellis.

Leave 2 spaces after full stop at end of sentence

7 Ask her. Ted is sad. Do go. She will.

D Practise word families

8 Wee; Weed; Feed; Reed; Seed; Deed; Greed

9 And; Sand; Wand; Rand; Send; Tend; Fend;

E Homophones *Use your dictionary to check the meaning*

10 altar alter; guessed guest; aught ought.

11 dear deer; aloud allowed; threw through.

F Apply the keys you know

12 Ask Ed Reid if we should join the Swede.

Check your posture

13 She was right. Dirk was jealous. Fine.

14 Flora would like to go; just state when.

Centred ruled tabulation with leader dots

The method used for typing leader dots in ruled tables is the same as that given on page 134 when typing unruled tables. Refer to the points given on page 134 before typing exercise 8.

8 Type the following table on A4 paper. (a) Centre the table vertically and horizontally on the paper. (b) Use centred style. (c) Double spacing. (d) Leave three spaces between the columns. (e) Rule horizontal lines by underline and vertical lines in ink. (f) Insert leader dots.

STAINLESS STEEL CUTLERY*

PRICE LIST - November 1988

Item No	Item	Price
		£
I	Soup spoon	4.25
II	Dessert spoon	4.00
III	Table fork	3.00
IV	Table knife	5.50
V	Fish fork	2.50
VI	Fish knife	3.50
VII	Bread knife	7.75
VIII	Salad servers, pair	9.00
IX	24 piece set (6 x 4 piece place sets)	75.00
X	42 piece set (6 x 7 piece place sets)	140.00
XI	Carving knife	13.50

* Guaranteed for a lifetime

Follow **Prepare to Type** on page 6 and instructions given at top of page 9.

Margins: 12 pitch 30, 10 pitch 22.
Spacing: single, with double between exercises.

A Review the keys you know

1 aA; sS; dD; fF; wW; eE; rR; Red; Gee; As

2 Ask Flo. See Roger. Tell Fred. Go in.

3 Ede had gone. Write to us. A fake jug.

Leave 2 spaces after full stop at end of sentence

B Practise left shift key

To make capitals for letters typed by the right hand:
(a) With left-hand little finger depress and hold left shift key well down.
(b) Strike right-hand capital letter.
(c) Remove finger from shift key and return all fingers to home keys.

4 jJa kKa lLa jUj kIk Judd Kidd Lode Hoad;   *Eyes on copy*

5 Ida Ken Len Jude Owen Hilda Oakes Usual;

Practise F to B back to F. Keep little finger on home key

C Practise [B] key—F finger

6 fff bbb fbf fbf bud fbf bus fbf but fbf;

7 fbf rob fbf sob fbf fob fbf hob fbf job;

D Practise word families

8 Nib Jib Lib Job Lob Hob Hail Jail Nails;

9 Jill Hill Kill Lill Tall Ball Fall Wall;

E Homophones *Use your dictionary to check the meaning*

10 break brake; bare bear; blue blew; suite

11 sweet; whether weather; road rode rowed;

F Apply the keys you know

12 She will be taking those salads to Jane.

13 Jill knows. Kit had to bluff Bob Green.

14 Fred will ask us to do those jobs again.

The same procedure is adopted when ruling centred tabulation as for blocked tabulation. Refer to page 136 and revise the points given before attempting the following exercises.

6 Type the following table on A5 portrait paper. (a) Centre the table vertically and horizontally on the paper. (b) Use centred style. (c) Double spacing. (d) Leave three spaces between columns. (e) Rule horizontal lines by underline and vertical lines in ink.

LONGMORE NATURE RESERVE

Birds	Flowers	Butterflies
Swan	Rose Bay Willowherb	Orange Tip
Nightingale	Purple Loosestrife	Brimstone
Dabchick	Dog Rose	Red Admiral
Tufted Duck	Harebell	Large White
Willow Warbler	Creeping Jenny	Wall Brown

7 Type the following table on A5 landscape paper. (a) Centre the table vertically and horizontally on the paper. (b) Use centred style. (c) Double spacing. (d) Leave three spaces between columns. (e) Rule horizontal lines by underline and vertical lines in ink.

EUROPEAN MONARCHS

Dates of Accession

Country	Sovereign	Date
Norway	Olav V	21 September 1957
Sweden	Carl Gustaf XVI	15 September 1973
Denmark	Margrethe II	14 January 1972
Great Britain	Elizabeth II	6 February 1952
The Netherlands	Beatrix	30 April 1980
Belgium	Baudouin	17 July 1951
Spain	Juan Carlos I	22 November 1975

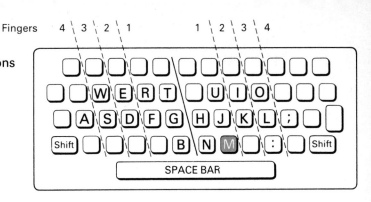

Follow **Prepare to Type** on page 6 and instructions given at top of page 9.

Margins: 12 pitch 25, 10 pitch 18.
Spacing: single, with double between exercises.
NOTE: Margin sets have changed.

A   Review the keys you know

1 fbf sws jnj ftf lol frf jhj Len Ken Hen Ian Win Go
2 Dan and Rob left.   He will go just now.   Ask Nell.
3 Lois and Earl will see June.   Go with Fred Bolton.

Leave 2 spaces after full stop at end of sentence

B   Practise ⬛M Key—J finger

4 jjj mmm jmj jmj jam jmj ham jmj dam jmj ram jmjmj;
5 jmj rum jmj hum jmj sum jmj mum jmj gum jmj strum;

Practise J to M back to J. Keep little finger on home key

C   Practise left and right shift keys

6 Ada Ben Dan East Fred Green Hilda Irwin James King
7 Lil Mark Nell Owen Rene Sara Todd Usher Wills Watt

Little fingers for shift keys

D   Practise word families

8 arm farm harm warm alarm art hart tart darts mart;
9 game name dame fame same lame home dome some foam;

E   Homophones   *Use your dictionary to check the meaning*

10 there their; moan mown; air heir; eminent imminent
11 missed mist; mail male; aid aide; morning mourning

F   Apply the keys you know

12 Most of the fame goes to John who had been working
hard for his father but he has now left the works.
I think he is now at home.

3 Type the following exercise on A5 landscape paper. (a) Use centred style of display. (b) Centre the table vertically and horizontally. (c) Double spacing. (d) Leave three spaces between columns.

BRITISH PRIME MINISTERS

1964 - 1979

Name of Prime Minister	Political Party	Dates in Office
Mr. J. H. Wilson	Labour	1964 - 1970
Mr. E. R. G. Heath	Conservative	1970 - 1974
Mr. J. H. Wilson	Labour	1974 - 1976
Mr. L. J. Callaghan	Labour	1976 - 1979

Typing column headings — Centred style

If the column heading is shorter than the longest item in the column (as in exercise 4 below), the column heading is centred over the longest item:

(a) Set left margin and tab stops as usual.
(b) Find the centre point of the column by tapping space bar once for every two characters and spaces in the longest column item, beginning from the point set for the start of the column. This will bring the printing point to the centre of the column.

(c) From the point reached in (b), backspace once for every two characters and spaces in the column heading. Type the column heading at the point reached.
(d) The column items will start at the tab stop already set for each column.

4 Type the following exercise on A5 landscape paper. (a) Use centred style of display. (b) Centre the table vertically and horizontally. (c) Centre headings over the longest item in each column. (d) Double spacing. (e) Leave three spaces between columns.

CAMBOURNE LEISURE CENTRE

Evening Activities

Monday	Tuesday	Wednesday	Thursday
Motor Club	Chess Club	Bridge Club	Craft Club
Table Tennis	Choir	Dog Training	Pressed Flowers
Weight Watchers	Wine Circle	Drama Group	Badminton
French Club	Pottery	CB Radio	Photographic Society

5 Type the following exercise on A5 portrait paper. (a) Use centred style of display. (b) Centre the table vertically and horizontally. (c) Double spacing. (d) Leave three spaces between columns.

PRICE LIST

Special Offers for January

Catalogue No	Description	Price
2468	Display Cleaning Kit	£9.90
3640	VDU Screen Filter	£48.00
8311	VDU/Micro Trolley	£99.00
2816	Acoustic Hood	£32.50

Improvement practice

Follow **Prepare to Type** on page 6 and instructions given at top of page 9. Margins: 12 pitch 25, 10 pitch 18. Spacing: single, with double between exercises.

A   *Improve control of home row keys*

1   add had jag gas ask ash sash dash glad flags flash
2   Dad has a flag. Sal had a sash. A lass asks dad.
3   A lass had had a jag. A glad lad. Ask a sad lad.

Leave 2 spaces after full stop at the end of sentence

B   *Improve control of* O *and* U *keys*

4   to go now out our hour tour sour would house shout
5   Ask Ruth if she would like to go to our house now.
6   Tell Flo we will start out on our tour in an hour.

C   *Improve control of carriage/carrier return*

7   I will go
     I will go soon
     I will go as soon as
     I will go as soon as I get there.

D   *Improve control of* W E R *and* T *keys*

8   we wet were west tree tell test where threw refers
9   We were all in here. I saw those trees last week.
10   She referred to the tests. Tell her to rest here.

E   *Improve control of shift keys*

11   He Ask Jon Sara Kite Dale Lord Ford Hall Iris Tait
12   Ask Miss Ford if she will see Mrs Tait in an hour.
13   Owen Dale and Gerald Reid are going to Harrow now.

No full stop after Mrs

Fully-centred tabulation

In previous exercises on tabulation all the tables were blocked. You should also become proficient in centring column work. The following points should be noted.

(a) Refer back to pages 80 and 81 for horizontal and vertical centring.

(b) The main heading and subheading (if there is one) are centred on the paper, ie, backspace once for every two characters and spaces from the centre of the paper.

(c) As in previous exercises on tabulation, back-space once for every two characters and spaces in the longest line in each column, plus half the number of spaces to be left between columns. Set your left margin at the point reached.

(d) Tap forward from left margin and set tab stops.

NOTE: Any one piece of tabulation must be blocked or centred—a combination of the two is unacceptable.

1 Type the following exercise on A5 portrait paper. (a) Centre the exercise vertically and horizontally. (b) The main heading and subheading should be centred on the paper. (c) Double spacing. (d) Leave three spaces between columns.

METHODS OF COMMUNICATION

<u>Written and Spoken</u>

Reports	Interviews	Lectures
Conferences	Announcements	Charts
Statistics	Accounts	Letters
Memoranda	Advertisements	Control Boards

Typing column headings—Centred style

If the column heading is the longest item in the column (as in exercise 2 below), the column items are CENTRED under the headings as follows:

(a) Type the column headings at the left margin and at the tab stops set.

(b) Find the centre of the heading by tapping the space bar once for every two characters and spaces in the heading, starting from the left margin or the tab stop set for the heading. This will bring the carriage/carrier to the centre point of the heading.

(c) From the point reached in (b), backspace once for every two characters and spaces in the longest line under the heading. This gives you the starting point for EACH ITEM in the column. Make a note of the point reached, then cancel the tab stop set for the heading and set another tab stop for the start of the column items.

2 Type the following exercise on A5 landscape paper. (a) Centre the exercise vertically and horizontally. (b) Centre the column items under the column headings. (c) Double spacing. (d) Leave three spaces between columns.

EUROPEAN CURRENCIES

<u>European Country</u>	<u>Monetary Unit</u>	<u>European Country</u>	<u>Monetary Unit</u>
France	Franc	USSR	Rouble
Italy	Lira	West Germany	Deutsche Mark
The Netherlands	Guilder	Irish Republic	Punt
Spain	Peseta	Great Britain	Pound

F Improve control of I and N keys

14 an is in into line infer night noise injure inside
15 Irene infers Nina was injured one night this week.
16 The noise is inside the inn. Neither one will go.

G Improve control when typing phrases

17 to go to us to see to ask to take to fill to write
18 I wish to see Wales. Ask her to fill in the date.
19 Leslie would like to take Jill to the new theatre.

Brisk, even strokes

H Improve control of B key

20 bid but bad best both able book begin about better
21 Both of us will be better off when he begins work.
22 Bob has been able to book a table for Bill and me.

I Improve control of M key

23 am me man seem make main must item them from might
24 I am making out a form for the main items we lost.
25 I must tell him that the amount seems to be right.

J Improve control of space bar

26 a w s e d r f t g b h j n u m k i o l f b j n m l.
27 is it if in as an at am on or of to go he me we be
28 He did go to tea. It is now time for us to go on.

Use right thumb and even strokes

Semi-blocked personal letter with home address blocked at right margin

When your home address is not printed on your stationery, you may wish to block it at the right margin. This is done in the same way as you backspaced for the date when typing it in exercise 1 on page 159; from the right margin backspace once for each character and each space in a line and, from the point reached, start typing that line. Before starting the first line of your address, turn up four single spaces and turn up two single spaces before typing the date.

6   Type the following letter on a sheet of plain A5 portrait paper. (a) Block the home address at the right margin. (b) Use margins of 12 pitch 13–63, 10 pitch 6–56. (c) Use open punctuation and semi-blocked style.

17 High Street
RUGBY
Warwickshire
CV22 5QE

27th October 1988

The Managing Director
Kenkott Scotia PLC
Langside
GLASGOW   G41 3DI

Dear Sir

    Your Rugby Branch installed fitted wardrobes for me at the end of September, and today I have received a second reminder that I have not paid the sum of £724.00.

    I have on 4 occasions pointed out to your Rugby Office Manager that I have no intention of paying this amount until your workman returns and puts the handles on the wardrobe doors!

    Please make arrangements immediately for the work to be completed.

       Yours faithfully

       Gladys Jackson (Mrs)

Centring the home address on the page

Another way of typing your home address on plain paper is to centre each line on the page in the same way that you displayed the notice on page 154 when you backspaced one for each two letters and spaces from the centre point of the paper. This style is acceptable for blocked or semi-blocked letters.

7   Type the above letter again, but this time centre the home address on the page. As usual, turn up four singles before the first line and two singles before typing the date at the right margin.

Check your work after each exercise

After returning the carriage/carrier at the end of an exercise, check your typescript carefully and circle any errors. **Always** check *before* removing the paper from the machine.

They have to leave early.

1 Each incorrect character is one error.	1 The(y) have to leave early.
2 Each incorrect punctuation is one error.	2 They have to leave early(?)
3 An extra space is one error.	3 They○have to leave early.
4 Omitting a space is one error.	4 They hav(et)o leave early.
5 When using a manual machine, a raised/lowered capital is one error.	5 (T)hey have to leave early.
6 When using a manual machine, an uneven left margin is one error.	6 ○They have to leave early.
7 Omitting a word is one error.	7 They have○leave early.
8 Inserting an extra word is one error.	8 They have to (to) leave early.
9 Inserting an extra letter is one error.	9 They have to leave(s) early.
10 Omitting a letter is one error.	10 They have to (l)ave early.

Half- or one-minute goals

1 Type the exercise. If any word causes you to hesitate, type that word three times.
2 Take a half- or one-minute timing.
3 If you reach the goal or beyond, take another timing and see if you can type the same number of words but with fewer mistakes.
4 If you do not reach the goal after three tries, you need a little more practice on the key drills. Choose the previous exercise(s) that gives intensive practice on the keys that caused difficulty.

NOTES:
(a) There is little to be gained by typing any one drill more than three times consecutively. When you have typed it three times, go on to another drill; then, if necessary, go back to the original drill.
(b) At present, techniques (striking the keys evenly and sharply, good posture, eyes on copy, returning the carriage without looking up) are very important and you should concentrate on good techniques. If your techniques are right, then accuracy will follow. However, if you have more than two errors for each minute typed, it could mean that you have not practised the new keys sufficiently and that you should go back and do further intensive practice on certain key drills.

Measure your speed

Five strokes count as one 'standard' word. In a typing line of 50 spaces, there are ten 'standard' words. The figures to the right of each exercise indicate the number of 'standard' words in the complete line, and the scale below indicates the number across the page. If in the exercise below you reach the word 'we' in one minute, your speed is 10 + 6 = 16 words per minute. You will now be able to measure your speed.

Type the following exercise as instructed under Nos 1–4 of 'Half- or one-minute goals'. Set left margin at 12 pitch 25, 10 pitch 18.

Goal—8 words in half a minute   16 words in one minute

We will take her to see our new house on the north   10

side of the new estates and we shall ask George to   20

join us at that time. (SI 1.04)   24

```
1  |  2  |  3  |  4  |  5  |  6  |  7  |  8  |  9  |  10  |
```

Memoranda

Revise the points given on page 76 about the typing of memos. The layout of the printed forms used for memos varies considerably, but the same rules for typing them apply. It is preferable to leave two clear character spaces after the words in the printed headings before typing the insertions, and to use the variable linespacer to ensure their alignment. Never type a full stop after the last word of an insertion, unless it is abbreviated and full punctuation is being used. A memo form with printed heading is given in the *Handbook and Solutions Manual*, and copies may be duplicated.

4 Type the following memo on a printed A4 memo form. (a) Use margins of 12 pitch 13–90, 10 pitch 11–75. (b) Take a carbon copy and address an envelope. (c) Use full punctuation and semi-blocked style.

PERSONAL   MEMORANDUM

From   Gerry Wells   **Ref** BW/tel/12/PW

To   Mr. J. Barclay   **Date** 14 December 1988

                    ← TELEPHONES AND ACCESSORIES

As requested in your memo dated 8 December, I have obtained copies of a variety of catalogues and enclose them with this memo.

TONE RINGER

This is a portable plug-in unit that works well where there is a lot of noise and distraction: it has a distinctive high-pitch ring which makes it easier to hear in noisy locations like workshops. It would seem eminently suitable for the Works Manager's office.

PHONE SOCKETS

It would seem wise to remove the permanent phones from a number of points and have the phone sockets fitted so that we can take a phone to whichever room is in use for a meeting. These sockets can be fitted easily by qualified engineers.

EXTENSION CORD

Handy when you have to move about the desk area to find information. There is a plug at one end & a specially designed casing at the other. The standard length is 3 metres.

5 Type the following memo on a printed memo form. Use suitable margins and semi-blocked style.

To   Gerry Wells   **From**   John Barclay

Date 15 Dec 88   **Reference** JB/AM

Thank you for yr memo dated 14 Dec. Please order 2 Tone Ringers + 2 Extension Cords.

Insert heading - Telephones + Accessories

Follow **Prepare to Type** on page 6 and instructions given at top of page 9.

Margins: 12 pitch 25, 10 pitch 18.
Spacing: single, with double between exercises.

A Review the keys you know

1 jmj fmj kmk fmf lml am; Mat Tom Ham Sam Lamb Farm;
2 Mrs Lamb would like to take on the job we offered.
3 None of them would go with Job down the long road.

Eyes on copy

B Practise C key—D finger

4 ddd ccc dcd dcd cod dcd cot dcd cob dcd cog dcdcd;
5 dcd cut dcd cub dcd cur dcd cud dcd cab dcd cat cd

Practise D to C back to D. Keep little finger on home key

C Practise Y key—J finger

6 jjj yyy jyj jyj jay jyj hay jyj lay jyj bay jyjyj;
7 jyj say jyj day jyj ray jyj may jyj gay jyj way jj

Practise J to Y back to J. Keep other fingers on home keys

D Practise word families

8 sty try fry dry cry wry dice rice mice nice trice;
9 shy sky sly try sty slay stay fray gray dray stray

Brisk, even strokes

E Homophones *Use your dictionary to check the meaning*

10 sealing ceiling; council counsel; cent sent scent;
11 stationery stationary; creak creek; cereal serial;

F Apply the keys you know

Goal—8 words in half a minute   16 words in one minute

12 He is not able to find a nice jacket which he says   10

   he lost on the way to your farm. He will send you   20

   his bill in a week or so. **(SI 1.08)**   25

1 | 2 | 3 | 4 | 5 | 6 | 7 | 8 | 9 | 10 |

Displayed matter in semi-blocked letters

The usual method for displaying matter in semi-blocked letters is to arrange for the longest line of the matter to be centred in the typing line. To do this:

(a) Find the centre point of the body of the letter by adding together the points at which the left and right margins are set and divide by two.

(b) Bring printing point to this scale point and backspace once for every two characters and spaces in the longest line of the displayed matter. This is the starting point for all items.

(c) ALWAYS leave one clear space above and below displayed matter.

 With computers, word processors and electronic typewriters you could use the automatic centring device and/or the temporary second margins.

3 Type the following letter from Eastways Developments (UK) Ltd (use A4 letterhead paper) in semi-blocked style with full punctuation. (a) Take a carbon copy and centre the subject heading and displayed portion. (b) Margins: 12 pitch 22–82, 10 pitch 12–72.

Our Ref LAB/PAC/398

Your Ref CCS/MA

9 September 1988

J. Holland & Co. Ltd.,
64 Durham Road,
Central Estate,
HARTLEPOOL,
Cleveland.   TS24 7RQ

Dear Sirs,

                    INTERIOR LIGHTING

      Enclosed please find our interior lighting booklet
giving you details about our wide selection of lighting for
showrooms. We feel sure you will find many useful ideas and
projects, and would draw your attention to the following
sale items:

          747/88   Triple Spotlight Circular   £17.40
          785/88   Double Spotlight Bar   £10.85

      Our products are listed in 12 sections and you should use
the section numbers on page 3 for easy reference when looking
for a particular project.

      We will be pleased to quote you for your special needs.

                    Yours faithfully,

Backing sheets

These can be used for the following purposes:

(a) To prevent damage to the cylinder of the typewriter.

(b) To hold the paper in place when typing near the bottom of a page, and prevent the bottom lines from 'running off' the sheet.

(c) To help you find the horizontal and vertical centre of the page by drawing a vertical line down the centre and a horizontal line across the centre.

(d) To remind you to leave an inch clear at the top of a page by drawing a heavy horizontal line one inch from the top.

Follow **Prepare to Type** on page 6 and instructions given at top of page 9.

Margins: 12 pitch 25, 10 pitch 18.
Spacing: single, with double between exercises.

Fingers   4 \ 3 \ 2 \ 1   1 \ 2 \ 3 \ 4

A   Review the keys you know

Eyes on copy

1 dcd jyj dcd fbf jhj fgf lol yet coy yes call come.
2 Her mother had brought a new kind of jersey cloth.
3 He sent us a ticket for the jumble sale on Monday.

B   Practise **P** *key — ; finger*

Practise ; to P back to ;. Keep J finger on home key and other fingers curved

4 ;;; ppp ;p; ;p; cap ;p; lap ;p; rap ;p; jap p;p;p;
5 ;p; pip ;p; dip ;p; sip ;p; hip ;p; lip ;p; nip p;

C   Practise **V** *key — F finger*

Practise F to V back to F. Keep little finger on home key

6 fff vvv fvf fvf vow fvf van fvf vat fvf vet fvfvf;
7 fvf eve fvf vie fvf via fvf very fvf give fvf live

D   Practise word families

8 tup cup pup sup lop pop fop hop cop top tops mops;
9 live jive hive dive give rave pave save wave gave;

E   Homophones   *Use your dictionary to check the meaning*

10 canvas canvass; reviews revues; patients patience;
11 principle principal; presents presence; site sight

F   Apply the keys you know

Goal—9 words in half a minute   17 words in one minute

12 She moved a pink jug away from the very back shelf   10

    where it had been hidden from sight. It now shows   20

    up better on that top shelf. **(SI 1.15)**   26

    1 | 2 | 3 | 4 | 5 | 6 | 7 | 8 | 9 | 10 |

UNIT 15   Measure your speed—17 wpm
Keys: P and V

23

Semi-blocked letters with attention line, enclosure and subject heading

The **attention line** and **enclosure** are typed in the same style and position as in fully-blocked letters (see pages 59–60).

Turn up two single spaces after the salutation and centre the subject heading over the body of the letter. To do this:

(a) Add together the points at which the left and right margins are set and divide by two.

(b) Bring the printing point to the scale point found when you divided by two and back-space once for every two characters and spaces in the subject heading.

(c) Type heading.

(d) Turn up two single spaces before starting the body of the letter.

2 Type the following letter from Eastways Developments (UK) Ltd (use A4 letterhead paper) in semi-blocked style, taking a carbon copy. (a) Use full punctuation. (b) Margins: 12 pitch 22–82, 10 pitch 12–72.

Our Ref RLJ/RJ   9th September, 1988

Your Ref LAB/PAC

NOTE: A comma may be inserted after the month

FOR THE ATTENTION OF MS. H. W. HOGAN

F. K. Gilbertson & Co. Ltd.,
38 Westoe Road,
SOUTH SHIELDS,
Tyne and Wear.
NE33 1AA

Dear Sirs,

DAMAGED GOODS

Further to our telephone conversation of this morning, the Three-in-one Electronic Inflator was returned to you by parcel post on 4 August, 1988, as it was found to be damaged when it was delivered to our warehouse.

NOTE: To be consistent, insert comma after month

As you say you have received the Inflator but cannot trace your having invoiced us for this item, we enclose a copy of your invoice No 23489/88.

Rather than send us a credit note, please let us have a replacement for the damaged Inflator.

Yours faithfully,

R. L. JAKEMAN

Enc.

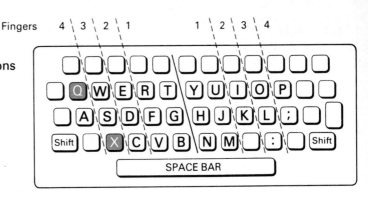

Fingers 4 3 2 1   1 2 3 4

Follow **Prepare to Type** on page 6 and instructions given at top of page 9.

Margins: 12 pitch 25, 10 pitch 18.
Spacing: single, with double between exercises.

A Review the keys you know

1 ;p; fvf ftf jhj dpf apf kpf pot van cop map eve p;
2 Jack was glad my family all moved to North Avenue.
3 Daniel may have to give back a few paper journals.

Fingers curved

B Practise **X** key—S finger

4 sss xxx sxs sxs tax sxs lax sxs pax sxs wax sxsxs;
5 sxs sex sxs hex sxs vex sxs rex sxs cox sxs vox sx

Practise S to X back to S. Keep first finger on home key

C Practise **Q** key—A finger

6 aaa qqq aqa aqa quad aqa aqua aqa equal aqa quick;
7 aqa quin aqa quit aqa quite aqa equal aqa query qa

Practise A to Q back to A. Keep first finger on home key

D Practise word families

8 qua quad squad quit quip quins quill quint quilts;
9 fox cox mix fix nix axe lax pax wax tax taxi taxed

E Homophones *Use your dictionary to check the meaning*

10 accede exceed; accept except; access excess; stake
11 steak; checks cheques; choir quire; coarse course;

F Apply the keys you know

Goal—9 words in half a minute   17 words in one minute

12 Joe quickly moved the gross of new boxes for which   10
   you had paid and then took an extra box of the red   20
   quilts and sheets you wanted. **(SI 1.15)**   26

   1 | 2 | 3 | 4 | 5 | 6 | 7 | 8 | 9 | 10 |

UNIT 16 Measure your speed—17 wpm
Keys: X and Q

24

Semi-blocked letters

The following points should be noted when typing semi-blocked letters

(a) *Date*: This ends flush with the right margin. To find the starting point, backspace from right margin once for each character and space in the date.

(b) *Reference*: Type at left margin on same line as the date.

(c) *Body of letter*: The first word of each paragraph is indented five spaces from the left margin. Tap in and set tab stop for paragraph indent.

(d) *Complimentary close*: Start this approximately at the centre of the typing line.

(e) *Signature*: As in fully-blocked letters, turn up a minimum of five single spaces to leave room for signature. Type name of person signing, starting at the same scale point as the complimentary close.

(f) *Designation*: Begin to type official designation (if any) at the same scale point as complimentary close, ie, immediately below the name of person signing.

(g) *Punctuation*: Semi-blocked letters may be typed with open or full punctuation.

1 Type the following semi-blocked letter from Eastways Developments (UK) Ltd, on headed A5 portrait paper. (a) Margins: 12 pitch 15–60, 10 pitch 10–55. (b) Use open punctuation.

```
Our ref AK/HS                    6 September 1988

Miss W M Burgess
19 Trafalgar Street
TRURO
Cornwall
TR1 2DN

Dear Miss Burgess

        You have been a valued customer for a
number of years, and we hope you will find
time to study the catalogue sent to you
last week.

        We are offering a superb range of fur-
nishings and kitchen co-ordinates in our
sale and there are also bargains in ready-
assembled units and microwaves.

        May we look forward to being of service
to you?

                Yours sincerely




                Amir Khan
                Sales Manager
```

Set tab stop for paragraph indents at 20(15)

Start approximately at the centre of the typing line

See Practical Typing Exercises, Book One, page 57, for further exercises on

Follow **Prepare to Type** on page 6 and instructions given at top of page 9.

Margins: 12 pitch 25, 10 pitch 18.
Spacing: single, with double between exercises.

A   Review the keys you know

1 axs aqa fxf fcf axs xaj sex vex tax quit aqua quad
2 Just have one box of new grey mats packed quickly.
3 With extra help Clive found many quite black jugs.

B   Practise **Z** *key—A finger*

Practise A to Z back to A. Keep first finger on home key

4 aaa zzz aza aza zoo aza zinc aza zeal aza azure za
5 aza zip aza zero aza size aza gaze aza jazz aza za

C   Practise **,** *key—K finger*

Practise K to , back to K. Keep little finger on home key

6 kkk ,,, k,k k,k l,k a,k s,k j,k d,k f,k hj,k g,f,k
One space after comma

7 at, it, is, or, if, one, can, yes, may, for, cross

D   Practise word families

8 daze haze gaze laze maze, lazy hazy crazy, puzzle.
9 zeal zero zest zone, size prize, buzz fuzz, azure.

E   Homophones   *Use your dictionary to check the meaning*

10 affect effect; style stile; deference difference;
11 born borne; complement compliment; miners minors;

F   Apply the keys you know

Goal—9 words in half a minute   18 words in one minute

12 We do hope the right size is in stock; yes, it is;   10

Feet apart, firmly on floor

    we have just a few boxes, but the colour, although   20

    quite pretty, is not the same. **(SI 1.15)**   26

    1 | 2 | 3 | 4 | 5 | 6 | 7 | 8 | 9 | 10 |

Follow instructions given at the top of page 42. Margins: 12 pitch 22–82, 10 pitch 12–72. Single spacing, with double between exercises.

A Review alphabet keys

1   We saw the five models at the waxworks, which were just amazing, as the exact resemblances to folks in the past were quite remarkable.

B Language arts—agreement of subject and verb (See explanation on page 182)

2 A new set of wheels and axles <u>has</u> been fitted to my old van.
3 My friend and neighbour <u>has</u> moved to 4 High Street, Falkirk.
4 Neither of the golfers <u>was</u> prepared to play in the new year.

Skill measurement 30 wpm   5 minutes   Not more than 5 errors

SM40   Have you ever 'met' a person for the first time over   10
the telephone? How did you know what kind of person she/he   22
was? By the voice, of course! Was it gruff or pleasant,   34
calm or excited? How do you appear over the telephone? You   46
cannot be seen, only heard, and your voice will convey your   57
personality.   59

      You should speak clearly and distinctly, and be tactful   70
and logical in expressing your thoughts. The good telephon-   82
ist will handle all telephone calls courteously and intelli-   94
gently by speaking in a well-modulated voice, enunciating   105
distinctly, choosing words that convey her thoughts clearly,   117
and expressing through her tone sincere interest in the per-   129
son calling. How well you represent your employer on the   140
telephone will depend on your telephone technique. **(SI 1.45)** 150

   1 | 2 | 3 | 4 | 5 | 6 | 7 | 8 | 9 | 10 | 11 | 12 |

Record your progress 5 minutes

R31   A low, well-controlled voice carries better and is more   11
pleasant to listen to than one pitched high. Your voice   22
should not be raised above normal; if anything, talk in a   34
lower tone than you are accustomed to use in speaking.   45

      One of the great advantages of using the telephone is   55
the saving of time. This advantage is lost unless your con-   67
versation is to the point and concise. Avoid sounding curt,   79
and avoid using jargon or slang expressions such as 'O.K.',   91
'Yeah', etc. If you are cut-off during a call initiated by   103
you, it is your place to ring again. This accepted proced-   115
ure ensures that both parties are not simultaneously ringing   127
each other and finding the lines engaged.   134

      To save time, list frequently used numbers in an alpha-   145
betic index which should be kept up to date. When a client   157
notifies you of a change of address and/or telephone number   169
amend your records immediately. Also, to save time, use a   181
standardized form for taking messages. **(SI 1.40)**   189

   1 | 2 | 3 | 4 | 5 | 6 | 7 | 8 | 9 | 10 | 11 | 12 |

Improvement practice

Follow **Prepare to Type** on page 6 and instructions given at top of page 9.
Margins: 12 pitch 25, 10 pitch 18. Spacing: single, with double between exercises.

A Improve control of carriage/carrier return

1 Type the following lines exactly as shown.
Repeat the exercise and see if you can type it in one minute

```
It was good
It was good to see
It was good to see you
It was good to see you today
```

Return carriage/car-rier without looking up

B Improve control of B and M keys

```
2  mob bump brim Mabel blame bloom climb bombs became
3  Blame Mabel.   The mob climbed in through a window.
4  My rose bloom became well known.   I bumped my car.
```

Leave 2 spaces after at end of sentence

C Improve control of punctuation

```
5  I shall tell Wilfred.   No, he may be rather angry.
6  We are pleased to hear from you; but we cannot go.
7  John, Mary and Elsie are going.   You may come too.
```

ONE space after ; and ,

D Improve control of C and Y keys

```
8  cry city clay copy cozy carry yacht comply certify
9  We certify that this is a correct copy made today.
10 Cathy must comply with the order.   The yacht left.
```

E Improve control of space bar

```
11 at it up on to we an be go of so am by do as no he
12 Go to her.   It is up to us.   I am here.   Tell him.
13 If you go to the shop now, he will still be there.
```

Use right thumb and even strokes

Indented paragraph headings

See guide given on page 49 for paragraph headings. The paragraphs may be indented and the headings typed in either of the forms given on page 49. A full stop may be typed after the paragraph heading, two spaces being left after the full stop.

2 Type the following on A5 landscape paper. (a) Single spacing, with double between paragraphs. (b) Indented paragraphs. (c) Underline the paragraph headings and type a full stop after each, as shown. (d) Margins: 12 pitch 13–90, 10 pitch 11–77. (e) Make your own line-endings. (f) Centre the main heading.

VISITING HONG KONG

Indent ——→ <u>Identity.</u> Hong Kong law requires a resident to carry an identity card. Visitors should carry some means of identification such as a passport.

<u>Airport Tax.</u> You have to pay 120 Hong Kong dollars when checking in at the airport.

<u>Police.</u> A red flash indicates that (s)he is proficient in English. The patrolling police are always very willing to help.

Shoulder headings

See guide given on page 50 for shoulder headings. The paragraphs that follow the shoulder headings may be indented.

3 Type the following exercise on A4 paper. (a) Double spacing. (b) Indented paragraphs. (c) Suitable margins. (d) Centre the main heading. (e) Type the shoulder headings at the left margin in capitals.

TRAVELLERS' NOTES

EXCURSIONS

The visit to China offers excellent value in th. the majority of excursions are included in the tour price. The excursions described are representative of the type of programme in ea. city.

ACCOMMODATION

You will not know the name of yr hotel until you arrive in ea. city

The accommodation is based on twin-sharing, first-class rooms. International bookings may be made & sharing wl be arranged by yr. tour escort.

TRAINS

Overnight accommodation in the train wl be in soft-class, 4-berth sleeping compartments.

VISAS & PASSPORTS

Every person shd. be in possession of a valid passport. Entry & exit visas are required.

F Improve control of [P] and [V] keys

14 pave prove vapour provide private prevent provoked
15 I will provide a private plane. We will prove it.
16 Prevent Peter from provoking Val and Victor Payne.

G Improve control of shift keys

17 Sal Joe Fay Ida Roy Lee Don Gay Bob Your Mary Hall
18 Tell Joe, Fay, Lee and Marie to call on Roy Young.
19 Edna Kelly and Nan Peters will visit Olive Walker.

Hold shift key well down with little finger

H Improve control of [Q] and [X] keys

20 mix tax vex exit next taxi; quay quiz quite quiet;
21 A taxi will be at the quay exit; expect him there.
22 Keep quite quiet in that queue for this next quiz.

I Improve control of phrases

23 to go, to ask, to see, to pay, to hear, to let him
24 I am pleased to hear that you are going to see me.
25 Remember to go and to ask her to pay for the flat.

J Improve control of [Z] and [;] keys

26 zip, size, lazy, zeal, zone, prize, dozen, amazed,
27 I was amazed, quite amazed, to see a dozen prizes.
28 We gazed at the zebra, also a gazelle, in the zoo.

K Apply the keys you know

Goal—9 words in half a minute   18 words in one minute

29 The whizzing of a jet plane across the sky had now   10

  become such a normal event that it won but a quick   20

  glance from the young boys in the crowd. (SI 1.14)   28

    1 | 2 | 3 | 4 | 5 | 6 | 7 | 8 | 9 | 10 |

Headings centred in the typing line

To centre headings in the typing line, find the centre point of the line by adding the two margins together and dividing by two. Then backspace from this point, one space for every two characters and spaces in the heading.

Examples: Margins set at 12 pitch 22–82   22+82=104÷2=52 (centre point)
                          10 pitch 12–72   12+72=84 ÷2=42 (centre point)
                          12 pitch 13–63   13+63=76*÷2=38 (centre point)

* When dividing by two, ignore any fractions.

Main headings centred

See guide given on page 48 for main headings. Centred headings may be used with indented or blocked paragraphs. The heading is centred in the typing line.

Subheadings centred

See guide given on page 48 for subheadings. If the main heading is centred, it is usual to centre the subheading in the typing line.

Enumerated items—Roman numerals blocked to the right

See information given on pages 99 and 124 about enumerated items. As well as being blocked to the left, roman numerals may be blocked to the right with or without full stops. Full stops are never used with brackets. There are two spaces after the full stop, bracket and after the figure without a full stop. With open punctuation, there is no full stop after an enumeration. As indented paragraphs are used in the exercise below, the roman numeral with the most characters **iii** starts at the indent, which means that from the indent there are two spaces before the **i**, one space before the **ii**.

1   Type the following exercise on A4 paper in double spacing. (a) Margins: 12 pitch 18–88, 10 pitch 15–75. (b) Indented paragraphs (turn up two singles only between paragraphs). (c) Centre the main heading and subheading in the typing line. (d) Make your own line-endings.

CHINA'S INTERNATIONAL TRAVEL SERVICE

Beijing Branch

Beijing is the capital of the People's Republic of China and is renowned for its quaint customs and numerous historical sights. It is situated at the northwest edge of the great North China Plain, and was first built to guard the fertile plains of northern China against marauding tribes 3 thousand years ago.

The Chinese International Travel Service (CITS) was founded in 1958 and has contributed a great deal to the understanding and friendship between the Chinese and people all the world over.

The Beijing Branch will handle

   i   individual or family package tours

  ii   group package tours

iii   hotel reservations for individuals and groups.

The Branch employs 500 well-trained travel guides who speak 12 different languages.

Open punctuation

Many businesses and most examining bodies prefer this style for business documents. It means that the full stop is omitted from an abbreviated word (except at the end of a sentence) and is replaced by a space. Example: Mr (space) J (space) Smith, of W M Smith & Co Ltd, will discuss the terms of payment, etc, with Mrs U E St John-Browne.

Where an abbreviation consists of two or more letters with a full stop after each letter, the full stops are omitted and no space is left between the letters, but one space (or comma) after each group of letters. Example: Mrs G L Hunt, 21 South Road, will call at 7 pm today. She requires past examination papers from several bodies, eg, LCCI, RSA and UEI.

Grammatical punctuation must still be used.

The major part of this book is written in open punctuation, ie, no full stops are given in or after abbreviations.

Improve your typing technique

If a technique is faulty, check with the following list and carry out the remedial drill.

Faulty technique   *Remedy*
Manual machines

Faulty technique	Example	Remedy
Raised capitals caused by releasing shift key too soon.	I˚ may go.	Drills 4–9 page 16; drills 4–9, page 17.
Uneven left margin, caused by faulty carriage return.	I may go.	Return carriage without looking up. Any 'Apply the keys you know'.
Heavy strokes, caused by not releasing keys quickly.	I **ma**y go.	Practise finger movement drills. Any 'Apply the keys you know'.
Light strokes, caused by not striking the keys hard enough.	I may go.	Practise finger movement drills. Any 'Apply the keys you know'.

Manual, electric, and electronic machines

Faulty technique	Example	Remedy
Omitting or inserting words (looked up from the copy).	may I go	Eyes on copy always. Page 25—lines 1, 2 and 3 backwards.
Extra spaces, caused by your leaning on the space bar.	I may go.	Right thumb slightly above space bar. Drills 5–7, page 14.
Omitting spaces, caused by poor wrist position.	I maygo.	Say 'space' to yourself each time you tap space bar. Drills 5, 6 and 7, page 14. Drills 26, 27 and 28, page 20.
Fingers out of position.	I ,au go.	Return fingers to home keys. Any 'Apply the keys you know'.
Turning letters around—eyes get ahead of fingers.	I may og.	Eyes on copy always. Say each letter and space to yourself as you type. Any preceding drills.
Extra or wrong characters caused by accidentally depressing keys.	KKK may go.	Keep all fingers slightly above home keys—especially with electronics.

Skill measurement

Practice routine for all skill measurement exercises:

1 Type a copy of the exercise.
2 Check and circle all errors.
3 Compare your errors with those shown above.
4 Practise the remedial drills.
5 Type as much of the exercise as you can in the time suggested.
6 Check and circle any errors.

7 On your Skill measurement table record actual number of words typed in a minute and number of errors, if any.
8 If you made more than the stipulated number of errors, continue with the timed practice and aim for accuracy.
9 If your errors were below the tolerance given, type the exercise again (timed) and endeavour to type a little faster.

Set left margin at 12 pitch 25, 10 pitch 18

Skill measurement   *19 wpm*   *One minute*   *Not more than one error*

SM1 As those shoes are too small, you should take them   10

back and have them changed for the right size. **(SI 1.00)**   19

1 | 2 | 3 | 4 | 5 | 6 | 7 | 8 | 9 | 10 |

Follow instructions given at top of page 42. Margins: 12 pitch 22–82, 10 pitch 12–72. Single spacing, with double between exercises.

A Review alphabet keys *(Indent first line)*

1   The quiz was ranked as being very difficult requiring a great deal of thought and adjustment on the part of the contestants, who were of mixed ability.

B Language arts—agreement of subject and verb *(See explanation on page 182)*

2   The works is to be closed from 1800 hours on 23 August 1986.
3   A pair of shoes is missing from the stockroom in the office.
4   The committee is to prepare its final report by 14 December.

Skill measurement *30 wpm   5 minutes   Not more than 5 errors*
(Use indented paragraphs for Skill measurement and Record your progress)

SM39   Input is the data prepared by the author and entered   10
into the system by means of the keyboard. The input may be   21
in the form of typed or handwritten drafts, or shorthand/   33
audio dictation. Whatever kind of input you work from, pre-   45
paring correspondence and reports will be your task. You   56
must use: the correct paper for the printout - letterhead,   68
memo, plain bond, and, of course, bank paper for the carbon   80
copies; the preferred house style; accurate spelling, gram-   92
mar, and punctuation. You must proofread thoroughly, making   103
any corrections on the soft copy before printout.   113

        You should follow instructions precisely, use your time   124
wisely, apply common sense and initiative, and type mailable   136
copy, within a given time, ready for approval, signing and/   148
or comment. **(SI 1.48)**   150

  1 | 2 | 3 | 4 | 5 | 6 | 7 | 8 | 9 | 10 | 11 | 12 |

Record your progress *5 minutes*

R30   Any document which is not 'mailable' is not acceptable.   11
By mailable copy we mean: the contents must make sense; no   23
omissions; no uncorrected errors (misspellings, incorrect   34
punctuation, typing errors, etc); no careless corrections   46
(if part of the wrong letter(s) is showing, the correction   57
is not acceptable); no smudges; no creases.   65

        With your VDU screen it is fairly easy to text edit a   76
document that has been amended by the author. The data is   88
retrieved from the file and displayed on the screen. The   99
backspace-strikeover method is normally used to correct typ-   111
ing errors and, with the use of the function keys, text-   123
editing techniques are used to change information in the   134
text. If the text on the VDU looks hazy, you should clean   146
the screen or adjust the luminous intensity.   155

        While corrections and amendments are easily made on   165
the VDU screen, these changes may take up a lot of time   176
which could better be spent on other work. Try to produce a   188
correct copy on the first printout. **(SI 1.43)**   195

  1 | 2 | 3 | 4 | 5 | 6 | 7 | 8 | 9 | 10 | 11 | 12 |

Each line or sentence in the lettered exercises should be typed three times and, if time permits, type each complete exercise once. For **Skill measurement** follow instructions on page 28, and for **Record your progress** follow instructions on page 30. Single spacing, with double between exercises. Left margin: 12 pitch 25, 10 pitch 18.

A Review alphabet keys

1 Five excellent school prizes were awarded and Jamy
   qualified for the best work in his group.

B Practise  (hyphen) key—; finger

2 ;-; ;-; p-; p-;-; blue-grey, one-fifth, part-time,
3 Over one-third are part-time day-release students.
4 Her father-in-law asked for all-wool yellow socks.

Position of hyphen varies on different machines. Find it on your machine and practise drills

No space before or after hyphen

C Practise [?] key—; finger

5 Now? When? Where? May she? Must we? Will you?
6 Who said so? What is the time? Is it late? Why?

Position of ? varies on different machines. Find it on your machine and practise drills

Leave 2 spaces after ? at end of a sentence

D Practise [:] (colon) key—; finger

7 ;;; ::: ;;; a:; l:; s:; k:; d:; j:; f:; hj:; gf:;a
8 Delivery Period: One month. Prices: Net ex Works.

Depress left shift key .
One space after colon

E Homophones   *Use your dictionary to check the meaning*

9   board bored; sight cite; chute shoot; birth berth;
10 recover re-cover; hair hare; key quay; peace piece

Skill measurement   20 wpm   One minute   Not more than one error

SM2 If you are good at figures, and are keen to have a   10
     job in our firm, we should like you to call on us.   20
                                            (SI 1.05)

SM3 I wish that you could have been with us on Tuesday   10
     to see the new office machines which were on view.   20
                                            (SI 1.15)

     1 | 2 | 3 | 4 | 5 | 6 | 7 | 8 | 9 | 10 |

Horizontal centring—All lines centred

Follow the points give for horizontal centring on page 44, but do not set a left margin, and centre each line, not just the longest one. For this purpose set a tab stop at the horizontal centre point of the paper and backspace one space for every two characters and spaces as before.

Vertical centring

To centre the matter vertically on a sheet of paper, follow the points (a) to (f) as given on page 45.

6   Type the following notice on A5 landscape paper. Set a tab stop at the horizontal centre point of the page, eg, 12 pitch 50, 10 pitch 41, and centre each line horizontally and the whole notice vertically.

WEYMOUTH - LODMOOR COUNTRY PARK

2 clear spaces

Children's Playground and Games

Beach Barbecue

New Self-service Restaurant and Gift Shop

LANDSCAPED PICNIC AREAS

2 clear spaces

A splendid family outing with lots to do

7   Type the following notice on A5 portrait paper. Set a tab stop at the horizontal centre point, eg, 12 pitch 35, 10 pitch 29, and centre each line horizontally and the whole notice vertically.

T H E   A L P I N E   H O T E L

CONFERENCE MENU

22 November 1988

2 clear spaces

Chilled Honeydew Melon

York Ham
Roast Norfolk Turkey
Roast Rib of Beef
Roast Chicken

Selection of Vegetables and Potatoes

Fresh Fruit Salad and Cream
Fresh Cream Gâteau

Coffee

These drills have been specially prepared for corrective practice on keystroking errors made when typing the **Record your progress** exercises. For further information about the drills, read the information below and the introduction to **Personalized remedial drills** on page 173.

Record your progress exercises

In the fifth edition of *Typing First Course*, each **Record your progress** exercise will contain *all the letters* of the alphabet.

Instructions for all **Record your progress** exercises:

(a) Type the exercise *once* as practice.
(b) Check and circle any error.
(c) Record the individual letter errors on your **Personalized remedial drill sheet** — see *Handbook and Solutions Manual* for a copy.
(d) Turn to the **Individual letter drills** on pages 173–177 and type (at least once) the appropriate words and sentences for each letter on which you made a mistake.

   NOTE: If you made no errors, turn to the **Individual letter drills** and type the words and sentences for any letters that cause you difficulty.

(e) Return to the **Record your progress** exercise and type as much of the passage as you can in the time allotted.
(f) Record the number of words typed and the number of errors (if any) in the second typing, on your **Record your progress chart** — see *Handbook and Solutions Manual* for a copy.

   NOTE: Over a period of time you will see from the **Personalized remedial drill sheet** which finger reaches initially caused difficulties and have now been mastered, and which reaches still require concentrated practice.

Record your progress   *One minute*

```
R1   I know you will be pleased to hear that Zola Coles      10

     joined this firm on a part-time basis.  Chris said      20

     I must give her a quick test next week.  (SI 1.08)      28

         1  |  2  |  3  |  4  |  5  |  6  |  7  |  8  |  9  |  10  |
```

4 Type the following exercise on A4 paper. (a) Margins: 12 pitch 22–82, 10 pitch 12–72. (b) Although the exercise is set out in single spacing, please type it in double spacing. (c) Make your own line-endings. (d) Open punctuation. (e) Indented paragraphs. (f) Note the use of abbreviations.

```
TYPING MEASUREMENTS

     When typing measurements, always use the small 'x' for the
multiply sign, and leave one space either side of the 'x', eg,
20½ (space) ft (space) x (space) 10¼ (space) ft = 20½ ft x 10¼ ft.
The same spacing is necessary when using metric measurements, eg,
1 m = 100 cm; 1 m = 1000 mm; 1 m x 1000 = 1 km.

     You can also use the sign for feet and inches, eg, 9 ft
10 5/16 in x 15 ft 9 7/12 in = 9' 10 5/16" x 15' 9 7/12".  You
will see that, when using the signs, there is no space between
the figure and the sign, but there is one space after the sign.

     Do not add 's' to the plural of ft, in, lb, m, kg, etc.  In
imperial measurements a full stop is used after an abbreviation
when using full punctuation, but in metric measurements full
stops are never used after symbols even with full punctuation,
except at the end of a sentence, eg, 210 mm x 197 mm.
```

Note the use of apostrophe for feet and double quotation marks for inches

5 Type the following exercise on A4 paper. (a) Margins: 12 pitch 22–82, 10 pitch 12–72. (b) Double spacing. (c) Full punctuation. (d) Blocked paragraphs.

TYPEWRITING THEORY

As a typist in a business, or in a typewriting exam, you wl be expected to remember & apply certain points of theory. [When writing to individuals, a courtesy title is essential.]

If you do not know whether a lady is Mrs. or Miss, type Ms. A man shd be addressed as Mr. or Esq., never both. If you use the courtesy Dr. or Rev., do not use (title) Mr. or Esq.

(Leave a space of at least 1½" wide here)

(single spacing)

It is normal practice to hv the left margin slightly wider than the right—except in display & tabulation work—& when using A4 paper have a left margin of not less than 1 inch (25 mm) and a right margin of about half an inch (13 mm).

[If a name & address appear in one line in a heading or in 'run on' text & you are typing in open punctuation, it shd be typed w. 2 clear spaces (or commas as in full punctuation) btwn ea. item e.g., Mr. J. Cornforth, 2 North Road, Bury, BL8 2BG.

UNIT 53 See Practical Typing Exercises, Book One, page 52, for further exercises on Paragraphing—Blocked, indented and hanging

153

Each line or sentence in the lettered exercises should be typed three times and, if time permits, type each complete exercise once. For **Skill measurement** follow instructions on page 28, and for **Record your progress** follow instructions on page 30. Single spacing, with double between exercises. Left margin: 12 pitch 25, 10 pitch 18.

A   Review alphabet keys

1 The taxi ranks were busy because of a sizeable jam

   which caused very long queues of cars up the hill.

Shift-lock key

When you need to type several capital letters one after the other, the shift lock must be used. When it is depressed, the shift key remains engaged until the lock is released, and you will be able to type capitals without using the shift key. The following steps should be practised:

(a) Depress shift lock, using 'A' finger of left hand.
(b) Type capital letters.
(c) Depress left-hand shift key to release shift lock.

B   Practise shift-lock key

2 BEFORE lunch please ring me in LUDLOW next MONDAY.

3 MEETINGS held in LONDON, LIVERPOOL and MANCHESTER.

4 Both LAURA and KATHLEEN were present at the party.

Skill measurement   21 wpm   One minute   Not more than one error

SM4 We trust that the hints we gave for the removal of   10

     stains will be found to be of great help to all of   20

     you.   **(SI 1.09)**   21

       1 | 2 | 3 | 4 | 5 | 6 | 7 | 8 | 9 | 10 |

Record your progress   One minute

R2 At what time does the Zurich bus arrive? You must   10

    equip yourself with: extra shoes, raincoats, brown   20

    socks, a warm jumper, a large torch, and the maps.   30
                                              (SI 1.23)

       1 | 2 | 3 | 4 | 5 | 6 | 7 | 8 | 9 | 10 |

Paragraphing

Paragraphs are used to separate the different subjects or sections. This breaks the writing into short passages to facilitate reading and understanding. There are three different forms of paragraphing, viz, indented, hanging and blocked.

Indented paragraphs

When using indented paragraphs, the first line of each paragraph is indented five spaces from the left margin. This indentation is made by setting a tab stop five spaces to the right of the point fixed for the left margin. When using indented paragraphs, two single or one double is turned up between paragraphs, whether typing in single or double spacing.

1   Type the following on A5 landscape paper. (a) Margins: 22–82, 12–72. (b) Single spacing, with double between each paragraph. (c) Set a tab stop at 27 (17) for the paragraph indentation.

> ──→Your employer, and certain examining bodies, may ask
> you to use indented paragraphs. This means that, before you
> start typing, you must set a tab stop 5 spaces to the right
> of your left margin.

Return carriage
twice on single

> ──→Each time you start a new paragraph you should use the
> tab bar or key to move to the beginning of the first line.

 Some word processors and software for computers have pre-set tab stops so that you do not have to set a tab for a standard paragraph indent.

Hanging paragraphs

When using hanging paragraphs, the second and subsequent lines of each paragraph start two spaces to the right of the first line. This type of paragraph is often used in display work to draw attention to particular points.

2   Type the following exercise on A5 landscape paper. (a) Margins: 22–82, 12–72. (b) Single spacing, with double between each paragraph. (c) Hanging paragraphs as shown.

> If your hanging paragraph is long, you may wish to set a tab
> Indent ──→stop for the start of the first line and set your left
> margin for the beginning of the indented lines.

> When you start a new paragraph, you should then use the mar-
> gin release key to move out to the tab stop. This will
> Indent ──→ensure that you do not forget that the second and subse-
> quent lines are indented.

Blocked paragraphs

3   Type the following on A5 landscape paper. (a) Margins: Left 51 mm (2 inches), right 38 mm (1½ inches). (b) Make your own line-endings. (c) Single spacing, with double between paragraphs. (d) Block each paragraph at the left margin.

> As you have already learnt, in blocked paragraphs all lines start at the
> same scale-point.

> When single spacing is used, as in this exercise, you turn up 2 single
> spaces between the paragraphs.

> However, when double spacing is used, you should turn up 2 double spaces
> between each paragraph.

Each line or sentence in the lettered exercises should be typed three times and, if time permits, type each complete exercise once. For **Skill measurement** follow instructions on page 28, and for **Record your progress** follow instructions on page 30. Single spacing, with double between exercises. Left margin: 12 pitch 25, 10 pitch 18.

A Review alphabet keys

1 You will of course realize it is very important to

   acquire excellent skills; you may well be rejected

   for a post yet again.

B Practise ▬ (*dash key*)—*; finger*

2 ; - ; ; - ; Call today - no, tomorrow - after tea.
3 The book - it was his first - was a great success.
4 It is their choice - we are sure it will be yours.

— key
Practise ; to —
back to ;. Keep
first finger over
home key

ONE space *before*
and *after* dash

Upper and lower case characters

Characters requiring use of shift key are called UPPER CASE characters. Characters not requiring use of shift key are called LOWER CASE characters.

C Homophones *Use your dictionary to check the meaning*

5 ascent assent; carat caret carrot; incite insight;

6 dependent dependant; incidence incident; rap wrap;

Skill measurement *22 wpm One minute Not more than one error*

SM5 We want a first-class employee: one who has a good 10

     knowledge of accounts. She must be able to manage 20

     a section. **(SI 1.32)** 22

     1 | 2 | 3 | 4 | 5 | 6 | 7 | 8 | 9 | 10 |

Record your progress *One minute*

R3 No charge will be made for any extra copies of the 10

    GAZETTE: but their account must be paid at the end 20

    of the quarter. Will this suit Kate? James would 30

    like to have your reply. **(SI 1.20)** 35

    1 | 2 | 3 | 4 | 5 | 6 | 7 | 8 | 9 | 10 |

SKILL BUILDING

Follow instructions given at top of page 42. Margins: 12 pitch 22–82, 10 pitch 12–72. Single spacing, with double between exercises.

A Review alphabet keys

1 I saw the grey squirrel relax by the very old trees and then jump with zest from one piece of bark to another.

B Language arts—agreement of subject and verb (See explanation on page 182)

2 Neither the lecturer nor the students <u>are</u> going to the park.
3 The typists, as well as the manager, <u>are</u> attending the game.
4 None of the travellers <u>is</u> willing to pay for the extra trip.
5 One of Ms Mitten's cars <u>is</u> not in use because it is damaged.

Skill measurement 30 wpm 5 minutes Not more than 5 errors

SM38

When you apply for your first post, how should you look? Is	12
the prospective employer going to say to himself, "This per-	24
son is smart looking and I will be pleased to introduce her	36
to the office staff." Or will he feel that your clothes are	48
"way out", your hair is too startling and unkempt, and your	60
finger nails look dirty. Make certain that your appearance	72
is suitable for the job you are seeking, and forget about it	84
until after the interview.	89
At an interview you will be required to answer and ask ques-	101
tions. The interviewer will have your application form and	113
will perhaps ask you questions that you have answered on	124
paper; however, he wishes to have the information repeated	136
orally. When answering questions, speak clearly and do not	147
bite your words. **(SI 1.37)**	150

  1 | 2 | 3 | 4 | 5 | 6 | 7 | 8 | 9 | 10 | 11 | 12 |

Record your progress 5 minutes

R29

The interviewer will give you details about the business and	12
he will give you a chance to ask questions, so see that you	24
have one or 2 points in mind. You will certainly want to	35
know, for example, starting and finishing times, holidays,	47
salary, lunch breaks, etc.	52
The interviewer will usually indicate when the interview is	64
at an end. Say "thank you" and leave the room without undue	76
haste, and do not forget to take all your belongings with	88
you - it can be embarrassing if you have to return for an	99
item. On the way out, remember to thank the receptionist.	111
On the evening of the same day in which you had your inter-	123
view, write a short thank you note to the person who saw	135
you. This follow-up technique is important because it will	146
show that you have an interest in the prospects of working	157
for the organization. All persons present at an interview	169
are usually nervous. There is no reason to be frightened,	180
just treat the interviewer with respect. **(SI 1.39)**	188

  1 | 2 | 3 | 4 | 5 | 6 | 7 | 8 | 9 | 10 | 11 | 12 |

Each line or sentence in the lettered exercises should be typed three times and, if time permits, type each complete exercise once. For **Skill measurement** follow instructions on page 28, and for **Record your progress** follow instructions on page 30. Single spacing, with double between exercises. Left margin: 12 pitch 25, 10 pitch 18.

A Review alphabet keys

1 The freezer was stocked with pork, bread, six game
   and veal pies, and some quince jelly.

B Practise key—use A finger

(NOTE: If your typewriter does not have a figure 1 key, use small 'L'.)

2 We require 11 pairs size 11; also 11 pairs size 1.
3 Add up 11 plus 11 plus 11 plus 11 plus 11 plus 11.
4 On 11 August 11 girls and 11 boys hope to join us.
5 After 11 years, 11 of them will leave on 11 March.

C Practise  key—use S finger

6 sw2s sw2s s2ws s2ws s2s2s s2s2s s2sws s2sws 2s2ws.
7 22 sips 22 seas 22 skis 22 sons 22 spas 22 sets 2.
8 We need 2 grey, 2 blue, 2 red, and 22 orange ties.
9 The 12 girls and 12 boys won 122 games out of 212.

D Practise key—use D finger

10 de3d de3d d3ed d3ed d3d3d d3d3d d3ded d3ded 3d3ed.
11 33 dots 33 dips 33 dogs 33 dads 33 dyes 33 duds 3.
12 Send 313 only to 33 Green Road and to 3 West Road.
13 Type the numbers: 3, 2, 1, 11, 12, 13, 32, 31, 23.

Skill measurement   23 wpm   *One minute*   *Not more than one error*

SM6 If you feel some day that you would like a trip in   10
     the country, perhaps you could drive out to a farm   20
     to pick fruit. **(SI 1.09)**   23

SM7 Do you wish to take a holiday? Now is the time to   10
     take one of our out-of-season vacations. Send for   20
     our brochure. **(SI 1.26)**   23

     1 | 2 | 3 | 4 | 5 | 6 | 7 | 8 | 9 | 10 |

Record your progress   *One minute*

R4 The gavels which Liz Max saw last July are now out   10
    of stock, and we would not be able to replace them   20
    for some weeks - perhaps a month - when we hope to   30
    receive a further quota. **(SI 1.23)**   35

    1 | 2 | 3 | 4 | 5 | 6 | 7 | 8 | 9 | 10 |

TYPIST — Please re-type correcting the circled words + typing any abbreviations in full.

CONDITIONS OF ADMISSION

(ATTTENDANCE)   Students are expected to be in (there) classes 5 (minutes') before the scheduled starting time. Regular attendance is required if satisfactory results are to be obtained.

(STUDENTS) PROPERTY   The College cannot accept responsibility for (personnal) property. It is (advisible) not to bring items of value to the College.

FEES   The award of a place at the College is on the understanding that the full course wl be completed, & therefore the payment of the fee, in full, is required before students commence their course of study. The fees for the present year are given below:

TYPIST: Please leave 2" here (51 mm) for the later insertion of fees.

ENTRY (REQUIRMENTS)   Prospective students shd have passed the General Certificate of Education at 'O' level in at least 3 subjects including English Language.

Word processor operator: Key in Document 5 (filename ADMS) for 12-pitch print-out. Embolden main heading. When complete, turn to page 181 and follow instructions for text editing.

NOTICE TO STAFF

Examination Entry Lists

TYPIST: One top + one carbon copy, please

In addition to the individual entry forms, each class teacher must submit a list of candidates for each examination. [The entry lists must contain the following information:

(Inset 5 spaces)

(1) Examining Body concerned
(2) Type of Examination
(3) Date + time of examination
(4) Room req'd
(5) Group taking examination
(6) Name of each candidate in alphabetical order
(7) Any special requirements

I should be glad if the above is strictly adhered to.

Word processor operator: Key in Document 6 (filename EXAMS) for 12-pitch print-out. Embolden main heading. When complete, turn to page 181 and follow instructions for text editing.

Each line or sentence in the lettered exercises should be typed three times and, if time permits, type each complete exercise once. For **Skill measurement** follow instructions on page 28, and for **Record your progress** follow instructions on page 30. Single spacing, with double between exercises. Left margin: 12 pitch 25, 10 pitch 18.

A Review alphabet keys

1 The jam that he bought tasted of exotic fruit like quince, guava and pomegranate, and May ate it with zeal.

B Practise 4 key—use F finger

2 fr4f fr4f f4rf f4rf f4f4f f4f4f f4frf f4frf 4f4rf.
3 44 furs 44 fish 44 firs 44 feet 44 figs 44 fans 4.
4 The 4 men, 4 women, 24 boys and 4 girls go by car.
5 We ordered 434 sets and received 124 on 14 August.

C Practise 7 key—use J finger

6 ju7j ju7j j7uj j7uj j7j7j j7j7j j7juj j7juj 7j7uj.
7 77 jugs 77 jars 77 jigs 77 jets 77 jags 77 jaws 7.
8 The 7 boys and 77 girls sent 77 gifts to the fund.
9 Take 4 from 47, then add 27 plus 7 and you get 77.

D Practise 8 key—use K finger

10 ki8k ki8k k8ik k8ik k8k8k k8k8k k8kik kik8k 8k8ik.
11 88 keys 88 kits 88 kids 88 kinds 88 kilts 88 kings
12 Type 38, 83, 28, 848 and 482 with alternate hands.
13 The 8 men, 28 women, 8 boys and 78 girls are here.

Skill measurement   24 wpm   One minute   Not more than one error

SM8 The account for May should now be paid, and I must   10
ask you to let me have your cheque for the sum due   20
as soon as you can. **(SI 1.04)**   24

SM9 When you leave the office at night you should make   10
sure that your machine is covered up and that your   20
desk is quite clear. **(SI 1.12)**   24

    1 | 2 | 3 | 4 | 5 | 6 | 7 | 8 | 9 | 10 |

Record your progress   One minute

R5 Our parents are fond of telling us that, when they   10
were quite young they were expected to work harder   20
than we do today; however, we will, no doubt, tell   30
our lazy children the same joyful tale. **(SI 1.29)**   38

    1 | 2 | 3 | 4 | 5 | 6 | 7 | 8 | 9 | 10 |

Cork Secretarial College

Principal: Patricia Kerry   BA   HDipEd   CTG   TDT

11 St Patrick's Hill
CORK

Telephone 021 507027

REPORT

Student ..Margaret O'Brien...

Course ..Secretarial Studies.............. Session ...1988/89.......

SUBJECT	Attendance hours		Marks %			Remarks
	Possible	Actual	Prep	Class	Exam	
COMMUNICATION	33	30	80	84	86	A high standard
SHORTHAND	110	107	82	79	75	Excellent work
TYPEWRITING	80	78	–	81	81	Excellent
SEC DUTIES	33	30	74	68	65	Good
BUSINESS ADMIN	33	30	62	67	60	Good
WORD PROCESSING	33	30	–	78	70	Very good
ACCOUNTS	33	30	76	72	71	Very good standard

General Remarks ..Margaret has worked conscientiously during.. her first term and achieved excellent results. With continued effort she should reach a very high standard by the end of the course and be capable of obtaining an interesting and rewarding secretarial post.

Principal .... Date ....

Next term begins on ......9 January 1989.........................

Each line or sentence in the lettered exercises should be typed three times and, if time permits, type each complete exercise once. For **Skill measurement** follow instructions on page 28, and for **Record your progress** follow instructions on page 30. Single spacing, with double between exercises. Left margin: 12 pitch 25, 10 pitch 18.

A   Review alphabet keys

1   The brightly coloured liquid was mixed in the jug, and given to the lazy patients for sickness.

B   Practise 9 key—use L finger

2   lo9l lo9l l9ol l9ol l9l9l 99 laws 99 logs 99 lids.
3   Type 29, 39, 49, 927 and 939 with alternate hands.
4   Joe is 99, Bob is 89, Jim is 79, and George is 49.

C   Practise 0 key—use right little finger

(If your machine does not have a 0 key, use capital 'O' and 'L' finger.)

5   101 201 301 401 701 801 901 10 left 10 look 10 lie
6   The 40 men, 70 women, 80 boys and 90 girls remain.
7   See the dates: 10 March, 20 July, 30 June, 10 May.

D   Practise 5 key—use F finger

8   fr5f fr5f f5rf f5rf 55 fill 55 flit 55 fled 55 fit
9   5 firs, 15 furs, 25 fish, 35 figs, 45 fewer, 515 5
10 25 January 1525; 15 August 1535; 15 December 1545.

E   Practise 6 key—use J finger

11 jy6j jy6j j6yj j6yj 66 jump 66 jerk 66 jest 66 jam
12 6 jars, 16 jets, 26 jabs, 36 jots, 46 jolts, 616 6
13 We need 656 green and 566 red by 16 February 1986.

Skill measurement   25 wpm   One minute   Not more than one error

SM10   I have just moved to my new house and, when I have   10
       put it straight, I would be glad if you could then   20
       spend a few days with me. **(SI 1.00)**   25

SM11   I am delighted to tell you that we have now joined   10
       the team. We had hoped to do so last year, but we   20
       were then not old enough. **(SI 1.12)**   25

       1 | 2 | 3 | 4 | 5 | 6 | 7 | 8 | 9 | 10 |

Record your progress   One minute

R6   I was sorry to find that my cheque - sent to Suzie   10
     on Monday - had not been received. I think it has   20
     just gone astray in the post. Shall I ask my bank   30
     to stop it now? Please excuse the delay. **(SI 1.18)**   38

     1 | 2 | 3 | 4 | 5 | 6 | 7 | 8 | 9 | 10 |

TYPIST— One top + one carbon copy, please

MEMO

To All Staff

From Ms P Kerry

Ref PK/Staff/PB

Date 23.8.88

ABSENTEEISM + GENERAL BEHAVIOUR OF STUDENTS

With the new academic yr commencing, I bel. we are all anxious not to have a repeat of the rather indifferent attitude of several students during last session.   + regulations

I shd be very glad if teaching staff wd make sure that all students are def. aware of our rules.   Be particularly firm if students are late.

I have been asked for a number of refs for last year's students, + I shd be glad if you wd let me have, as soon as possible, an up-to-date list of any appts. That the students have been offered.

CORK SECRETARIAL COLLEGE

Examinations — 1988 (APRIL)

Name of Student	Class	Subject
Anna Kennedy	B1	Typewriting – Stage II
Ann O'Hara	C4	Commerce – Intermediate
Catherine O'Leary	B1	Word Processing – Stage I
Bridie Joesbury	C2	Accounts – Intermediate
Mary Leam LEAM	B1	Typewriting – Stage III
June Flynn	B1	Word Processing – Stage I
Eamonn Devlin	C2	Accounts – Intermediate
Michael O'Dwyer	C2	Commerce – Intermediate

TYPIST – Double spacing

Each line or sentence in the lettered exercises should be typed three times and, if time permits, type each complete exercise once. For **Skill measurement** follow instructions on page 28, and for **Record your progress** follow instructions on page 30. Single spacing, with double between exercises. Left margin: 12 pitch 25, 10 pitch 18.

A Review alphabet keys

1 A small quiet boy who lives next door to Jack came
   out of the gate and went down the zigzag path.

Placement of certain characters

As already mentioned on previous pages, the placement of the hyphen and question mark varies with the make of the machine. This also applies to a few of the signs, symbols, and marks keys such as the oblique and quotation marks. When practising these keys, make sure you know whether or not you have to use the shift key, decide on the correct finger, and then practise the reach from the home key; then type the drills given.

B Practise quotation marks   NO space after initial " NO space before closing "

2 "Go for 30 days." "Call at 12 noon." "Ring now."
3 "I am going," he said. "It is already very late."
4 Mary said, "Mr Bell is here." "Ring me tomorrow."

C Practise brackets (ONE space before NO space after
)   NO space before One space after

5 (1 (2 (3 (4 (5 (6 (7 (8 (9) 10) 11) 12) 13) 14) 8)
6 (22) (23) (24) (25) (26) (27) (28) (29) (30) (31).
7 Mail: (a) 2 pens; (b) 3 pins; (c) 1 tie; (d) 1 hat

D Practise apostrophe   NO space before or after in middle of a word

8   It's Joe's job to clean Dad's car but he's unwell.
9   Don't do that; it's bad for Mary's dog; he's nice.
10 Bill's 2 vans are with John's 8 trucks at Reading.

Skill measurement   25 wpm   1½ minutes   Not more than 2 errors

SM12 Just a year ago we said that you should be given a   10
      trial as a clerk in sales and, as one of the staff   20
      will leave next week, I would like you to take his   30
      place. Let me know if this will suit you. **(SI 1.08)** 38

      1 | 2 | 3 | 4 | 5 | 6 | 7 | 8 | 9 | 10 |

Record your progress   1½ minutes

R7 Many thanks for your note about the dozen desks we   10
    ordered. They are not required right away, but if   20
    we have them on Thursday you may expect our remit-   30
    tance quite soon. We will adjust our records when   40
    we receive your invoice and the amount is paid.   49
                                              (SI 1.29)

    1 | 2 | 3 | 4 | 5 | 6 | 7 | 8 | 9 | 10 |

Ref PK/FT

23 August 1988

Mr Patrick Cassidy
12 Waterford St
CORK

TYPIST— Take a carbon please — and don't forget the envelope

Dear Mr _____

I am pleased to offer you a permanent part-time appt w us, to take effect from 1 Sept 1988, as a lecturer of Business Administration. [The hours wl be as follows:

Inset 1½"

Mondays and Fridays	0900 – 1230 hours
Tuesdays	0900 – 1100 hours
Wednesdays	0900 – 1100 hours
Thursdays	0900 – 1000 hours

You wl be resp. for teaching B _____ A _____ to 3 groups of twenty students, leading to a final examination at Stage II to be taken in June of each yr.

Holidays wl be taken during the normal College vacation, + it wl be necy to give one full term's notice on either side of any termination of this appt.

In the advert. for this post it was stated that the starting salary wd be £4,250 per annum, but in view of yr past experience I am pleased to be able to offer you £4,750 per annum. [I hope very much that you wl accept this invitation to join the staff of the College, + that you wl enjoy many happy yrs with us.

Yours sincerely

Principal

Word processor operator: Key in Document 1 (filename APPTS) for 12–pitch print-out. When complete, turn to page 181 and follow instructions for text editing.

Follow instructions given on page 36. Single spacing, with double between exercises. Margins:
12 pitch 25, 10 pitch 18.

A   Review alphabet keys

1   The boy did just give a quick answer, but he could
    not find words to explain the amazing story.

Backspace key

Locate the backspace key on your machine. This is usually on either the top left or top right of the
keyboard. When the backspace key is depressed, the carriage/carrier will move back one space at a time.
On most electric and electronic machines the carriage/carrier will continue to move for as long as the
backspace key is depressed.

Underscore key — underline function

Before underscoring a short word, backspace once for each letter and space in the word to be
underscored. For longer words, or several words, use carriage release lever. After you finish underscoring,
always tap space bar. Use shift lock when underscoring more than one character. A final punctuation mark
may or may not be underscored. If you are using an electronic keyboard, follow instructions given for
underscoring (underlining) in manufacturer's handbook. With word processors, it is not possible (on most
systems) to underscore a heading, or words, in the normal way because a special underline function is
available. If you need to rule a horizontal line on a word processor, depress the underscore key in the usual
way. In offices today, there is a tendency to use the word **underline** instead of the word **underscore**.

B   Practise underling (underscore key)

2   Please send them 29 only - not 9 - by air-freight.
3   John Brown, Mary Adams and Janet Kelly are coming.

C   Practise £ sign

4   Buy 5 at £15, 8 at £68, 17 at £415 and 30 at £270.
5   £1, £2, £3, £4, £5, £6, £7, £8, £9, £10, £20, £30.

D   Practise ampersand (&)   ONE space before and after

6   Jones & Cutler Ltd, 67 & 68 North Street, Falkirk.
7   Mr & Mrs Weston, 18 & 19 Main Street, Cirencester.

E   Practise oblique (/)   NO space before or after

8   I can/cannot be present.   I do/do not require tea.
9   Jim Minett will take an aural and/or written test.

Skill measurement   25 wpm   2 minutes   Not more than 2 errors

SM13 There must be little imps who sleep until we begin   10
      to work and then they come to our office and start   20
      to harass and try us. We must all try to keep our   30
      minds on the work we have to do, and avoid letting   40
      our thoughts move away from our immediate labours.   50
      (SI 1.22)

        1 | 2 | 3 | 4 | 5 | 6 | 7 | 8 | 9 | 10 |

Record your progress   2 minutes

R8   There seems to be quite an amazing lack of simple,   10
      and easy-to-follow guides to operate the more com-   20
      plicated machines; in fact, we looked at 2 or 3 of   30
      the books and felt they made the operations seem a   40
      little hard - indeed, they were not. We read just   50
      one foreign text that gave a lucid account of what   60
      had to be done. **(SI 1.30)**   63

        1 | 2 | 3 | 4 | 5 | 6 | 7 | 8 | 9 | 10 |

Cork Secretarial College

TYPING POOL – REQUEST FORM

Typist's log sheet

This sheet contains instructions which must be complied with when typing the documents. Read the information carefully before starting, and refer back to it frequently.

Originator **Ms Patricia Kerry Principal**   Department **—**   Date **23·8·88**   Ext No **2**

> Typists operating a word processor, or electronic typewriter with appropriate function keys, should apply the following automatic facilities: top margin; carrier return; line-end hyphenation; underline OR bold print (embolden); error correction; centring; any other relevant applications.

Remember to (a) complete the details required at the bottom of the form; (b) enter typing time per document in appropriate column; and (c) before submitting this Log sheet and your completed work, enter TOTAL TYPING TIME in last column so that the typist's time may be charged to the originator.

Document No	Type of document and instructions	Copies – Original plus	Input form¶	Typing time per document	Total typing time ¥
1	Letter to Mr Cassidy with an envelope	1 original + 1 carbon	MS		
2	Memo to Staff	1 original + 1 carbon	MS		
3	List of examination candidates	1 original	MS		
* 4	Completion of Report Form	1 original	MS		
5	Extract from the Conditions of Admission	1 original	AT		
6	Notice to Staff	1 original + 1 carbon	MS		
				TOTAL TYPING TIME	

TYPIST – please complete:

Typist's name: Date received: Date completed:
                         Time received: Time completed:

> If the typed documents cannot be returned within 24 hours, typing pool supervisor should inform the originator. Any item that is urgent should be marked with an asterisk (*).

¶ T = Typescript   AT = Amended Typescript   MS = Manuscript   SD = Shorthand Dictation   AD = Audio Dictation
¥ To be charged to the originator's department.

Follow instructions given on page 36. Single spacing, with double between exercises.
Margins: 12 pitch 25, 10 pitch 18.

A Review alphabet keys

1 The day dawned quiet and warm, and the lazy foxes
   enjoyed a feast at the back of the undergrowth by
   Valerie Peter's farm.

B Practise at key (@) ONE space before and after, in continuous text

2 f@f f@f d@d j@j 9 @ 10p; 8 @ 11p; 7 @ 12p; 3 @ 8p.
3 Please send 44 @ £5; 6 @ £7; 13 @ £8; and 28 @ £9.
4 Order 420 @ £12, 50 @ £5, 40 @ £6 and 5 @ £8 each.

Numeric keypads

Some machines with electronic keyboards have a numeric keypad, usually placed to the right of, and
separate from, the alphabet keyboard. This keypad may be used in addition to, or instead of, the figure keys
on the top row of the keyboard. When using the 10-key pad, employ the **4 5 6** as the home keys on which
you place the **J K L** fingers. The fingers and thumb will then operate the keypad as follows:

J = 1 4 7   **K** = 2 5 8   **L** = decimal point 3 6 9
Thumb = 0   **Little finger** = enter comma minus

The layout of the keypad will differ from one machine to another. Study your keyboard and, if you have a
keypad, note any differences from the layout above and the characters to which the suggested fingering
applies.

C Practise typing figures on the numeric keypad

5 456 654 147 258 369 041 520 306 470 508 906 159 02
6 417 528 639 159 350 256 107 369 164 059 378 904 38
7 4.5 6.9 4.1 4.7 5.2 5.8 4,655 3,987 2,541 8,465 79

Skill measurement   25 wpm   2½ minutes   Not more than 3 errors

SM14 We were all happy to hear that you are now back at   10
      work, and we hope that your long rest by the lakes   20
      will have restored you to good health. As soon as   30
      you can, please call and see us. You will observe   40
      that we have moved to a house quite near to Rugby,   50
      and I am sending you a map of the area so that you   60
      will find us. (SI 1.11)   62

      1 | 2 | 3 | 4 | 5 | 6 | 7 | 8 | 9 | 10 |

Record your progress   2½ minutes

R9 Have you ever thought of taking one of our out-of-   10
    season holidays? A quiet winter break - January -   20
    may be just what you would enjoy. In our brochure   30
    you will find a wide choice of 122 cities to which   40
    you can go. Write to: Sun Traveller Ltd, Leighton   50
    Buzzard, and we will be pleased to send you one of   60
    our up-to-date guide books telling you, in detail,   70
    about our exotic holidays. (SI 1.30)   75

    1 | 2 | 3 | 4 | 5 | 6 | 7 | 8 | 9 | 10 |

Fully-blocked letter with full punctuation and display

Letter display is exactly the same as given on pages 56–58 for open punctuation. However, when using full punctuation, note the following points:

(a) Full stop after the abbreviation Ref. but no punctuation in the reference.

(b) Note the punctuation and spacing in the 'For the attention of . . .' line, with no full stop at the end.*

(c) The points for typing the name and address

of the addressee are the same as those for typing envelopes given on page 144.

(d) Always type a comma after the salutation.

(e) Always type a comma after the complimentary close.

(f) Always type full stop after abbreviations Enc./Encs.

* If the last word were abbreviated (Esq.), then a full stop would be necessary.

6 Type the following letter in fully-blocked style using full punctuation. (a) A4 letterhead paper (Kenkott Scotia PLC). (b) Suitable margins. (c) Follow display. (d) Type a C6 envelope.

```
Our Ref.  BL/MAD


8 December 1988


FOR THE ATTENTION OF MRS. K. WALKER


E. L. Appleby & Co. Ltd.,
34 Lincoln Road,
NEWARK,
Notts.       NG22 1AA


Dear Sirs,


SECURITY LOCKINGS


Further to our Mail Order Catalogue which we sent to you last
Tuesday, 6 December, we now have a special offer as follows:


Locking Window Bolts    Packs of 4    £15.99
Deadlocks and Sashes    5 Lever       £14.99


The security of your premises is of paramount importance, and our
Rugby Branch has stocks of these items which can be delivered within
12 hours of receipt of your order.  We enclose an order form.


Order this week, and you can have the locks fitted before you
close for your Christmas vacation.


Yours faithfully,


BRIAN LUCKNOWE    SALES MANAGER    ENC.
```

Extra points to note when typing letters with either full or open punctuation, blocked or semi-blocked

(a) Whether using full or open punctuation, 'st', 'nd', 'rd', 'th' may be used in dates. Similarly a comma may follow the month;
    eg, 21st August, 1988.

(b) If a date appears in the body of a letter, then it should be in the same form as that used at the head of the letter.

(c) Whether using full or open punctuation, the date may be typed on the same line as the reference and backspaced from the right margin.

(d) The words 'Our ref' may already appear in a printed letter heading. If this is the case, it is necessary to type the reference after it, irrespective of its position in the heading.

(e) The words 'Your ref' may also appear. This is the reference of the firm to whom you are writing, and if their reference is given, then it must be inserted.

Standard sizes of paper

In the office you will have to use different sizes of paper. The standard sizes are known as the 'A' series and are shown below. The most common of these sizes are: A4, A5 and A6.

420 mm	420 mm	**Sizes** 25 mm = 1"

A3 (297 mm × 420 mm)
A2 (594 mm × 420 mm)
A5 (148 mm × 210 mm)
A4 (297 mm × 210 mm)
A7 (74 mm × 105 mm)
A6 (148 mm × 105 mm)

Sizes   25 mm = 1"

A2 420 × 594 mm

A3 420 × 297 mm

A4 297 × 210 mm (landscape)   11¾" × 8¼"

A4 210 × 297 mm (portrait)   8¼" × 11¾" (approx)

A5 210 × 148 mm (landscape)   8¼" × 5⅞" (approx)

A5 148 × 210 mm (portrait)   5⅞" × 8¼" (approx)

A6 148 × 105 mm   5⅞" × 4⅛" (approx)

Vertical linespacing

6 single vertical lines = 25 mm (1")

Number of single-spaced lines in the full length of A4 and A5 paper:

A4 landscape paper — 50 single-spaced lines
A4 portrait paper — 70 single-spaced lines
A5 landscape paper — 35 single-spaced lines
A5 portrait paper — 50 single-spaced lines

Horizontal spacing

The three most usual typefaces are:

10 characters to 25 mm (1") — known as 10 pitch
12 characters to 25 mm (1") — known as 12 pitch
15 characters to 25 mm (1") — known as 15 pitch

Number of horizontal characters in full width of A4 and A5 paper

	10 pitch	**12 pitch**	**15 pitch**
A4 landscape	117 (centre point 58)	141 (centre point 70)	176 (centre point 88)
A4 portrait	82 (centre point 41)	100 (centre point 50)	124 (centre point 62)
A5 landscape	82 (centre point 41)	100 (centre point 50)	124 (centre point 62)
A5 portrait	59 (centre point 29)	70 (centre point 35)	88 (centre point 44)

The guide to the addressing of envelopes given on page 102 applies with the exception of inserting punctuation after abbreviations and at line-ends. It should be noted that Miss is not an abbreviation and, therefore, does not require a full stop. Examples:

Mr. M. James   Dr. O. Coleman   Messrs. W. O. Horne & Sons   Ms. N. Gray

```
Mrs. W. Fallon,          E. P. Freeman, Esq., M.A., B.Sc.,
24 St. John's Street,    T. R. Beach & Co. Ltd.,
BOSTON,                  2 Herne Bay Road,
Lincs.                   BANBURY,
PE21 6AA                 Oxon.       OX16 8LB
```

Points to note:

(a) Full stop after an initial followed by one clear space.

(b) Comma at the end of each line except for the last line before the postcode, which is followed by a full stop.

(c) NO punctuation in postcode.

(d) Comma after surname, followed by one space before Esq.

(e) Full stop and NO space between the letters of a degree, but a comma and space between each group of letters.

(f) Notice recognized abbreviation for Oxfordshire.

3   Type each of the following lines twice in single spacing. (a) Use margins of 12 pitch 20–80, 10 pitch 11–71. (b) Notice that there is NO full stop in the 24-hour clock.

```
Ms. W. K. Fleming will see you at 9 a.m. or 2 p.m. tomorrow.
Address the letter to P. W. St. John-Lloyd, Esq., M.D., B.A.
Miss U. B. Wallace will meet Mrs. L. V. Stait at 1400 hours.
```

4   Address C6 size envelopes to the following. Use blocked style and full punctuation. Mark the envelope to Ms. Hewitt 'CONFIDENTIAL', and the envelope to K. C. Brennan P.L.C. 'FOR THE ATTENTION OF MR. G. MADDEN'. Do not copy the single quotation marks.

```
Ms. A. I. Hewitt, O.B.E., 17 Park Road, SWINDON.   SN2 2NR
K. C. Brennan P.L.C., 3 High Street, SEASCALE, Cumbria.   CA20 1PQ
Mr. T. Morgan, NAGROM, Bond Street, CRAWLEY, W. Sussex.   RH10 0ND
Mrs. L. M. Mulligan, 8 New Street, OMAGH, Co. Tyrone.   BT78 1AA
K. S. Mulcahy & Sons, 10 Carlow Street, WEXFORD, Irish Republic.
Mr. W. Chisholm, 5 High Street, LOSSIEMOUTH, Morayshire.   IV31 6AA
F. J. Jones p.l.c., Llangawsai, ABERYSTWYTH, Dyfed.   SY23 1AA
```

Half-space corrections

You can squeeze in an extra letter, eg, type four letters where there were originally three, or spread a word with a letter less than the incorrect word, eg, type a four-letter word where there were five letters before. Inserting a word with an extra letter: (a) Erase incorrect word. (b) Move carriage to second letter of the erased word. (c) Depress backspace key, hold it down and type first letter of new word; release backspace key and tap space bar once; hold down backspace key, type second letter, and repeat process. Inserting a word with a letter less: (a) Erase incorrect word. (b) Move carriage to third letter of the erased word. (c) As in (b) above. Alternatively: By means of the paper release lever, move the paper so that the printing point is half a space to the left of the erased word, or place printing point half a space to the right so that $1\frac{1}{2}$ spaces precede and follow the word.

Electric/electronic keyboards: Some of these keyboards have a half-space key, and some manual machines have a half-space mechanism on the space bar.

5   Type lines 1, 2, 3 and 4 exactly as shown; then squeeze the word **them** in each of the two blank spaces in line two and spread the word **her** in each of the two blank spaces in line four. Use margins of 12 pitch 22–82, 10 pitch 12–72.

```
1  I told her that I will call.  I told her that I will call.
2  I told     that I will call.  I told     that I will call.
3  I told them that I will call.  I told them that I will call.
4  I told     that I will call.  I told     that I will call.
```

See Practical Typing Exercises, Book One, page 50, for further exercises on
Forms of address with full punctuation — Addressing envelopes,

Linespace selector

The linespace selector is a lever or knob which may be situated at the left- or right-hand end of the paper table or to the left or right of the keyboard. Most machines can be adjusted for single and double spacing and may also have the facility for 1½, 2½ and treble spacing. The selector controls the distance between the lines of typing. In previous exercises you have been typing in single spacing — the linespace selector has been set on '1'. You can also type in double (one clear space between each line of typing) or treble spacing (two clear spaces between each line of typing).

	Single spacing (type on every line)	Double spacing (type on every second line)	Treble spacing (type on every third line)
	I am	I am	I am
	going	*(space)*	*(space)*
	to	going	*(space)*
	the	*(space)*	going
	market	to	*(space)*
	today	*(space)*	*(space)*

6 single-line spaces equal 25 mm (1 inch) — 25 mm

Blocked paragraphs

Paragraphs are used to break up the writing into short passages to facilitate reading and understanding. There are three different styles of paragraph but, for the time being, we will deal with the **blocked** paragraph where all lines start at the left margin.

When typing **blocked** paragraphs in **single** spacing, turn up two **single** spaces between each paragraph, ie, leave one blank space between each paragraph.

1   Type the following paragraphs on A5 landscape paper. (a) Margins: 12 pitch 22–82, 10 pitch 12–72. (b) Leave 25 mm (one inch) clear at the top of the page, ie, turn up 7 single spaces — for explanation of alignment guide, see page 4. (c) Single spacing.

We are sure you will have noticed that laser printers cut down on print costs and noise.

You can achieve a high quality finish in a wide variety of typestyles.

When typing **blocked** paragraphs in **double** spacing, turn up two **double** spaces between each paragraph, ie, leave three blank spaces between each paragraph.

2   Type the following paragraphs on A5 landscape paper. (a) Margins: 12 pitch 22–83, 10 pitch 12–73. (b) Leave 25 mm (one inch) clear at the top of the page, ie, turn up seven single spaces. (c) Double spacing.

As you have already learnt, when using blocked paragraphs all

lines start at the same scale-point.

Return twice on double

When typing a blocked paragraph in double spacing, you should

turn up twice between paragraphs, so that it is clear to the

reader where one paragraph ends and the next one begins.

(b) Used with figures only:

Open punctuation   *Full punctuation*

am	a.m.	ante meridiem—before noon
pm	p.m.	post meridiem—after noon
in	in.	inch(es)
ft	ft.	foot (feet)
g	g	gram(s)
kg	kg	kilogram(s)
mm	mm	millimetre(s)
m	m	metre(s)
km	km	kilometre(s)

Punctuation is NEVER used in metric abbreviations

(c) Abbreviations always used:

Open punctuation   *Full punctuation*

eg	e.g.	exempli gratia—for example
etc	etc.	et cetera—and others
ie	i.e.	*id est*—that is
NB	N.B.	*nota bene*—note well
viz	viz.	*videlicet*—namely
Esq	Esq.	Esquire
Messrs	Messrs.	Messieurs—Gentlemen
Mr	Mr.	
Mrs	Mrs.	
Ms	Ms.	

NOTE:
There is no space in the middle of an abbreviation

NOTE:
Miss is not an abbreviation and does not require a full stop

1   Type the following sentences on A5 landscape paper. (a) Note the use of abbreviations. (b) Margins: 12 pitch 22–82, 10 pitch 12–72. (c) Blocked paragraphs. (d) Single spacing, with double between each group of sentences. (e) Open punctuation.

Mr & Mrs A T Goulde were told to see Dr H Patridge at St Augustine's Hospital at 3.00 pm.

The cars, motor bikes, vans, etc, were all parked in a small area which measured only 600 sq ft.

Parker & Browne PLC is a large company, but F S Dodwell & Co Ltd is more well known, although employing fewer staff.

Leave a top margin of 25 mm, and a left margin of 38 mm, when typing the report for Ms J Farmer, BSc.

2   Type the following sentences on A5 landscape paper. (a) Margins: 12 pitch 22–82, 10 pitch 12–72. (b) Blocked paragraphs. (c) Single spacing, with double between each group of sentences. (d) Full punctuation. (e) On completion compare with the previous exercise.

NOTE: One space after a full stop at the end of an abbreviation, unless it occurs at the end of a sentence when you leave two spaces. No space after a medial full stop within an abbreviation.

Mr. & Mrs. A. T. Goulde were told to see Dr. H. Partridge at St. Augustine's Hospital at 3.00 p.m.

The cars, motor bikes, vans, etc., were all parked in a small area which measured only 600 sq. ft.

Parker & Browne P.L.C. is a large company, but F. S. Dodwell & Co. Ltd. is more well known, although employing fewer staff.

Leave a top margin of 25 mm, and a left margin of 38 mm, when typing the report for Ms. J. Farmer, B.Sc.

Fractions

3   Find the ½ key and the % key on your keyboard and make certain you know whether or not you have to use the shift key. Type each of the following lines three times. Margins: 12 pitch 22–82, 10 pitch 12–72.

```
;;;  1 1 1   ;;;  1 1 1  ;½;  ;½;  1½;  2½;  3½;  4½;  5½;  6½;  7½;  8½;  90½;
     2 2 2        2 2 2
;;;  %%%   ;;;  %%%  ;%;  ;%;  ½%;  2%;  3%;  4%;  5%;  6%;  7%;  9%;  19%;
```

NOTE: In addition to the ½, most typewriters have keys with other fractions. Examine your machine to find what fractions it has. These are all typed with the ; finger. Some will require the use of the shift key. Practise the reaching movement from the home key to the fraction key you wish to type. Remember: ALWAYS return your finger quickly to the home key.

Sloping fractions

When fractions are not provided on the typewriter, these should be typed by using ordinary figures, with the oblique, eg, 2 fifteenths = 2/15; 3 sixteenths = 3/16. Where a whole number comes before a 'made-up' fraction, leave a clear space (NOT a full stop) between the whole number and the fraction. Fractions already on the keyboard and sloping fractions may both be used in the same exercise.

4   Type the following on A5 landscape paper. (a) Double spacing. (b) Margins: 12 pitch 22–82, 10 pitch 12–72.

```
2½, 3¼, 6 2/5, 2 5/16, 3 7/8, 4 8/9, 8 2/9, 17 3/7, 16 3/10.
The following widths are in inches: 7½, 5 3/8, 16¾, 17 1/10.
```

Decimals

(a) Use full stop for decimal point. This is usually typed in the normal position of the full stop.
(b) Leave NO space before or after decimal point.
(c) No punctuation required at the end of figures except at the end of a sentence.
(d) Always insert the number of decimal places required by using zero.
       Examples: 2 decimal places: type 86.40 not 86.4.
                      3 decimal places: type 95.010 not 95.01.

5   Type the following sentences three times

```
Add up 12.54, 13.02, 24.60, 6.75 and 0.20 and you get 57.11.
The sheet measures 1.200 x 5.810 x 2.540 m; the gross weight
is approximately 50.802 kg and the net weight is 38.102 kg.
```

Sums of money in context

(a) If the sum comprises only pounds, type as follows: £5, £10 or £5.00, £10.00.
(b) If only pence, type: 10p, 97p.
       NOTE: No space between figures and letter p, and no full stop after p (unless, of course, it ends a sentence).
(c) With mixed amounts, ie, sums comprising pounds and pence, the decimal point and the £ symbol should always be used, but NOT the abbreviation p.
       Example: £7.05.
(d) If the sum contains a decimal point but no whole pounds, a nought should be typed after the £ symbol and before the point.
       Example: £0.97.

6   Type the following exercise in double spacing

```
We have purchased goods to the value of £200.50, and we must

send our cheque for this amount; however, we still await a

credit note for £61.49 which means the cheque should be for

£139.01.   The latest discount we were offered was 2½% and

not 3½% as stated in their letter.
```

Open punctuation

Up to this point in the book all the exercises have been displayed with open punctuation. This means that full stops have not been inserted after abbreviations, and business and personal letters have been typed with the omission of commas after each line of the address, and after the salutation and complimentary close. The modern trend is to omit punctuation in those cases as it simplifies and speeds up the work of the typist. However, punctuation is always inserted in sentences, so that the grammatical sense is clear.

Full punctuation

It is also acceptable to insert punctuation after abbreviations and after each line of an address as well as after the salutation and complimentary close. Grammatical punctuation is always inserted. Open and full punctuation must NEVER be mixed: a document must be typed in either open or full punctuation.

Abbreviations

In typewritten work abbreviations should not, as a rule, be used. There are, however, a few standard abbreviations that are never typed in full, and others that may be used in certain circumstances. Study the following lists, so that you will know when not to use abbreviations and when it is permissible to use them. You must always be consistent in their use.

NOTE: In the Royal Society of Arts Typewriting Skills, Examination Paper, Stage I, full stops are inserted after certain abbreviated words to indicate that those words *must* be typed in full, the aim being to make sure that the candidate is able to spell the words correctly. Full stops are not inserted after any other abbreviation in the Royal Society of Arts Typewriting Skills, Examination Paper, Stage I.

(a) Used in the cases indicated:

Open punctuation	Full punctuation	
Ltd	Ltd.	Limited. Abbreviation used in names of private limited companies and companies limited by guarantee. It must be typed in full if that is how it appears in the printed letterhead or in the exercise being copied.
PLC or plc	P.L.C. or p.l.c.	Public Limited Company. Abbreviation used in names of public limited companies. It may be typed in full or abbreviated. Follow the style used in the exercise being copied.
Co	Co.	Company. Abbreviation used only in names of companies. It must be typed in full if that is how it appears in the printed letterhead or in the exercise being copied.
OHMS	O.H.M.S.	On Her Majesty's Service. Usually abbreviated but occasionally typed in full. Follow the style used in the exercise being copied.
PS	PS.	Postscript. Abbreviation used only at the foot of a letter.
v	v.	Versus. May be abbreviated or typed in full. Follow the style used in the exercise being copied.
&	&	And, known as the 'ampersand'. Abbreviation used in names of firms, such as Smith & Brown, and in numbers such as Nos 34 & 35 (Nos. 34 & 35).
@	@	At. Abbreviation used only in invoices, quotations and similar documents.
%	%	Per cent. May be abbreviated or typed in full. Follow the style used in the exercise being copied.
Bros	Bros.	Brothers. Abbreviation used only in the names of companies.

SKILL BUILDING

Each line or sentence in the lettered exercises should be typed three times and, if time permits, type each complete exercise once. For **Skill measurement** follow instructions on page 28, and for **Record your progress** follow instructions on page 30. Single spacing, with double between exercises. Margins: 12 pitch 22–82, 10 pitch 12–72.

A Review alphabet keys

1 The bold pilot was unable to land the jet owing to extremely thick fog which quite covered the whole zone.

B Improve control of space bar

2 as is so or be in am if an me go my do he by us ask may you.
3 It is so. Ask me to go. You must be in time. I may do so.
4 Who is she? He can go home on 6 May. It is a 65-page book.

C Improve control of down reaches

5 Ac lack back rack hack jack track crack brace vacant accents
6 Ab cabs dabs tabs jabs able table gable sable labels enables
7 Ask Jack to bring back the labels for that one vacant table.

Spelling

Employers suggest that the greatest impediment to a typist is uncertainty about spelling. We all find difficulty in spelling certain words and, from now on, there will be spelling drills on each skill-building page. When typing these, look carefully at each word and note the sequence of the letters. Practise these drills as often as possible.

D Spelling skills   Correct the one misspelt word in each line (see page 182 for answers)

8 view untill merge awful chaos quiet forty really absorb centre
9 lose occur gauge audio among receive develop seperate account
10 We have received your cheque and will book the accomodation.

Skill measurement   25 wpm   3 minutes   Not more than 3 errors

SM15 We have not yet been able to send the goods you ordered last	12
week as they are not stock lines, but we shall do all we can	24
to let you have some of the goods, if not all, by Tuesday of	36
next week. We trust that you will excuse the delay in send-	48
ing your requirements, and that we may look forward to meet-	60
ing your requests more promptly in the future. We enclose a	72
new price list. **(SI 1.21)**	75

1 | 2 | 3 | 4 | 5 | 6 | 7 | 8 | 9 | 10 | 11 | 12 |

Record your progress   3 minutes

R10 Have you ever followed modern machine manuals in any detail?	12
They seem to be written in a complex language which contains	24
a great deal of jargon - quantity rather than quality with a	36
lack of easy-to-follow wording. I did read 3 books in which	48
the message was plain, and one told me how to produce clear,	60
dazzling graphics in a simple way. Students using this book	72
would find it easy to follow because there are many diagrams	84
and notes that are very clear. **(SI 1.37)**	90

1 | 2 | 3 | 4 | 5 | 6 | 7 | 8 | 9 | 10 | 11 | 12 |

SKILL BUILDING

Follow instructions given at top of page 42. Margins: 12 pitch 22–82, 10 pitch 12–72. Single spacing, with double between exercises.

A Review alphabet keys

1 The thick haze over the lake meant that Jacques would not be expected to visit his good friends living nearby.

B Language arts—agreement of subject and verb
(See explanation on page 182)

2 The box of 12-pitch printwheels is no longer in that drawer.
3 Both the report and the letter are almost ready for posting.
4 Every name and address on the printout is being scrutinized.
5 Each boy and girl is ready to study the 'Electronic Office'.

Skill measurement 30 wpm 4½ minutes Not more than 4 errors

SM37 Before your employer leaves on a business trip, obtain from   12
her/him instructions as to what business or private letters   24
may be opened and what correspondence should be forwarded by   36
mail. If you decide to send on the actual letters, make a   47
copy of each as a safeguard against loss or damage in the   59
post. When posting, make sure that the envelope used is of   71
a suitable size and that it is addressed to the town your   83
employer will have reached by the time the letter arrives.   94

Mark the letter/package clearly TO AWAIT ARRIVAL, and state   106
your business address to which the letter should be returned   118
if not claimed within a certain time. You must also record   130
the date of posting mail. **(SI 1.35)**   135

    1 | 2 | 3 | 4 | 5 | 6 | 7 | 8 | 9 | 10 | 11 | 12 |

Record your progress 4½ minutes

R28 The storage medium used on a word processor (and some elec-   12
tronic typewriters) is referred to as a floppy disk or disk-   24
ette because it is made from flexible materials, as distinct   36
from hard disks which are much larger and used more in com-   48
puter memories. Floppy disks are usually 8 inch or 5¼ inch   60
in size (adequate for 120 and 75 A4 pages) and you can even   72
buy smaller ones known as minidisks. There are also single-   84
and double-density disks - the double-density disk will hold   96
more data. Disks are in a jacket-type cover.   105

When using a floppy disk, you will have a disk drive into   117
which you insert the disk. Inside the drive, the disk spins   129
at high speed and when keying in information, the data will   140
be transferred to the disk by a device called a head. This   151
head will also read data from the disk and transfer it to a   163
screen or thin window display. **(SI 1.38)**   169

    1 | 2 | 3 | 4 | 5 | 6 | 7 | 8 | 9 | 10 | 11 | 12 |

Display

Some types of matter such as notices, menus and advertisements are much more attractive if items are displayed on separate lines and good use is made of capital letters, small letters, the underscore and bold print.

In its simplest form, and to save time, decide on a *suitable* left and top margin depending on the length of the longest line and the actual number of lines to be typed. Then type each line at the left margin, leaving extra lines between items as required, for emphasis.

Spaced capitals

Important lines may be given prominence by using spaced capitals, ie, leave one space between each letter and three spaces between each word.
NB   When using closed capitals, it is usual to leave only one space between each word.

Notice the use of spaced capitals, closed capitals and the underline to stress important lines in the exercises that follow.

Electronic machines

If you are using an *electronic machine*, you may be able to make use of the **bold** function key. This key is depressed before typing the chosen line, eg, **modern office technology**. The line will then appear in a heavier print than the others in the exercise, and so be given prominence. To save time, you can also use the **automatic underline** feature if your electronic machine has this particular function.

The margins have been decided for you in the following two exercises. As A5 portrait paper is being used, a one inch margin is adequate. As the exercises contain only 12 lines each, a two inch top margin will make your completed exercise more pleasing to the eye.

1   Display the following notice on A5 portrait paper. (a) Leave 51 mm (2 inches) at the top of the page. (b) Left margin: 12 pitch 13, 10 pitch 11. (c) Copy the exercise line for line.

			Turn up 13 single spaces
1	Line 1	I N T R O D U C T I O N	
2	Space		Turn up 2 single spaces
3	Line 2	to	
4	Space		Turn up 2 single spaces
5	Line 3	MODERN OFFICE TECHNOLOGY	
6	Space		Turn up 3 single spaces
7	Space		
8	Line 4	by	
9	Space		Turn up 2 single spaces
10	Line 5	J J Grainger	
11	Line 6	and	Type the last 3 lines in single
12	Line 7	F P Simpson	spacing

3   Type the following letter from Eastways Developments (UK) Ltd, on A4 letterhead paper.
    (a) Margins: 12 pitch 22–82, 10 pitch 12–72. (b) Take a carbon copy. (c) Mark the letter
    PERSONAL.

Our ref Pm/PW/127/Appt

21 June 1988

(leave 9 lines clear for name & address to be inserted later)

Dear (leave blank)

DEPARTMENTAL CLERICAL OFFICER

With ref to yr recent interview, I confirm yr appointment
as Departmental Clerical Officer in the Maintenance Dept
at our Southampton Branch. [The appt is to date from
4 July 1988 & yr salary wl commence at £8,000 per
annum.

I enclose a list of the duties you wl be expected to
perform & sh be glad to receive yr acceptance of this
appt.) in writing,

Yrs sincerely

Personnel Manager

4   Type the following on A4 paper. (a) Single spacing. (b) Set a tab stop at 12 pitch 18, 10
    pitch 15 for side headings. (c) Margins: 12 pitch 31–88, 10 pitch 28–72.

BANK SERVICES

Banks provide many services other than the current and deposit account facilities.
For example –

NIGHT SAFE   The customer is issued with a special container for cash. After the
FACILITIES   bank has closed,the customer can deposit this, using the special trap
               door in the outer wall of the bank.

FOREIGN   Foreign currency may be obtained through the bank where overseas travel
CURRENCY   is involved. I give below today's Exchange Rates.

               (leave 4 clear lines here for the rates to be inserted later.)

VALUABLES*   It is possible to hire private, steel safes in the bank's premises, or
               locked deed boxes, or sealed packages can be handed to the bank for
               safe keeping.

* Title deeds, jewellery, or any precious possession

2   Type the following exercise on A5 portrait paper. (a) Leave 51 mm (2 inches) at the top of
    the page. (b) Left margin: 12 pitch 13, 10 pitch 11. (c) Copy the exercise line for line.

<u>FULL-TIME SECRETARIAL COURSE</u>   Turn up 13 single spaces

                                                       Turn up 3 single spaces

S U B J E C T S   S T U D I E D
                                                       Turn up 2 single spaces

Shorthand
Typewriting
Word Processing   Type these 5 lines in single spacing
Economics
Secretarial Skills
                                                       Turn up 2 single spaces

<u>Course commences - September 1988</u>

Effective display

If the previous two exercises had been centred on the page, most readers would agree that they would
look more effective. In order to do this you will need to use the backspace key, and follow the points
given for horizontal and vertical centring.

Backspace key

Refer to page 37 and locate the backspace key on your machine.

Horizontal centring — Blocked style

When centring a piece of display in the full width of the paper, take the following steps:
(a) See that the left edge of the paper is at 0 on the paper guide scale.
(b) Move margin stops to extreme left and right.
(c) Divide by two the total number of spaces between 0 and the scale point reached by the right-
     hand edge of paper; this gives the centre point of the paper.
(d) Bring carriage/carrier to the centre point.
(e) Locate the backspace key and backspace once for every two characters and spaces in the longest line.
     Ignore any odd letter left over.
(f) Set the left margin at the point reached.
(g) All lines in the exercise start at the left margin.

 On electronic keyboards there is usually an automatic centring function which will centre the typed line
when you press the appropriate key(s).

3   Display the following notice on A5 landscape paper. (a) Leave 51 mm (2 inches) at the top
    of the page. (b) Centre the longest line horizontally. (c) Set the left margin and start all lines
    at this point.

                                                                    Turn up
                                                                    13 single spaces

DIFFERENT TYPES OF BUSINESS ORGANIZATIONS

                                                                    3 single spaces

Partnership
                                                                    2 single spaces

Sole Trader
                                                                    2 single spaces

Limited Company
                                                                    2 single spaces

Public Corporation
                                                                    2 single spaces

Co-operative

The left margin will be set at 12 pitch 30, 10 pitch 41.

Allocating space

In examinations and in business, you may be given instructions that will require you to leave a certain amount of blank space in a typewritten document for the insertion, at a later date, of further information. For example, you may be asked to leave room for the name and address of the addressee in a circular letter, to leave a specified top margin of, say, 51 mm (2 inches), or to leave a certain amount of space in the middle of a document for the later insertion of a diagram, photograph, etc.

In an examination you will be told how much space to leave, either as a measurement, eg, leave 25 mm (one inch), or as a number of linespaces, eg, leave seven single lines clear.

It is important to remember that if an instruction states 'leave seven lines *clear*', you must turn up *one* extra space, ie, turn up eight single spaces and type on the eighth line, so leaving seven clear. If the instructions asks for a space of '*at least* 51 mm (2 inches)', it is wise to leave a little extra space rather than risk not leaving sufficient space. If the words 'at least' are not used, then the amount of space left must be exact.

2   Type the following on A4 paper. (a) Single spacing. (b) Margins: 12 pitch 22–82, 10 pitch 12–72.

Leave a top margin of at least 38 mm (1½")

THOMAS HARDY
1840-1928   , the great novelist & poet,*
Thomas Hardy was born near Dorchester in Dorset at 8 o'clock in the morning on 2 June 1840.

Leave 12 single lines clear for a photograph of Thomas Hardy to be inserted later.

Hardy was a sensitive child who loved reading & the countryside.
Later he became an architect, & made frequent visits to the National Gallery, concerts, theatres, & literary readings. In 1874 Thomas Hardy married Emma Gifford, & by 1880 Hardy was regarded as a major novelist. The Mayor of Casterbridge was published in 1883 & Tess of the D'Urbervilles in 1891. Hardy's marriage to Emma was not a happy one, & she died in 1912. His marriage to Florence Dogdale in 1914 proved to be much more successful, & he had several yrs of happiness with her prior to his death on 11 Jan 1928.

*   Hardy wrote over 1,000 poems.

Vertical centring

To centre matter vertically on a sheet of paper, take the following steps:

(a) Find the number of vertical single spaces on the paper.

(b) Count the number of lines and blank spaces between the lines in the exercise to be typed.

(c) Deduct (b) from (a).

(d) Divide answer in (c) by two to equalize top and bottom margins (ignore fractions).

(e) Insert paper with left edge at 0 on paper scale. See that the top edge of the paper is level with the alignment scale.

(f) Turn up the number of spaces arrived at in (d) PLUS ONE EXTRA SPACE.

4 Display the following on A5 landscape paper. (a) Centre the notice vertically. The vertical spacing at the side of the notice and the calculation below are given as a guide. (b) Centre the longest line horizontally. (c) Set the left margin and start all lines at this point.

1	Line 1	CLANFIELD COLLEGE OF FURTHER EDUCATION	Turn up
2	Space		2 spaces
3	Line 2	Department of Business and General Education	
4	Space		3 spaces
5	Space		
6	Line 3	offers the following full-time courses	
7	Space		2 spaces
8	Line 4	Secretarial Studies	1 space
9	Line 5	Shorthand-Typists	1 space
10	Line 6	Audio-Typists	1 space
11	Line 7	Personal Assistants	1 space
12	Line 8	Executive Secretaries	

The left margin will be set at 12 pitch 28, 10 pitch 19.

The calculations for the vertical centring in the above exercise are as follows:

(a) Number of lines on A5 landscape paper = 35

(b) Number of lines and spaces in exercise = 12

(c) Deduct (b) from (a)   35 − 12 = 23

(d) Divide answer in (c) by two for top and bottom margins (ignore fractions) 23 ÷ 2 = 11.

(e) Turn up 12 single spaces and type the first line of the notice. As you wish to leave 11 clear spaces, it is necessary to turn up the extra space as you will type on the 12th line, so leaving 11 clear.

Side headings

These headings are typed to the left of the set left margin. Side headings are usually typed in closed capitals with or without the underline, but lower case may also be used.

The following steps should be taken:

(a) First decide on left and right margins.

(b) Set right margin.

(c) Set a tab stop at the point where you intended to set the left margin.

(d) From the tab stop set in (c) tap in once for each character and space in the longest line of the side headings, plus three extra spaces.

(e) Set the left margin at this point.

(f) To type the side headings, use the margin release and bring typing point to tab stop set in (c).

 NOTE: If you are using an electronic keyboard, you may have the facility for setting a second left margin instead of using the tabular mechanism.

1   Type the following on A4 paper. (a) Double spacing. (b) Set a tab stop at 12 pitch 18, 10 pitch 15 for the side headings. (c) Margins: 12 pitch 28–88, 10 pitch 25–72.

PROTECT YOUR HOME

Defy the burglar

WINDOWS   Make sure all windows are securely fastened when you go out. Key-operated window locks are very effective.

DOORS   Fit mortice locks to outer doors, and bolts at the top and bottom of back and side doors. Lock all exterior doors before leaving the house.

LADDERS   Do not leave a ladder outside the house - keep it locked in the garage or shed.

MONEY   Never keep more money in the house than you require. Keep your cheque book and banker's card in a safe place.

Spaced capitals

To centre words that are to be typed in spaced capitals:
Say the letters and spaces in pairs, backspacing once for each complete pair, including the two extra spaces between words, eg, S space P space A space C space E space D space space space C space A space, etc. DO NOT backspace for the last letter in the final word.

$$\widehat{S\ P}\ \widehat{A\ C}\ \widehat{E\ D}\ \widehat{\ \ C}\ \widehat{A\ P}\ \widehat{I\ T}\ \widehat{A\ L}\ S$$

Remember to leave three spaces between each word.

5   Display the following notice on A5 landscape paper. (a) Centre the whole notice vertically.
(b) Centre the longest line horizontally.

B R I T I S H   T E L E C O M

GUIDELINES

Cricketline
Discline
Timeline
Recipeline
Storyline
Sportsline

Leave 2 clear spaces here,
ie, turn up 3 single spaces

Leave 2 clear spaces here,
ie, turn up 3 single spaces

6   Display the following notice on A5 portrait paper. (a) Centre the whole notice vertically.
(b) Centre the longest line horizontally.

WORD PROCESSORS

F U N C T I O N   K E Y S

Edit
Merge
Display Advance
Menu
Line delete
Justify

Leave 2 clear line spaces here,
ie, turn up 3 single spaces

Leave 2 clear line spaces here,
ie, turn up 3 single spaces

7   Display exercise 1 on page 43, on A5 landscape paper. (a) Centre the whole notice vertically. (b) Centre the longest line horizontally.

8   Display exercise 2 on page 44, on A5 landscape paper. (a) Centre the whole notice vertically. (b) Centre the longest line horizontally.

Follow instructions given at top of page 42. Margins: 12 pitch 22–82, 10 pitch 12–72. Single spacing, with double between exercises.

A Review alphabet keys

1 The brightly coloured liquid was mixed in a jug and given to the lazy patient for sickness.

B Improve control of figure keys

2 aqla sw2s de3d fr4f fr5f hy6h ju7j ki8k lo9l ;p0; 1234 56789
3 The certificates were numbered 123/456/7890 and 489/267/134.
4 Find me invoices numbered: 9195, 19153, 59191, 27846, 72864.
5 24 May 1987, 30 June 1988, 17 July 1989, 15 May 1987, 6 June

C Language arts—agreement of subject and verb
(See explanation on page 182)

6 Keyboarding is the entering or keying in of text or numbers.
7 Function keys are special keys on most electronic keyboards.
8 You were our first employee when we started business in May.
9 He agrees with me, I agree with you, and they agree with us.

Skill measurement 30 wpm 4 minutes Not more than 4 errors

SM36 Please note that as from 2 October there will be an increase   12
of 9% in air fares because of higher landing charges, a drop   24
in the value of sterling, and a surge in the price of fuel.   36

May we again remind you that you must comply with police and   48
immigration regulations at the points of arrival and depar-   60
ture and at any place along the route. Your journey may be   72
broken at most stops (except on package tours) with no extra   84
charge, provided you complete your journey within the dates   96
stated. As there are a number of formalities, the check-in   107
time quoted is the time you must register at the check-in   119
desk. (SI 1.37)   120

1 | 2 | 3 | 4 | 5 | 6 | 7 | 8 | 9 | 10 | 11 | 12 |

Record your progress 4 minutes

R27 We were very glad to learn from your letter of 16 April that   12
the prospects we discussed when you visited us some 3 months   24
ago are now materializing. You inform us that you have pur-   36
chased a new truck for business purposes and that you intend   48
saving storage charges by housing it in your factory; doubt-   60
less you have calculated well and the truck will cut down on   72
your expenses.   75

Have your insurance brokers reviewed your policies since you   87
bought the truck? We do venture to suggest that you go over   99
your insurance cover with your brokers to make sure that you   111
have comprehensive protection. The fact that you have this   123
truck in your works may change the rates and may invalidate   135
the policies. (SI 1.39)   137

1 | 2 | 3 | 4 | 5 | 6 | 7 | 8 | 9 | 10 | 11 | 12 |

Follow instructions given at top of page 42. Margins: 12 pitch 22–82, 10 pitch 12–72. Single spacing, with double between exercises.

A Review alphabet keys

1   The exquisite butterflies flew past, and Kathy could see the amazing colours of jade, blue, and mauve on their wings.

B Build speed on fluency drills

2   Did for the key all dog why see you put car ask new her site
3   She did not see the new bus. Ask her for all the old shoes.
4   Tom has won the new car. Buy all the tea you can. See May.
5   Put out the cat and the dog now. You may see him for a day.

C Build speed on phrase drills

6   to me to go to ask to see to get to the to her to him to us.
7   I am to ask you to see if you can go to the game on Tuesday.
8   I will talk to him as soon as he is ready to go to the play.
9   In order to get to them, you must come to me for a road map.

D Improve control of up reaches

10   Ki kick kirk kite kind king skim skips taking asking napkin.
11   Aw awed laws saws paws yawn Shaw shawl crawls brawls straws.
12   He is taking the skips of straw to Crawley on Monday 3 June.

E Spelling skill   Correct the one misspelt word in each line. (See page 182 for answer)

13   guard recur queue pursue govern beleive tariff fulfil humour
14   modern cancell except access genius serial unique transferred
15   The video recorder was out on tempoary loan until Thursday.

Skill measurement   26 wpm   One minute   Not more than one error

SM16   In spite of the rain all of us thought it had been an excel-   12
       lent evening; but the guests could not travel till the storm   24
       had passed.   **(SI 1.15)**   26

    1 | 2 | 3 | 4 | 5 | 6 | 7 | 8 | 9 | 10 | 11 | 12 |

Record your progress   One minute

R11   Enclosed please find our price lists. When you have studied   12
      the range of goods, you will be amazed at the quality of the   24
      vast majority of the articles. Our agent will keep in touch   36
      and you may expect a visit.   **(SI 1.31)**   41

    1 | 2 | 3 | 4 | 5 | 6 | 7 | 8 | 9 | 10 | 11 | 12 |

Blocked tabulation—Horizontal and vertical ruling

In addition to the horizontal lines, a boxed table has vertical lines and the left and right sides may or may not be closed in by vertical lines. The vertical lines between the columns must be ruled exactly in the middle of each blank space. It is therefore advisable to leave an odd number of spaces between the columns—one for the vertical ruling and an equal number on either side of the ruling. If the outside verticals are to be ruled, the horizontal lines must extend two spaces to the left and right of the typed matter.

To rule the vertical lines, take the following steps:

(a) First set left margin and tab stops.

(b) From last tab stop, tap space bar once for each character and space in the longest line of the last column plus two spaces, and set right margin at point reached.

(c) After typing main heading and subheading (if there is one), turn up two single spaces and return carriage to left margin.

(d) Press margin release key and backspace two. This gives you the starting point for the horizontal lines which will extend to the right margin.

(e) Move to first tab stop and backspace two; at this point make a pencil mark for the first vertical line.

(f) Move to the next tab stop and backspace two; at this point make a pencil mark for the second vertical line.

(g) Continue in the same way for any additional columns.

(h) When you have typed the last horizontal line, mark in pencil the bottom of each of the vertical lines.

(i) Horizontal lines may be ruled by underscore and the vertical lines in matching colour ink.

(j) Do not allow the vertical lines to extend above or below the horizontal lines. They must meet precisely.

NOTE: When marking the top of the vertical lines, make a note of the scale points at which they have to be drawn so that when you have typed the bottom horizontal line, you will know exactly where to make the pencil marks.

7 Type the following table on A5 landscape paper. (a) Centre the table vertically and horizontally on the paper. (b) Leave three spaces between columns. (c) Rule horizontal lines by underscore and vertical lines in ink.

CAPITAL CITIES

Approximate Population

Town	County	Population
Belfast	Co Antrim	417,000
Cardiff	S Glam	274,000
Dublin	Co Dublin	915,000
Edinburgh	Lothian	419,000
London	Greater London	7,000,000

8 Type the following table on A5 portrait paper. (a) Centre the table vertically and horizontally on the paper. (b) Leave three spaces between columns. (c) Rule horizontal lines by underscore and vertical lines in ink.

CASA DE EUROPA PLC - Figures in £m

	1985	1986	1987
Profit before interest	54.4	55.7	110.7
Profit before taxation	47.0	45.5	92.0
Profit after taxation	29.6	26.5	55.6

Types of display headings

Main headings

The main heading, the title of a passage, is blocked at the left margin when using blocked display. Unless otherwise instructed, turn up seven single spaces, 25 mm (one inch), from the top edge of the paper before starting the main heading. It may be typed in:

(a) Closed capitals — leave one space between each word.

(b) Spaced capitals — leave one space between each letter and three spaces between each word.

(c) Lower case with initial capitals.

(d) These headings may be underlined. Generally it is wise to follow the display indicated in the exercise to be copied. Lower case headings, particularly, can be given greater emphasis by the use of underlining. The underline must not extend beyond the typing.

(e) Bold print.

1   Type the following exercise on A5 landscape paper. (a) Single spacing. (b) Margins: 12 pitch 22–83, 10 pitch 12–73.

TYPING TECHNIQUE   *Turn up 7 single spaces*

Turn up 2 single spaces

Good posture is a very important habit to develop from the start of your typewriting training. Make sure you are sitting comfortably, with your back supported and your feet flat on the floor.

Turn up 2 single spaces

Always check that you are sitting centrally to the typewriter about a handspan away from the machine.

Subheadings

The main heading may be followed by a subheading which further clarifies the contents of the passage. Turn up two single spaces after typing the main heading and then type the subheading.

2   Type the following exercise on A5 landscape paper. (a) Single spacing. (b) Margins: 12 pitch 22–82, 10 pitch 12–72.

SHORTHAND EXAMINATIONS   *Turn up 7 single spaces*

Turn up 2 single spaces

Preparation

Turn up 2 single spaces

Do not enter for a shorthand speed examination unless you are capable of writing at least 10 words a minute above the speed of the test you are taking.

Turn up 2 single spaces

Arrive in the examination room in good time, and sit as near to the front as possible so that you can be sure of hearing the dictation clearly.

Blocked tabulation — Horizontal ruling

A neat and pleasing appearance may be given to column work by ruling in ink or by the use of the underscore key. An 'open' table has no ruled lines, its main use is for displayed columns of items in the body of a letter or report. A 'ruled' table has the column headings separated from the column items by horizontal lines above and below the headings, and below the last line in the table.

When typing a ruled table proceed as follows:

(a) Find vertical starting point by calculating number of typed lines and spaces— remember to count the horizontal lines.

(b) In the usual way, backspace to find the left margin.

(c) From the last tab stop, tap space bar once for each character and space in the longest line of the last column, and set right margin at point reached.

(d) Type main heading and subheading (if there is one) at left margin. Turn up two single spaces and return carriage to left margin.

(e) Type underscore from margin to margin.

(f) Remember to turn up TWICE after and ONCE before a horizontal line.

5   Type the following table on A5 landscape paper. (a) Use blocked style and centre table vertically and horizontally on the paper. (b) Leave three spaces between columns. (c) Rule by underscore.

1 Line 1	WEEKEND BREAKS	
2 Space		
3 Line 2	_____	
4 Space		
5 Line 3	Town Hotel Address	
6 Line	_____	
7 Space		
8 Line 5	Betws-y-coed Grand Holyhead Road	
9 Line 6	Connemara Phoenix Roundstone	
10 Line 7	Dunfermline King's Lodge Queensferry Road	
11 Line 8	_____	

NOTE: Do NOT underline column headings in a ruled table

Blocked tabulation with columns of figures

When columns in a table contain figures, care must be taken to see that units come under units, tens under tens, etc. Where there are four or more figures, these are grouped in threes starting from the unit figure, a space being left, or a comma inserted, between each group. When typing blocked tabulation, the £ symbol is placed above the first figure in the longest line.

NOTE: When typing continuous matter, it is preferable to insert a comma between the groups, rather than leave a clear space.

6   Display the following table on A5 landscape paper in blocked style. (a) Centre vertically and horizontally on the paper. (b) Leave three spaces between columns and rule by underscore. (c) Insert leader dots.

DEPARTMENTAL TURNOVER

Department	1985	1986	1987
	£	£	£
Domestic Utensils	1,985,240	995,985	1,172,248
Ladies' Wear	3,112,300	4,002,755	4,384,973
Men's Wear	998,275	992,831	883,467

Apart from the main heading and the subheading at the beginning of a passage, paragraph headings are used to give emphasis to the first few words of a paragraph. In blocked style the paragraph heading starts at the left margin as in exercise 3 below. They may be typed in upper case, with or without underlining, or in lower case with underlining. The heading may be followed by a full stop and two spaces, or just the two spaces without the full stop, and may also run straight on into the following words of the paragraph but may be emphasized by using capitals, underlining, and/or bold print.

3   Type the following exercise on A5 portrait paper. (a) Single spacing. (b) Margins: 12 pitch 13–63, 10 pitch 6–56.
    NOTE: The figure in blue after the paragraph heading, indicates the number of character spaces to be left and should not be typed.

DATAPOST	Turn up 7 single spaces
	Turn up 2 single spaces
An Overnight Courier Service	Turn up 2 single spaces

SCHEDULED DATAPOST^2 This is a service for those
who need to send urgent packages regularly for
delivery the next morning. Charges vary depending on weight, frequency of service, etc.

ON DEMAND DATAPOST^2 This service is available for
those who do not have regular requirements but do
demand urgent and secure delivery. Packets must
be handed in at a post office, items being paid
for at the time of posting.

Blocked exercises typed in double spacing

NB   If the text is typed in double spacing, it is wise and easier for the reader, if an extra space, or spaces, is left after the headings. As stated on page 40, it may be easier for you to return twice on double, but three single spaces are equally acceptable.

4   Type the following exercise on A5 portrait paper. (a) Double spacing. (b) Margins: 12 pitch 13–63, 10 pitch 6–56.

T O W N T W I N N I N G	Turn up 7 single spaces
EXCHANGE TRIPS	Turn up 1 double space
	Turn up 2 double spaces

Town twinning has, over the years, given many

people the opportunity of experiencing a culture

and lifestyle very different from their own.

Turn up 2 double spaces

Young people, particularly, benefit enormously

from these exchange trips.

Leader dots

(a) Leader dots (full stops) are used to guide the eye from one column to another. There are four methods of grouping but, for the moment, we will use only continuous leader dots.

(b) Leader dots must be typed at the same time as you type the horizontal line to which they apply.

(c) There must always be one clear space between the last word and the first dot or the last dot and the vertical line, ie, leader dots must never be typed right up to the preceding or following word or line. No word or letter must be allowed to extend beyond the last leader dot, although leader dots may extend beyond the last word.

(d) Leader dots must always finish at the same point on every line, although the longest line may not have any leader dots—all dots on the other lines finish at the last letter of the longest line.

(e) In the exercises below, the leader dots finish at the last letter of the longest line and, to ensure that you do not type them beyond this point, tab in to the tab stop *after* the leader dots and backspace four. Then type one full stop. This will be the last leader dot. The others can be filled in when you have completed the details up to this point. Remember to leave one space before typing the first leader dot.

3 Type the following on A5 portrait paper. (a) Centre vertically and horizontally. (b) Insert leader dots between first and second columns. (c) Retain all abbreviations.

TYPING: TWO-IN-ONE COURSE

by Archie Drummond
and Anne Coles-Mogford

C O N T E N T S

Subject	Page No
Effective Display	35
Typing from Manuscript	44
Business Letters	56-61
Envelopes	62 & 63
Carbon Copies	64
Tabulation	96

4 Type the following on A5 landscape paper. (a) Centre vertically and horizontally. (b) Insert leader dots. (c) Retain all abbreviations.

STATIONERY ORDER

l.c. Price-List as at 1 January 1989

Ref No	Description	Price*
F/2/6	12 Rulers	£1.50 per doz
T/6A	10 Reams A4 Bond Typewriting Paper......	£2.10 per ream
135	2 doz Shorthand Notebooks..........	18p each
28C	68 Bottles Typewriting Correction Fluid	£2.00 per half doz
528	1 doz Felt Tip Pens (Black).	30p each

* Correct at time of going to Press.

Shoulder headings

When this form of heading is used, it is typed at the left margin and may be in closed capitals or in lower case with initial capitals, with or without the underline and/or bold print. It is preceded and followed by one blank line when using single spacing. When using double spacing, it is preceded by three blank lines and followed by one.

5   Type a copy of the following on A5 landscape paper. (a) Blocked paragraphs. (b) Single spacing. (c) Margins: 12 pitch 22–82, 10 pitch 12–72.

MOREBY TECHNICAL COLLEGE

Turn up 2 single spaces

Secretarial Studies Section

Turn up 2 single spaces

LOCATION

Turn up 2 single spaces

It is accommodated in the Secretarial Suite of rooms on the 8th floor. The college is approximately one mile from the railway station, and close to the bus stop to take you to the city centre.

Turn up 2 single spaces

EQUIPMENT

The Section has a suite of rooms containing electronic type-writers, word processors and micro-computers.

RESIDENTIAL ACCOMMODATION

Unfortunately the college does not have residential accommodation for students.

6   Type a copy of the following on A5 portrait paper. (a) Blocked paragraphs. (b) Double spacing. (c) Margins: 12 pitch 13–63, 10 pitch 6–56.

T H E   P O S T   O F F I C E

Turn up 1 double space

A BRIEF HISTORY

Turn up 2 double spaces

Letter Carriers

Turn up 1 double space

Initially mail was carried by coaches, payment

varying greatly, with some people refusing to pay

when the mail was delivered.

Turn up 2 double spaces

Postage Stamps

Turn up 1 double space

On 1st May 1840 the first postage stamps were sold.

These were the famous Penny Blacks.

Later Developments

The first postcards were introduced in 1870.

Blocked tabulation with single-line column headings

Refer to Unit 38, pages 79 to 82 for the method to be used when arranging items in columns.

Footnotes

Refer to Unit 46, page 120, for the method to be used when typing footnotes.
NOTE: It is not usual to type a line above the footnote when it occurs after a table.

1 Type the following on A5 landscape paper. (a) Centre the whole table vertically and horizontally. (b) Leave three spaces between columns. (c) Double spacing, but single spacing for items taking more than one line.

```
CHILDREN'S PLAY PRODUCTS

Built to last

Product           Size                          Price*

Garden Slide      Height: 3' 8 3/16"
                  Length: 8' 9½"                £34.95

Playframe         Height: 6' 9"
                  Base area: 7' 6" x 6' 7"      £43.75

Garden Swing      Height: 7 1/9' 2 1/9'
                  Base area: 5' 4" x 4' 9"      £17.85

    * Plus postage and packing
```

2 Type the following on A4 paper. (a) Centre the whole table vertically and horizontally. (b) Leave three spaces between columns. (c) Single spacing, with double between items, after the column headings and before the footnote.

```
ELECTRIC BLANKETS

Finding a Fault*

Symptom               Fault                 Action

No heat               Fuse blown            Fit new fuse

No heat or            Loose flex            Reconnect
intermittent heat     connections at
                      plug

                      Broken flex       ⎫   Return to
                      between plug and  ⎪   manufacturer
                      switch, or switch ⎬
                      and blanket       ⎪
                                        ⎪
                      Faulty switch     ⎪
                                        ⎪
                      Faulty element    ⎭

    * WARNING  Remove plug from socket before attempting
      any repairs.
```

Follow instructions given at top of page 42. Margins: 12 pitch 22–82, 10 pitch 12–72. Single spacing, with double between exercises.

A Review alphabet keys

1 The examination was very difficult for the lazy boy who just managed to complete the first question; but unfortunately he did not gain many marks.

B Review hyphen key

2 full-time, up-to-date, blue-grey, 48-page, re-cover, co-opt.
3 Full-time students wore pin-striped blue-grey ties. He considered that the up-to-date 248-page document was now ready.

C Build accuracy on punctuation review

4 "Is John - John Mann, not John Green – here, please?" "No."
5 I think (in fact I'm sure) that Mrs Laing will arrive today.
6 Send me the documents immediately; I cannot wait any longer.
7 Call me tomorrow. May I borrow 3 or 4 books? Ask Mrs Tait.
8 We require: 2 daisywheels, 6 carbon ribbons, 10 small disks.

D Improve control of out reaches

9 Ga game gape gave gates gales garlic galley baggage Algarve.
10 Up upon sups cups upset soups couple duplex couplet superior
11 The superior baggage belongs to the couple going to Reigate.

E Spelling skill Correct the one misspelt word in each line. (See page 182 for answer)

12 quay basic weird losing prefer mislaid necessery acknowledge
13 paid weigh truley height eighth ascends recommend sufficient
14 I will definitely recommend that they alter this stationary.

Skill measurement 26 wpm 1½ minutes Not more than 2 errors

SM17 As a good typist you must be fast, accurate, and able to set   12
out all kinds of documents. In your first post there may be   24
some forms of layout that are not clear. If that is so, you   36
may need help. **(SI 1.18)**   39

  1 | 2 | 3 | 4 | 5 | 6 | 7 | 8 | 9 | 10 | 11 | 12 |

Record your progress 1½ minutes

R12 Dear Hazel, It is exactly 6 months since you moved from this   12
Sales Office to join our Accounts Section; therefore, as you   24
now qualify for a transfer and your work is highly regarded,   36
we would be happy to discuss the future with you. May I see   48
you one day soon? **(SI 1.31)**   51

  1 | 2 | 3 | 4 | 5 | 6 | 7 | 8 | 9 | 10 | 11 | 12 |

SKILL BUILDING

Follow instructions given at top of page 42. Margins: 12 pitch 22–82, 10 pitch 12–72. Single spacing, with double between exercises.

A Review alphabet keys

1 The pretty girl gave a cry of terror as those ravens quickly seized the jewels from the box.

B Improve control of double-letter words

2 programmes possible running supply arrive proof agrees added
3 difficult football baggage accept excess rubber attend carry
4 Is it possible to supply a proof of the football programmes?
5 We agree that it was difficult to accept the excess baggage.

C Improve control of jump reaches

6 cr cry crop crush crown creep crash secret concrete decrease
7 ni nib nice niece night ninth niche united finished animated
8 Before nightfall I finished mixing the concrete we required.
9 My niece told me that the United Club held a secret meeting.

D Language arts—use of apostrophe (See explanation on page 182)

10 Mary's mother spent 2 weeks' holiday at her niece's cottage.
11 It's time that the bird was released from its new enclosure.
12 Remember that the word 'accommodation' has 2 c's and 2 m's.
13 She said, 'I don't think we will have time to call tonight.'

Skill measurement 30 wpm 3½ minutes Not more than 4 errors

SM35 You get basic tax relief on most mortgages by paying less to   12
     the society who lent you the money, so no allowance is made   24
     in your code. If you pay higher rate tax, your code will be   36
     adjusted to give the extra relief due. If you pay interest   48
     in full on mortgages or other loans for such things as home   60
     improvements, an estimate of the amount of interest payable   72
     will be given in your code. If you have a mortgage on prop-   84
     erty that you let for a commercial rent (during 6 months of   95
     each year) interest will be allowed as a deduction. (SI 1.33)   105

     1 | 2 | 3 | 4 | 5 | 6 | 7 | 8 | 9 | 10 | 11 | 12 |

Record your progress 3½ minutes

R26 The number of guide cards used and their arrangement depend   12
     on the filing system; however, the purpose of the guide card   24
     is the same in all systems: to guide the eye when filing and   36
     finding papers, and to support the folders. Guide cards can   48
     be bought in all standard sizes, as well as for special sys-   60
     tems such as fingerprint, medical, and insurance classifica-   72
     tions. Most guide cards have a tab along the top edge, and   84
     the space contains a plain and clear reference to the folder   96
     behind. It is important that this reference should be easy   107
     to read, and the marker show the exact order of the folders.   119
     These cards, quite rightly, justify their existence. (SI 1.36)   129

     1 | 2 | 3 | 4 | 5 | 6 | 7 | 8 | 9 | 10 | 11 | 12 |

Personal letters

As the name implies, these are written by you to personal friends and it is acceptable practice today to type them, except in very personal circumstances such as a special birthday or anniversary. If you are not using stationery with your home address printed on it, then type on a plain sheet of paper and place your address about 13 mm (half an inch) from the top of the page and block each line at the left margin. After the last line of your address, turn up two single spaces and type the date. After the date turn up two singles and type the salutation; turn up two singles and start the first paragraph. From the example below, you will see that all lines start at the left margin — this is called **fully-blocked**, or **blocked**, style.

If you wish to give your personal letter a more intimate tone, handwrite the salutation (Dear George, Mary, etc) and the complimentary close (Sincerely, Love, Kindest regards, etc) and add a handwritten friendly message at the end.

Certain **formal personal letters** will be a little more reserved. When writing to a person much older than yourself, or to whom you owe respect, or with whom you are not on familiar terms, the salutation and complimentary close would be more formal. An example is given below in **fully-blocked** style. It is also in **open punctuation** which means that there is no punctuation in the sender's address, date and salutation (Dear Ms Walterson), nor in the complimentary close (Yours sincerely). When the recipient is not familiar with your handwriting, it is a good plan to type your name five single-line spaces below the complimentary close.

1   Type the following formal personal letter on plain A5 portrait paper. (a) Use margins of 12 pitch 13–63, 10 pitch 6–56. (b) Leave one clear space between the two halves of the postcode. (c) Follow the layout and capitalization precisely.

Turn up 4 single spaces

Sender's home
address

```
17 High Street
RUGBY
Warwickshire
CV22 5QE
```

Turn up 2 single spaces

```
14 September 1988
```

Turn up 2 single spaces

```
Dear Ms Walterson
```

Turn up 2 single spaces

```
I am sorry that Margaret has been unable to attend
school for the past 3 days.  As she had a high
temperature on Saturday last, I asked the doctor
to call, and he prescribed a course of antibiotics
and suggested she return to school on Monday next.
```

Turn up 2 single spaces

```
Margaret is now very much better and looks forward
to being in class on Monday morning.
```

Turn up 2 single spaces

```
Yours sincerely
```

Turn up 5 single spaces

```
Gladys Jackson
```

SELECTIVE LETTINGS LTD

TYPIST — Please re-type, correcting the words that are circled

We will be pleased to find a tenant for your property, but before doing so want to make sure that you are aware of the possible loopholes in letting and the legal requirments.

1   We will inspect and view the property to be let and advice you on the rent, taking into account furnishings, fittings and equipment.

2   The tenancy would be a fixed term agreement* depending on the length of time you wish to let your property.

3   On recieving an application from a prospective tenant we take up 3 referances, one bank and 2 business.

4   You should advise your insurance company that you intend to let the property. A tenants personal effects will be insured by him/her.

5   A full inventory is required. Two copies is handed to the tenant for signature, one being returned to us for retention in the office.

---

* For a period of 6 months or one year.

Word processor operator: Key in Document 5 (filename LEGAL) for 15–pitch print-out. Embolden main heading. When complete, turn to page 181 and follow instructions for text editing.

SELECTIVE LETTINGS LTD

22 WYNDHAM STREET

Three-bedroomed, detached House

Fitted Kitchen, Lounge, Bathroom

Separate WC, Gas Central Heating

Garage   Garden   NO PETS

£325 per calendar month

Property to be let

TYPIST — A5 paper

Word processor operator: Key in Document 6 (filename ADVT) for 12–pitch print-out. Embolden the address of the property but do not underline. When complete, turn to page 181 and follow instructions for text editing.

Personal business letter

The personal business letter, which you write to an organization or individual about a personal business matter, is displayed in the same way as the formal personal letter on the previous page, but with one addition: the name and address of the addressee (the organization or person to whom you are writing) is inserted and starts on the second single-line space after the date; then turn up two spaces and type the salutation. When typing her name at the end, a lady may, if she wishes, add the word Mrs, Miss, or Ms (in brackets) after her name.

2 Type the following personal business letter on plain A5 portrait paper. (a) Use margins of 12 pitch 13–63, 10 pitch 6–56. (b) Type the letter in fully-blocked style with open punctuation. (c) Follow layout and capitalization precisely.

Turn up 4 single spaces

Sender's home
address

```
46 Barrow Drive
Eglinton
GLASGOW
G41 5QE
```

Turn up 2 single spaces

```
14 September 1988
```

Turn up 2 single spaces

Name and
address
of addressee

```
Kenkott Scotia PLC
Byrnes Terrace
Langside
GLASGOW
G41 3DI
```

Turn up 2 single spaces

```
Dear Sirs
```

Turn up 2 single spaces

```
Thank you for your quotation number 02138, dated
13 September, for the sum of £724.00.

The measurement for the wardrobe in bedroom number
2 is not correct.  I asked for the top of this
unit to be flush with the ceiling, and the height
of the room is just 9 feet and you quote 8 feet.
Please let me have another quotation.
```

Turn up 2 single spaces

```
Yours faithfully
```

Turn up 5 single spaces

```
Mary Lynch (Mrs)
```

3 Type the following letter on a sheet of plain A5 portrait paper. Use margins of 12 pitch 13–63, 10 pitch 6–56. The letter is from Mrs Mary Lynch to Kenkott Scotia PLC; therefore, apart from the date, which should be 20 September 1988, follow layout and wording in the letter above, as far as the salutation, then type the following:

```
Thank you for your telephone call about the height
of the ceiling given in your quotation 02138, and
for letting me know that the 8 was a typist's mis-
take and should have read 9.

I accept your quotation for the sum of £724.00.
```

Type the complimentary close and Mrs Lynch's name as in the letter displayed in exercise 2 above.

TYPIST - A5 paper, please

INVENTORY ← St. caps please

22 WYNDHAM ST.   ALTRINCHAM

<u>Kitchen</u>	<u>Living Room</u>	<u>Bedroom One</u>	<u>Bedroom Two</u>
Table	Dining table	Double bed	Single bed
2 chairs	4 chairs	Dressing table	Writing desk
⊘ Gas cooker	2 easy chairs	Wardrobe	Single Wardrobe
Fridge	Settee	Double Chair	Chair
Washing machine	Television	2 bedside tables	Bedside table

To   Richard Williams, Lettings Department

From   Nigel Grant-Gough, Manager

53 BURY DRIVE   ALTRINCHAM

Mr Tonge wishes to let the above ~~premises~~ accom as soon as
possible. ~~I have~~ Two prospective tenants are interested
in the property & wish to take up residence in 2 weeks'
time. Before I can make a def. appt., it wl be necy
to take up refs, but I sh be attending a Conference
in Llandudno for the remainder of this week. Could
you please see to this for me?
I am attaching all relevant details.

Letters are ambassadors and advertisements for the organization that sends them; therefore, you must ensure that your letters are well displayed and faultlessly typed. Businesses have a variety of forms of display, and the examples that follow are in fully-blocked style with open punctuation, which you used in the letters on the previous page.

A business organization will always have paper with a printed letterhead and you should turn up a minimum of two single-line spaces after the last line of the printed heading before starting to type. The originator (writer or author) of a business letter will also have a reference at the top and this, in its simplest form, consists of the initials of the writer followed by an oblique and the typist's initials. It is also accepted practice, but by no means essential, to type the originator's name five single spaces after the complimentary close, with her/his designation (official position) typed underneath.

4 Type the following letter on A4 letterhead paper which will be found in the *Handbook and Solutions Manual*. (a) Use margins of 12 pitch 22–82, 10 pitch 12–72. (b) Follow the layout and capitalization given.

Printed heading

KENKOTT SCOTIA PLC
Registered Office: Byrnes Terrace Langside
GLASGOW   G41 3DI

Registered Number: 76558 (Scotland)   Freefone: 041–486 0669
Telephone: 041-486 2907   Telex: 23398   FAX: 041–486 4843

Turn up 2 single spaces

Our Ref AT/BWP

Turn up 2 single spaces

11 October 1988

Mrs M Lynch
46 Barrow Drive
GLASGOW
G41 5QE

Dear Mrs Lynch

Thank you for your letter dated 7 October about an estimate for designing and fitting a bedroom.

If convenient to you, Alasdair Millar, our Chief Estimator, will visit you on Tuesday, 18 October, at 10 am to consider your suggestions and offer his advice.

Please let us know if the suggested date and time are convenient to you.

Yours sincerely

Turn up 5 single spaces

A TOMKINSON
Department Manager

TYPIST — PLEASE INSERT THE HANDWRITTEN DETAILS ON TO A SKELETON FORM. MISS ARCHER WILL PAY 2 MONTHS' RENT IN ADVANCE.

SELECTIVE LETTINGS LTD
Barnett House
24 Main Street   ALTRINCHAM   Cheshire   WA16 2DN

TENANCY AGREEMENT FORM

Name of tenant *René Archer*   Mr/Mrs/Miss/Ms*

Present address *8 Langford Road*

North End

Portsmouth   Postcode *PO2 8HS*

Telephone number: Home *0705 4241*   Business *—*

Address of property you wish to rent *53 Bury Drive*
Altrincham
Cheshire   Postcode *WA12 0PN*

Length of time for which you wish to rent the property *One year*

Names and addresses of referees:

1 *Dr F P David*
   26 Broad Street Portsmouth PO1 2JD

2 *Mr L Childs   Personnel Manager*
   Drayton Engineering PLC   Arundel Street Portsmouth PO1 1NH

3 ....

....

I agree to abide by the Letting Terms and to pay two/three* months' rent in advance.

Signature of tenant ....

Date ....

*Delete as applicable

SKILL BUILDING

Follow instructions given at top of page 42. Margins: 12 pitch 22–82, 10 pitch 12–72. Single spacing, with double between exercises.

A Review alphabet keys

1 An extract from the magazine on the technique of painting in oils was requested by the majority of folk who were revising art.

B Improve control of shift key

2 Dear Sir, Yours faithfully, Mr J Brown, New York, Hong Kong.
3 Dear Mr Brown; Dear Mrs Green, Miss R Grey, Miss Jean R Dua.
4 Advanced Word Processing and the Electronic Office, by Joyce
5 and Derek Stananought is available from McGraw-Hill Book Co.

C Improve control of figure keys

6 ewe 323 woe 293 our 974 rye 463 you 697 tour 5974 writ 2485.
7 Type 1 and 2 and 3 and 4 and 15 and 16 and 17 and 80 and 90.
8 Drill: 10, 29, 38, 47, 56, 123, 456, 789, 010, 343, 678, 86.
9 Accounts: 00-11-2345, 00-12-6789, 00-13-5858, 00-14-2679-80.

D Improve control of jump reaches

10 Ve five live jive dive even vein pave have rave valve events
11 On lone zone cone tone hone bone fond only once bonus lesson
12 Five of these events have a once only bonus for the winners.

E Spelling skill   Correct the one misspelt word in each line. (See page 182 for answer)

13 cheque usable curser buffet format liaison referred business
14 debtor wholly reigns hungry choose develope exercise received
15 Choose 2 of the exercises referred to by my liason officer.

Skill measurement   26 wpm   2 minutes   Not more than 2 errors

SM18 Last May we had a chance to buy a large stock of fine cotton   12
sheets, and we are now selling these at a reduced price. If   24
your own stock of sheets is low, now is the chance to obtain   36
some of these goods at half price or less. Send an order by   48
July at the latest. (SI 1.13)   52

   1 | 2 | 3 | 4 | 5 | 6 | 7 | 8 | 9 | 10 | 11 | 12 |

Record your progress   2 minutes

R13 As requested, I give below the pay scales objected to at our   12
last 2 meetings. May I say that I am still quite puzzled by   24
the large increases suggested, and I feel that the new rates   36
should not be made effective at the present time. May I ask   48
you not to inform your staff before we next meet. (SI 1.26)   58

   1 | 2 | 3 | 4 | 5 | 6 | 7 | 8 | 9 | 10 | 11 | 12 |

TYPIST — Carbon copy & envelope, please. I have indicated those abbreviations to be typed in full by inserting a full stop after them.

Ref   NG-G/ *Your initials*

Today's date

Mrs F P Claxton
22 Wyndham St.
ALTRINCHAM
Cheshire
WA14 1EP

Dr. Mrs C ——————

LETTING OF 22 WYNDHAM ST.

With reference to yr. inquiry about letting the above ~~house~~ ~~property~~, I give below our letting terms.

1   LETTING ONLY (no management services) - 2 weeks' rental plus VAT.

2   INTRODUCTION OF TENANT ONLY - one week's rental plus VAT.

3   COMPLETE PACKAGE (for an initial period of one year, or pro rata for shorter tenancies) - £200 plus VAT.

Thank you for sending the inventory of furniture and fittings which will be left in the property for use by the tenants.

My co. has inserted an advert. in the local paper, and we shd. expect to be able to interview prospective tenants very shortly.

I shd. be glad if you wd. sign the attached form and return it to me at yr. earliest convenience.

Yrs. sincerely

NIGEL GRANT-GOUGH
Lettings Department

Word processor operator: Key in Document 1 (filename LETS) for 12–pitch print-out. Embolden subject heading and items numbered 1, 2 and 3.

PRODUCTION DEVELOPMENT

1   Type the following fully-blocked letter in open punctuation, from Kenkott Scotia PLC, on A4 letterhead paper. (See *Handbook and Solutions Manual*.) (a) Margins: 12 pitch 22–82, 10 pitch 12–72. (b) Keep to the spacing and layout indicated at this elementary stage in your learning process.

      NB   For an explanation of the numbered items see pages 59 and 60.

1 Reference	Our ref AT/BWP	*Turn up 2 single spaces*
2 Date	14 April 1988	*Turn up 2 single spaces*
4 Name and address of addressee	Mrs C Archer 46 Rosebank Drive Kirkintilloch GLASGOW G66 1JY	*Turn up 2 single spaces*
5 Salutation	Dear Mrs Archer	*Turn up 2 single spaces*
7 Body of letter	Thank you for visiting our shop.	*Turn up 2 single spaces*

We have noted your instructions about the built-in furniture you have asked us to install, and we have altered the plan and quotation accordingly.

Enclosed is a new acceptance sheet which shows the revised figures and amended calculations. Would you please sign the slip and return it with your deposit which will enable us to proceed with the order.

Turn up 2 single spaces

8 Complimentary close   Yours sincerely

Turn up 5 single spaces

10 Signatory   A TOMKINSON   *Turn up 1 single space*

11 Designation   Department Manager

Turn up minimum of 2 single spaces

12 Enclosure   Enc

2   Type the following fully-blocked letter in open punctuation, from Kenkott Scotia PLC, on A4 letterhead paper. (See *Handbook and Solutions Manual*.) (a) Margins: 12 pitch 22–82, 10 pitch 12–72. (b) The details as far as the salutation are exactly as those given in the letter above. (c) After typing the salutation, turn up two single spaces and then type the following paragraphs.

I refer to my letter mailed to you this morning.

I do apologize most sincerely for omitting to enclose the acceptance sheet showing the revised figures. I am now enclosing this sheet and should be most grateful if you would sign the slip and send it to me together with your deposit.

I confirm that we will start installing the furniture next Friday.

      (d) The complimentary close, etc, is the same as in the letter above.

SELECTIVE LETTINGS LTD

TYPING POOL – REQUEST FORM

This sheet contains instructions which must be complied with when typing the documents. Read the information carefully before starting, and refer back to it frequently.

Typist's log sheet

Originator **NIGEL GRANT-GOUGH** Department **Lettings**   Date **Today's**   Ext No **34**

 Typists operating a word processor, or electronic typewriter with appropriate function keys, should apply the following automatic facilities: top margin; carrier return; line-end hyphenation; underline OR bold print (embolden); error correction; centring; any other relevant applications.

Remember to (a) complete the details required at the bottom of the form; (b) enter typing time per document in appropriate column; and (c) before submitting this Log sheet and your completed work, enter TOTAL TYPING TIME in last column so that the typist's time may be charged to the originator.

Document No	Type of document and instructions	Copies – Original plus	Input form¶	Typing time per document	Total typing time Ŧ
* 1	Letter – 22 Wyndham St and envelope	1 original + 1 carbon	AT		
2	Tenancy Agreement Form for completion	1 original	MS		
3	Inventory	1 original	MS		
4	Memo & envelope	1 original	MS		
5	Requirements for letting – numbered list	1 original	AT		
6	Notice	1 original	MS		
				TOTAL TYPING TIME	

TYPIST – please complete:

Typist's name: Date received: Date completed:

Time received: Time completed:

If the typed documents cannot be returned within 24 hours, typing pool supervisor should inform the originator. Any item that is urgent should be marked with an asterisk (*).

¶ T = Typescript   AT = Amended Typescript   MS = Manuscript   SD = Shorthand Dictation   AD = Audio Dictation
Ŧ To be charged to the originator's department.

3 Type the following fully-blocked letter in open punctuation from Kenkott Scotia PLC on A5 letterhead paper. (a) Margins: 12 pitch 13–63, 10 pitch 6–56. (b) Insert today's date.
NB For an explanation of item number 6 see page 60.

Our ref TJB/OP

Turn up 2 single spaces

Miss F Y Maxwell
17 The Crofts
NEWTON ABBOT
Devon
TW12 5NA

Turn up 2 single spaces

Dear Miss Maxwell

Turn up 2 single spaces

6 Subject heading BONUS VOUCHERS

Turn up 2 single spaces

It is with great pleasure that the Directors have decided to offer a strictly limited number of Bonus Vouchers to certain of our valued customers.

The enclosed voucher entitles you to 15% discount on everything in our range, provided your order reaches us within the next 4 weeks.

Yours sincerely

T J BROOKSBANK
Marketing Manager

Enc

4 Type the following letter from Kenkott Scotia PLC on A5 letterhead paper. (a) Margins: 12 pitch 13–63, 10 pitch 6–56. (b) Insert today's date and enclosure notation.

Our ref YTS/FE

Mr K R Joesbury JP
90 Hillside Road
COLCHESTER
Essex
CO4 5BE

Dear Mr Joesbury

CREDIT VOUCHER

We have pleasure in enclosing a credit voucher giving the amount due to you in respect of goods returned 2 weeks ago.

As requested, we enclose a further catalogue, and look forward to your continued custom.

Yours sincerely

ACCOUNTS DEPARTMENT

5 Type the following circular letter on A4 letterhead paper (Kenkott Scotia PLC). (a) Use
   margins of 12 pitch 22–82, 10 pitch 12–72. (b) Turn up 10 single spaces so that the date
   and the name and address of the addressee may be inserted before a letter is sent out.
   (c) Take a carbon copy.

Our Ref INST/TR/BG

Dear Sir/Madam

SERVICE SCHEME CONDITIONS

This Agreement is made for a period of one year from the
date payment is received or the date of the service - whichever is the sooner.

Breakdown failure

U.C.   The company agree that, within a reasonable time of the owner   U.C.
        notifying them that the Appliance has broken down or failed
        during the period of this agreement, they will make any   U.C.
        repairs and fit any replacement parts, provided that:

        (a) The Owner will bear the labour charge and the cost of
             any parts of the Appliance which the Company consider
             it necessary to replace.

        (b) If any parts of the Appliance which the Company consider
             it necessary to replace become obsolete or unobtainable,
             the Company may supply and fit adequate replacement
             parts which are not the same as the parts being replaced.

        (c) The company sh. not be held resp. for any delay
             in the provision of spare parts by the suppliers.

Yours faithfully
KENKOTT SCOTIA PLC

Terry Richards
CONTRACT DEPARTMENT

6 File the carbon copy. Send the top copy to:
   Mr P O'Connor 47 Main Street Lurgan
   CRAIGAVON Co Armagh BT66 5AR. Insert
   date - 28 Nov. 1988 and delete the word 'Madam'.

5   Type the following letter from Kenkott Scotia PLC on A4 letterhead paper. (a) Margins: 12 pitch 22–84, 10 pitch 12–74.

    NB   For an explanation of the numbered items see pages 59 and 60.

Ref RAB/4PU/MA

Turn up 2 single spaces

20 May 1988

Turn up 2 single spaces

3 Special mark   FOR THE ATTENTION OF MR ADRIAN VAN SERTIMA

Turn up 2 single spaces

P Van Sertima & Sons
22 Main Road
GLASGOW
G32 5LL

Dear Sirs

12 ASH DRIVE DUMBARTON

Thank you for your letter of 17 May, in which you complain about the quality of the work carried out at your bungalow. Please accept our sincere apologies.

Our foreman has inspected the work and agrees that your complaints are entirely justified. We will make good all the defective work within the next few days, and regret the inconvenience you have been caused.

I wish to confirm that our workmen will be at your office premises in Main Road, Glasgow, on Monday, 30 May at 0830 hours, to commence the decorating and repair work you wish to be carried out there, and assure you that it will be completed as quickly and efficiently as possible.

Yours faithfully

Turn up 1 single space

9 Name of organization   KENKOTT SCOTIA PLC

R A Bushell (Ms)
BRANCH MANAGER

Circular letters

Circulars, or circular letters, are letters of the same contents which are sent to a number of customers or clients. The original is usually typed on a master sheet (stencil or offset litho) and a quantity is 'run off'. Alternatively, a circular letter may be stored on a disk and individual letters produced on a word processor.

Reference—in usual position.

Date—typed in various ways; eg, 21st July, 1988.

	July, 1988 (month and year only).
Follow instructions	Date as postmark (these words are typed in
or layout	the position where you normally type the date).

Name and address of addressee

(a) Space may be left for this and in that case the details are typed on individual sheets after they have been 'run off'. When preparing the master (or draft), turn up eight single spaces after the date (leaving seven clear) before typing the salutation.

(b) Very often the name and address of addressee are not inserted and, if this is so, no space need be left when the master is prepared. Turn up two single spaces after date.

Salutation

(a) Dear—the remainder of the salutation is typed in when the name and address are inserted.

(b) Dear Sir, Dear Madam, Dear Sir(s), Dear Sir/Madam.

Signature

The author may or may not sign the letter. If he or she is signing, type the complimentary close, etc, in the usual way. Should the author not wish to sign, type Yours faithfully and company's name* in the usual position, turn up two single spaces and type the name of the signatory, then turn up two single spaces and type the designation.

* If the company's name is not being inserted, turn up two single spaces after Yours faithfully and type the name of the signatory, then turn up two single spaces and type the designation.

4   Type the following letter on A4 letterhead paper (Kenkott Scotia PLC). (a) Use margins of 12 pitch 22–82, 10 pitch 12–72. (b) Leave three clear vertical spaces so that the date may be inserted whenever a letter is sent to a customer.

```
Our Ref FUR/BED/JC/GM
```

(Turn up 4 single spaces)

```
Dear Customer

FITTING PROCEDURE

The components for your bedroom furniture will arrive 3 days
before fitting, and, prior to this, our Transport Department
will telephone you to agree a time for the delivery of the
materials.

Our fitters are allocated sufficient time to ensure that we
maintain our high quality standards, and, in order to keep
our time schedule for each installation, it is important
that the room is ready before our fitter arrives.  If the
furniture is to be installed in a new property, please ensure
that there is a power supply on site.

Yours faithfully

James Castleford

MANAGER - INSTALLATION SERVICES
```

Open punctuation

1 No punctuation is inserted in the reference, date, name and address of addressee or the salutation.
2 In the body of the letter the points mentioned on page 28 apply.
3 No punctuation is inserted in the complimentary close, or in any of the wording that may follow it.

Printed letterhead

Letters are usually typed on the printed letterhead paper of the company that is sending the letter. Depending on the display of the letterhead and the length of the letter itself, it is usual to turn up anything from two to nine single spaces after the last line of the printed heading before commencing the letter.

Fully blocked

Every line of the letter is typed at the left margin, which may be set to line up with the printed letterhead — or if a short letter — the left margin may be anything from 25 mm to 51 mm (1 inch to 2 inches).

Linespacing

The example given on page 61 is suggested as a neat, compact style, pleasing to the eye. Note the linespacing between each item in the letter. There must always be *at least* one clear linespace between each individual part.

Parts of the letter

1 *REFERENCE* — Our ref, Your ref
   (a) Type at the left margin or in the space provided on the headed paper.
   (b) In their simplest forms they consist of the originator's/author's and typist's initials, eg, AMD/ACM.

2 *DATE*
   (a) Use the style that your employer prefers, but it is more usual to type it in the order of day, month, year, eg, 10 October 1988.
   (b) Even when using fully-blocked style of letter display some employers prefer the date to be typed at the right margin, for ease of reference.

3 *SPECIAL MARKS*, eg, FOR THE ATTENTION OF, URGENT, PRIVATE, PERSONAL
   (a) Usually typed in capitals with or without the underline, and/or in bold print.
   (b) All special marks are typed two single spaces above the name and address of the addressee. In a letter, for the attention of a particular person may be typed above *or* below the name and address, but the Post Office requires it to be placed ABOVE on the envelope; therefore, as the special marks MUST ALWAYS be typed on the envelope, and the typist usually copies the details from the letter, we suggest that for the attention of is typed above the name and address of the addressee.

4 *NAME AND ADDRESS OF ADDRESSEE*
   (a) Single spacing.
   (b) Each item preferably on a separate line.
   (c) It is usual to type the name of the post town in capital letters and the Post Office prefer it in this style when typing the address on the envelope.
   (d) The postcode is always typed in BLOCK CAPITALS. Do not use full stops or any punctuation marks between or after the characters in the code. Leave one clear space between the two halves of the code.

When roman numerals are used for enumerations, they may be blocked at the left. eg,

(i)[4]   Title of book   Leave four spaces after right bracket.
(ii)[3] Name of author   Leave three spaces after right bracket.
(iii)[2] Publisher   Always leave two spaces after right bracket in the *longest* number.

2   Type the following exercise on A4 paper. (a) Margins: 12 pitch 20–85, 10 pitch 10–75.
    (b) Single spacing. (c) Arabic figures in blue indicate the number of spaces to be left after
    the roman numeral, and are not to be typed.

AN ITINERARY

An itinerary is a programme of appointments and visits listed in date and/or time
order, so that it can be easily referred to. Itineraries vary in content but
may contain the following items:

I[4]   TITLE

The title usually consists of the name of the person travelling, and the general
destination.

II[3]   TRAVEL DETAILS

These must consist of exact times of departure and arrival, departure and arrival
points, transport arrangements, and facilities en route.

III[2] ACCOMMODATION

If applicable, the name, address, and telephone number of the hotel reservation.

IV[3]   ENGAGEMENTS

Complete list of engagements giving time, place, names of people involved, purpose
of visit.

3   Type the following on A5 landscape paper. (a) Margins: 12 pitch 22–82, 10 pitch 12–72.
    (b) Double spacing. NOTE: The text must always start at the same point on the scale.

TELEPHONE TECHNIQUES

Incoming Calls

(i)[4]   Always have a pencil and notepad handy.

(ii)[3]   Answer incoming calls promptly.

(iii)[2] Do not say "Hello".

(iv)[3]   Identify yourself or your company by name.

(v)[4]   Speak clearly and distinctly. Be brief, but pleasant.

(vi)[3]   Do not keep the caller waiting.

(vii)[2] If you need to pass on a message, write it down and
          deliver it immediately.

5 *SALUTATION*
As with all other items, the salutation is typed at the left margin with one clear linespace above and below it and no punctuation.

6 *SUBJECT HEADING*
May be typed in upper or lower case, but is easier to read and more clear to the reader if typed in all capitals or bold print. There is no need to underline when typed in capitals, but you should follow the exercise you are copying.

7 *BODY OF LETTER*
(a) Usually typed in single spacing with double between the paragraphs.
(b) Short letters may be typed in double spacing if preferred.

8 *COMPLIMENTARY CLOSE*
As with all other items, typed at left margin when using fully-blocked style of display. Only the first word has an initial capital.

9 *NAME OF ORGANIZATION SENDING THE LETTER*
This may be typed as part of the complimentary close.
(a) May be typed in upper or lower case, but capitals are preferable for clarity.
(b) Never underline.
NOTE: The practice of typing the organization's name after the complimentary close is less popular with the authors of today's business letters as these are much less formal and more personal. In any case, the name was really only inserted after Yours faithfully, never after Yours sincerely.
(c) If the name of the organization has to be put in, turn up one single space only after the complimentary close.
(d) ALWAYS follow the layout/instructions given to you by your employer/examiner.

10 *NAME OF SIGNATORY*
(a) Turn up five single spaces after the complimentary close (or name of organization if inserted) before typing the name of the person who will sign the letter.
(b) A lady may wish to insert her title (Mrs/Miss/Ms), usually after her name in brackets.

11 *DESIGNATION*
(a) After the name of the signatory, turn up one single space and type the designation (official position of the person signing the letter).
(b) May be typed in upper or lower case.

12 *ENCLOSURE*
(a) The inclusion of papers or documents in a letter must be indicated in some way, the most usual being the abbreviation Enc (or Encs if more than one).
(b) This abbreviation will not always appear on the examination paper and will rarely be dictated in the office. It is the responsibility of the typist to note if an enclosure is mentioned in the body of the letter and, if it is, to make sure the abbreviation is typed at the foot of the letter.

NOTE: Suitably printed letterheads and forms for this and other units are in the *Handbook and Solutions Manual*, and may be photocopied.

Roman numerals

Use of roman numerals

(a) For numbering tables or paragraphs instead of using ordinary (arabic) figures,
eg, Chapter IX Table XIII.

(b) Sometimes to express the year,
eg, 1988 MCMLXXXVIII.

(c) For designation of monarchs, forms and class numbers,
eg, George VI   Form V   Class IX.

(d) Small roman numerals are used for numbering prefaces of books, subparagraphs or sub-sections.

Examples of roman numerals

Study the following table. Note the seven symbols, 1 (one), V (five), X (ten), L (fifty), C (one hundred), D (five hundred) and M (one thousand). Note also that when a smaller numeral precedes a larger one, it is subtracted, eg, IX = 9; but when a smaller numeral follows a larger one, it is added to it, eg, XI − 11.

Roman numerals may be typed in upper or lower case. It is important to remember to use a capital or small I (i) to represent the figure one.

Arabic	Capital roman	Small roman	Arabic	Capital roman	Small roman
1	I	i	20	XX	xx
2	II	ii	30	XXX	xxx
3	III	iii	40	XL	xl
4	IV	iv	50	L	l
5	V	v	60	LX	lx
6	VI	vi	70	LXX	lxx
7	VII	vii	80	LXXX	lxxx
8	VIII	viii	90	XC	xc
9	IX	ix	100	C	c
10	X	x	500	D	d
			1000	M	m

NOTE: In the above example the roman numerals are blocked at the left.

1   Type the following exercise on A5 landscape paper. (a) Margins 12 pitch 22–82, 10 pitch 12–72. (b) Double spacing.

```
Refer to Section IX, Chapter II, Page 340, Paragraph 2(iii).

Read parts XVI, XVII, and XVIII, subsections ii, vi, and ix.

The boys in Forms VI and IX will take Stages I, II, and III.

Charles II, Henry VIII, George IV, James VI, and Edward III.
```

Our ref BL/TD

Your ref POR/46/TY

20 April 1988

<u>URGENT</u>

Mr L T Padbury
26 Forge Road
Bridgetown
GLASGOW
G40 1BU

Dear Sir

REPLACEMENT OF WINDOWS

We have pleasure in submitting our fixed price quotation
totalling £2,438, exclusive of Value Added Tax, to replace
the existing softwood windows to the front and rear of your
property.

This price includes taking out the existing windows, fitting
and glazing the new windows, as well as decorating the frames.
Any scaffolding required is also included in the price.

A deposit of £1,150 will be required prior to commencement of
the work, with the balance upon completion.

We enclose details of the designs for the windows, and look
forward to hearing from you.

Yours faithfully
KENKOTT SCOTIA PLC

BRIAN LUCKNOWE
Sales Manager

Enc

NOTE: This exercise contains all the
parts of a business letter.
Keep your copy and refer to it
when necessary.

Follow instructions given at top of page 42. Margins: 12 pitch 22–82, 10 pitch 12–72. Single spacing, with double between exercises.

A Review alphabet keys

1 Don't try to fix electrical equipment yourself. You may not
realize just how very dangerous this could be.

B Practise common letter combinations

2 it additional committee entitled definite credit remit visit
3 or transport effort report inform story order work word form
4 Your committee is entitled to free transport for the visits.
5 Make a definite effort to prepare an additional credit note.

C Improve control of up reaches

6 at bat hat cat sat that swat chat water elated patter lately
7 ju jug jut jury June Judy jump juice junior justice justify.
8 We were elated to see that June and Judy Judd were not late.
9 Pat Justin gave me a jug of water to quench my great thirst.

D Language arts — use of apostrophe (See explanation on page 182)

10 The man's computer terminal is on a desk in the main office.
11 The men's computer terminals were attached to the mainframe.
12 The child's personal computer was not really very expensive.
13 The children's personal computers were bought at cut prices.

Skill measurement 30 wpm 3 minutes Not more than 3 errors

SM34 When travelling in an aeroplane, make sure that none of your 12
hand luggage obstructs the aisle or seat areas. It should 24
be stored in the overhead lockers or under the seat in front 36
of you. Enjoy your flight! Sit back, relax, and make your- 48
self comfortable - the cabin staff will be pleased to attend 60
to your needs. Hot or cold meals will be served during the 72
flight, depending on the time of day and length of flight. 83
Radio and tape players may be used. (SI 1.27) 90

    1 | 2 | 3 | 4 | 5 | 6 | 7 | 8 | 9 | 10 | 11 | 12 |

Record your progress 3 minutes

R25 A wide range of tax-free goods is available on the aircraft, 12
and a list of the products, with prices and comparative UK 24
retail prices, will be found in the seat pocket. Your cabin 36
staff will let you know in good time as to when the tax-free 48
products will be on sale. For your guidance a list of items 60
you can hear on the audio channels is in the pocket - adjust 72
the sound to suit your needs, but keep the volume low. Some 84
flights have a film and you should select a suitable channel 96
to listen to the sound-track and channel 2 for quality jazz. 108
Your headset should be placed in the seat pocket before you 120
leave the aircraft. (SI 1.27) 124

    1 | 2 | 3 | 4 | 5 | 6 | 7 | 8 | 9 | 10 | 11 | 12 |

Follow instructions given at top of page 42. Margins: 12 pitch 22–82, 10 pitch 12–72. Single spacing, with double between exercises.

A Review alphabet keys

1 The breakfast Jackson requested was excellent even though it was cooked for him in a frying pan over a brazier.

B Improve skill on fluency drill

2 she her his him are not has had any our who did but was see.
3 they that week know time will days this here your food when.
4 They know that this food must have been left here some days.
5 Your team hope that they will have much more time this week.

C Build speed on phrases

6 to me, to go, to do, if it, if he, if we, do we, do it, out.
7 and the, for the, may the, can the, you are, you can, it is.
8 If you are late, you can get the last train to go from town.
9 If he calls, do we want him to do the work for the firm now?

D Improve control of in reaches

10 Ar are art ark lark dark park arch larch tartar barter March
11 Ou out our sour dour pour tour ounce pounce bounced trounced
12 It was dark in the park and the rain poured on the tourists.

E Spelling skill Correct the one misspelt word in each line. (*See page 182 for answer*)

13 media input argues omitted expenses priviledges inconvenient
14 diary depot misuse mislaid harassed comittees advertisement
15 The advertisment about this year's diaries had been omitted.

Skill measurement 27 wpm · One minute Not more than one error

SM19 The day was sunny but cool. After we had rested and had our   12
snack, we packed our bags and set out for the distant cliffs   24
some 2 miles off. **(SI 1.15)**   27

1 | 2 | 3 | 4 | 5 | 6 | 7 | 8 | 9 | 10 | 11 | 12 |

Record your progress One minute

R14 A thick haze covered the headland, and the wind, now at gale   12
force, was sharp and biting. I walked on and in a long time   24
I judged I had done only 3 miles. Anxious and quite worried   36
I sat down for a short time. **(SI 1.12)**   42

1 | 2 | 3 | 4 | 5 | 6 | 7 | 8 | 9 | 10 | 11 | 12 |

4   Type the following exercise on A4 paper. (a) Margins: 12 pitch 22–82, 10 pitch 12–72. (b) Double spacing. (c) Type each footnote in single spacing, with double spacing between each one.

ACCEPTABLE DISPLAY

Margin Settings   *specific*

Type para heading in upper case

Unless there are *specific* instructions to the contrary, NEVER set margins of less than one inch on the left and half an inch on the right when using A4, or A5 landscape paper.

portrait

With A5 paper, NEVER have margins of less than half an inch on either side. #

A4 PORTRAIT PAPER   Use margins of 12 pitch 13-63, 10 pitch 6-56.* [A4, AND A5 LANDSCAPE PAPER   As a rule, you should not use less than a 60-space typing line when the margins would be 12 pitch 22-82, 10 pitch 12-72. W. a 65-space typing line, you wd need margins of 12 pitch 20-85, 10 pitch 11-76. W. 12 pitch, you can hv a typing line of 70 and 75 w. margins of 18-88 and 13-90/95 ‡.

LETTERHEAD PAPER   If you are typing on letterhead paper, then you may wish to set the left margin in line w. the start of the heading. Of course, shd the heading start 2 inches in fr the left edge of the paper, then it wd be unwise to set a margin at th point.

MEMORANDA   Any of the settings for A4, and A5 landscape paper, may be used.

* Top and bottom margins on A5 portrait and landscape paper, min. of half an inch.

‡ Top and bottom margins on A4 paper, min of one inch. In this *text*, we hv set the *memoranda* margins at 12 pitch 13-90, 10 pitch 11-75.

Correction of errors

You should not correct errors when typing from the Skill building pages. From now on, you will probably want to correct all other typing errors, and the following are the methods you may use:

Rubber

(a) Turn up the paper so that the error is on top of the platen or paper table.

(b) Press the paper tightly against the platen or paper table to prevent slipping.

(c) Erase the error by rubbing gently up and down, blowing away rubber dust as you do so. (Too much pressure may cause a hole.)

(d) If you are using a new or heavily inked ribbon, erase first with a soft rubber and then with a typewriter eraser.

(e) Turn paper back to typing line and insert correct letter or letters.

(f) Always use a clean rubber.

NOTE: If the typewriter has a carriage, move it to the extreme right or left to prevent rubber dust from falling into the mechanism of the machine.

Correction paper

This specially coated strip of paper is placed in front of the printing point over the error, and the incorrect letter is typed again through the correction paper. The letter will then be covered with a film of powder, and the correct letter may be typed on top.

Correction fluid

Correction fluid is produced in various shades to match the typing paper and is applied with a small brush. The incorrect letter is obliterated and when the fluid is dry, the correct letter may be typed over the top. The liquid may be spirit- or water-based. If the spirit-based liquid is used, it is necessary to add thinner to the bottle as, after a time, the original liquid tends to thicken. Spirit-based liquid dries more quickly than water-based.

Correction ribbon

Some electric typewriters and most electronic typewriters are fitted with a correction ribbon. When making a correction with a correction ribbon, it is necessary to:

(a) Backspace to the error.

(b) Press the correction key—the error is then removed.

(c) Type the correct letter(s).

Correction on electronic typewriters/word processors

Electronic typewriters are equipped with a memory and may have a thin window display so that automatic corrections can be made—from a few characters to ten or more lines. The correction is made by backspacing the delete key and then typing in the correct character(s). The electronic typewriters may be fitted with a relocate key which, when depressed, returns the carrier to the last character typed before the correction was made.

NOTE: On those electronic typewriters that have visual display units, corrections are made by the use of the automatic overstrike, delete or erase functions.

Footnotes

1 Footnotes are used:
   (a) To identify a reference or person quoted in the body of a report.
   (b) For explanations that may help or interest a reader.
   (c) To give the source of a quotation cited in a report.

2 Each footnote is:
   (a) Preceded by the reference mark which corresponds to the reference mark in the text.
   (b) Typed in single spacing.

3 The reference mark may be a figure, asterisk, dagger or double dagger.

In the text:
   (a) It is typed as a superscript.
   (b) NO space is left between it and the previous character.

In the footnote:
   (a) It is usually typed as a superscript, but may be typed on the same line as the rest of the text. If the asterisk key on the typewriter is used, it will automatically be raised as a superscript. Therefore, any other reference mark in the footnote must be typed as a superscript.
   (b) ONE space is left between the reference mark and the first word.

4 The footnote is:
   (a) Usually placed on the same page on which the corresponding reference appears in the body of the text.
   (b) Typed in SINGLE spacing, with double between each footnote. If the main body of the text is typed in double spacing, the footnote is still typed in single spacing.
   (c) Separated from the main text by a horizontal line typed from margin to margin. The horizontal line is typed by using the underline, at least ONE single space after the last line of the text, and the footnote is typed on the second single space below the horizontal line.

NOTE: When the footnote has to be typed at the bottom of the first page, care must be taken to leave enough space at the bottom of the page for the footnote and, if a continuation page is needed, a clear space of 25 mm should be left after the footnote at the bottom of the page.

3 Type the following exercise on A5 landscape paper. (a) Margins: 12 pitch 22–82, 10 pitch 12–72. (b) Double spacing, except for the footnote which must be typed in single spacing.

THE EUROPEAN ECONOMIC COMMUNITY (EEC)

The Community was created in 1958 by the Treaty of Rome.

The 6 original members were Belgium, France, Germany,

Italy, Luxembourg, and the Netherlands. * The EEC has

various *aims* ~~objectives~~ one of them being the establishment of

common policies for agriculture and transport.

---

* Britain joined the Community in 1973, together with the Irish Republic and Denmark.

Proofreading

The most competent typist makes an error occasionally, but that error does not appear in the letter or document placed on the employer's desk for signature. Why? Because the typist has carefully proofread the work before it has been taken from the machine; the error has been detected and it has been corrected.

While proofreading has always been an integral part of the typist's training, it is now doubly important because if you wish to operate a word processing machine, your ability to check quickly and correct errors in typing, spelling, grammar, etc, is even more meaningful. Documents prepared on a word processing machine are often used over and over again, and you can well imagine the disastrous results if you typed the wrong figures, were careless in checking your finished work, and your original error is then repeated hundreds of times. When checking soft copy on the VDU screen, it can be helpful to use the cursor as a guide as you move it across the screen; a less time-consuming aid is to have the base of the screen for the line you are checking and using the vertical scroll to move the text up one line at a time. Adjusting the brightness of the soft copy can also be helpful.

1   In the exercise below, the sentences in COLUMN ONE have been repeated in COLUMN TWO. Those in column one are correct, but in each sentence in column two there is a typing error. Compare the sentences and see how quickly you can spot the errors. Then type the sentences correctly.

COLUMN ONE

1   Thank you for your letter.
2   Please book the accommodation.
3   Our cheque for £221.00 is here.
4   Ask to see that painting.
5   The book is on your desk.
6   His name is Mr B Edwardes.
7   Call in to see me on 12 May.
8   He took 3 years to write the book.
9   Send me £20.00.

COLUMN TWO

1   Thank you for your letter.
2   Please book the accomodation.
3   Our cheque for £212.00 is here.
4   Ask to see the painting.
5   The book is on your Desk.
6   His name is Mr B Edwards.
7   Call in to see me on 12 May
8   He took 3 year to write the book.
9   Send me £20.00p.

Further exercises on proofreading are on pages 178–180.

Typing from manuscript copy

You will have to type letters or documents from handwritten drafts. Take particular care to produce a correct copy. Before typing, first read the manuscript through to see that you understand it. Some words or letters, not very clear in one part, may be repeated in another part more clearly. Check the completed document and correct any errors *before* removing the paper from the typewriter.

2   Type the following paragraph on A5 landscape paper. (a) Read the whole passage through before you start to type. (b) From the top edge of the paper turn up seven single spaces. (c) Margins: 12 pitch 22–82, 10 pitch 12–72. (d) Single spacing. (e) Keep to the lines as in the copy.

THE CHAIRMAN'S ROLE AT MEETINGS

The Chairman of a committee must be knowledgeable about its functions and duties.   He or she must also see that the meeting is properly convened and correctly run. The minutes of the previous meeting must be signed by the chairman when they have been approved as a correct record.

It is the Chairman's responsibility to give decisions on points of order during the meeting.

1 Type a copy of the following exercise on A4 paper. (a) Make all the necessary corrections.
   (b) Margins: 12 pitch 22–82, 10 pitch 12–72. (c) Double spacing.

THE OFFICE ENVIRONMENT

Physical Conditions

✓ (a) Lighting Eye strain must be ~~avoided~~ *reduced*, and in many offices

it is necy to use artificial lighting, although it is important to

avoid glare.

lc (b) Heating It is important to keep an even heat to enable Staff

Run on   to produce their best work.

⌐The minimum temperature shd be 15.5°C.

(c) Ventilation Ventilation must be adequate to allow staff to

work at their full capacity. Many offices are air-conditioned.

NP [Noise can distract, causing loss of concentration, and this can

Trs increase the noise level (if windows have to be opened).

2 Type a copy of the following on A5 portrait paper. (a) Make all the necessary corrections.
   (b) Margins: 12 pitch 13–63, 10 pitch 6–56. (c) Single spacing.

OFFICE DIARIES

The secretary is resp for keeping 2 office diaries, one for herself,
and one for her employer.

Stet The secretary's diary wl def contain all the relevant ~~engagements~~ *appointments*
  ~~that are~~ entered in her employer's diary, as well as numerous daily
      reminders for herself.

Towards the end of the day the secretary shd check to make certain
that all matters have bn dealt with.
Run on
⌐It may not have bn possible, because of lack of time, to complete
all tasks on that day. If this is the case, they must be carried
forward to the next day.

All provisional engagements shd be entered in both diaries in pencil
trs so that they can be easily erased if necy.

3 Type the following paragraphs on A4 paper. (a) Read the paragraphs through carefully before you start to type. (b) From the top edge of the paper turn up seven single spaces. (c) Margins: 12 pitch 22–82, 10 pitch 12–72. (d) Double spacing. (e) Keep to the lines of the copy and correct any typing errors BEFORE removing paper from the machine.

PROOFREADING TYPEWRITTEN DOCUMENTS

An Important Technique

It is essential to proofread (check for errors) a document before you remove the page from the machine because it is not easy to realign the typing when the page is reinserted.

When proofreading, bear in mind the following types of errors: typographical errors – you struck the wrong key; word substitution – FROM for FORM, YOU for YOUR, etc; figures not typed in correct sequence; inconsistencies in use of capitals, in spelling, in spacing, etc.

4 Type the following exercise on A4 paper. (a) Read the paragraphs through carefully before you start to type. (b) From the top edge of the paper turn up seven single spaces. (c) Margins: 12 pitch 22–82, 10 pitch 12–72. (d) Double spacing. (e) Keep to the lines as in the copy and correct any typing errors BEFORE removing paper from the machine.

FURTHER PROOFREADING HINTS

Not only do you have to look for typing errors, you also have to read for sense; therefore, it is often necessary to read a document twice – once for typing errors and once for sense.

Useful Tips

Use the paper bail as a guide as you read each line, and make yourself focus on each letter of each word. You will not find your typing errors if you just scan the page, and you must give special attention to numbers and words that sound alike or look alike.

When the material contains statistical data and/or has to be duplicated or printed in some form, ask a colleague to help – one of you reading the original aloud while the other follows the copy.

Typewriting theory and conventions

Over the years certain conventions with regard to display and layout of typewritten documents have become accepted practice. While some examining bodies and employers do not worry unduly about layout as long as the document is clean, attractive and correct (no typing, spelling or grammatical errors), we do suggest that you use the 'theory'/conventions given in this textbook as a guide. In exercise 2 on page 40, it is necessary to leave at least two clear spaces between paragraphs typed in double spacing; however, it would not be 'wrong' if you left three clear, but it would be ridiculous if you left six. When you are familiar with the conventions and standards suggested in this textbook, then you can adjust the layout of a document to suit the contents, your employer or the examiner.

Proofreaders' marks

When amendments have to be made in typewritten or handwritten work of which fair copy is to be typed, these may be indicated in the original copy by proofreaders' marks. To avoid confusion, the mark may also be placed in the margin against the line in which the correction is to be made. The Royal Society of Arts use only the stet signs, ie, ⊘, in the margin, but other examining bodies may use any or all of the examples that follow.

Mark which may be in margin	Meaning	Mark in text	
lc	Lower case = small letter(s)	⟋	under letter(s) to be altered or struck through letter(s)
uc or CAPS	Upper case—capital letter(s)	⟋	under letter(s) to be altered or struck through letter(s)
ꝺ	Delete (take out)	⟋	through letter(s) or word(s)
NP or //	New paragraph	//or ⌐	placed before the first word of a new paragraph
Stet or ⊘	Let it stand, ie, type the word(s) that has been crossed out and has a dotted or broken line underneath	- - - -	under word(s) struck out
Run on	No new paragraph required. Carry straight on	⟿	
⋏	Caret—insert letter, word(s) omitted	⋏	placed where the omission occurs
⌣	Close up—less space	⌣	between letters or words
trs	Transpose, ie, change order of words or letters as marked		between letters or words, sometimes numbered
#	Insert space	⋏	

PONTYPOOL If a word is not clear in the text, it may have been written in the margin in capitals. The word should be typed in lower case, or as indicated in the original script.

We have reserved this unit for consolidation so that you have an opportunity to apply the practices and procedures introduced in the previous units thus enabling you to revise where necessary, or practise keyboard techniques and drills in order to type more accurately or more quickly.

The examiner, and your employer, will be interested in how many documents you type in a given time; therefore, in addition to accuracy and acceptable layout, we have set a Production target time for each exercise. At first you will reach this target only after concentrated practice.

If you make an error, stop and correct it. Of course, the more errors you make the more time you waste (!) in making corrections. When you have typed the complete exercise, check the whole document carefully and correct any errors you may find BEFORE removing the paper from the machine.

At the top of each page, type the date and the Production target.

Production target — 6 minutes

1   Type the following on A5 portrait paper.
    (a) Leave 25 mm (one inch) clear at the top of the page.
    (b) Double spacing.
    (c) Margins: 12 pitch 13–63, 10 pitch 6–56.

PRIVATE SECRETARY

Personal Qualities

As well as having a good general education and a

high standard of secretarial skills, together with

a wide business knowledge, a successful secretary

needs many personal qualities.

An employer will be looking for a secretary who is

neat in appearance, who will be punctual, reliable

and loyal, as well as being dedicated, helpful and

well-organized.

SKILL BUILDING

Follow instructions given at top of page 42. Margins: 12 pitch 22–82, 10 pitch 12–72. Single spacing, with double between exercises.

A Review alphabet keys

1 When we walked among the foxgloves and bluebells on that hot
   day in June, the crazy paving looked quite attractive.

B Improve control of down reaches

2 va vat vase vary vane oval rival canvas invade vacant valley
3 nk ink rank wink monk junk crank banker drinks unkind blanks
4 The vacant banker's house is near the taxi rank in Bankvale.
5 She did not charge VAT on the vase which was of great value.

C Language arts—use of apostrophe (See explanation on page 182)

6 The typist's workstation consisted of a screen and keyboard.
7 The typists' workstations were well laid out, and very tidy.
8 Our supervisor's office is at the end of the first corridor.
9 Their supervisors' offices were located on the fourth floor.

Skill measurement 30 wpm 2½ minutes Not more than 3 errors

SM33 The Chairman of the Board tells me that Tom Younger has been   12
      badly hurt in an accident on the M5, and points out that Tom   24
      will not be at work for at least 18 months. You are aware,   36
      no doubt, of the fact that he has a large number of speaking   48
      engagements in many different cities, and these will have to   60
      be cancelled at once unless we are able to engage someone to   72
      take over from him. (SI 1.25)   75

      1 | 2 | 3 | 4 | 5 | 6 | 7 | 8 | 9 | 10 | 11 | 12 |

Speed building

Speed is built up more easily on short, simple exercises and, as we have now reached 2½ minutes at 30 wpm, and will continue at 30 wpm with increased lengths of timing, we suggest that you use the earlier Skill measurement exercises as practice material for speed building. For example, to increase your speed from 30 wpm to 35 wpm, use SM12 on page 36. As a guide, we suggest that if you have more than one error for each minute typed, then you should strive for greater accuracy. With less than one error for each minute typed, you may wish to build your speed by using short exercises of low syllabic intensity.

Record your progress 2½ minutes

R24 When you arrive, you should follow the clearly marked black-   12
     on-yellow 'arrivals' signs to immigration. If you are going   24
     to take an onward flight, follow the signs to the 'Transfer   36
     Desk'. After clearing immigration, wait in the lounge until   48
     your flight number appears on the TV screen indicating which   60
     carousel in the Baggage Hall to go to. Just place your bag-   72
     gage on one of the unique, free-of-charge trolleys and go on   84
     through customs to the exit zone on the terminal concourse.   96
                                                        (SI 1.35)

     1 | 2 | 3 | 4 | 5 | 6 | 7 | 8 | 9 | 10 | 11 | 12 |

2 Type the following on A4 letterhead paper (Kenkott Scotia PLC). (a) Margins: 12 pitch 22–82, 10 pitch 12–72.

Ref DPB/FR

8 May 1988

Mrs F Fullilove CertEd PSDip
Department of Business Studies and General Education
James Watt Technical College
17 Paisley Road
HAMILTON
Lanarkshire   ML3 8NA

Dear Mrs Fullilove

CAREERS CONVENTION

On Wednesday, 9 July, from 7.30 pm to 9.30 pm, we shall be
holding an Open Evening for parents and trainees, and we are
inviting a panel of speakers. I should be very grateful if
you would be a member of the panel.

We suggest that members of the Forum should each speak for
about 10 minutes and then answer questions afterwards.

I do hope you will be able to attend.

Yours sincerely

D P BEAUMONT
Training Manager

3 Display the following notice on A5 landscape paper. (a) Centre the whole notice vertically.
  (b) Centre the longest line horizontally.

CENTRALIZED FILING SECTION

C L A S S I F I C A T I O N S

Alphabetical
Chronological
Geographical
Numerical
Subject

4 Type each of the following lines three times on A5 landscape paper. (a) Single spacing. (b) Margins: 12 pitch
   20–80, 10 pitch 18–78.

```
From afar there came to our ears the call "Cuckoo!  Cuckoo!"
They had spent $300 on presents and came home with only 90¢.
The asterisk (*) is used for a reference mark in a footnote.
250 ÷ 5 + 50 ÷ 4 = 25; 25 x 5 - 15 ÷ 2 = 55; $125 ÷ 5 = $25.
```

Brace

The brace is used by printers for joining up two or more lines. To represent the brace in typing, use continuous brackets as
shown in exercises 5 and 6 below.

5 Type the following on A5 portrait paper. (a) Centre horizontally and vertically. (b) Double spacing except for
   bracketed items which should be in single spacing. (c) Leave three spaces between columns.

```
COACH TIMETABLE

London to Oxford        Oxford to London

0715) Not Sundays       1745
0815)
0845)                   1755) Saturdays only
                        1815)
0915                    1835)

0935                    1855

0955) Saturdays only    1915) Not Sundays
1015)                   1935)
```

Handwritten or printer's bracket

This has to be replaced by the round brackets used in exercise 5 above. Where lines of unequal length are bracketed together,
the brackets are typed immediately after the last characters in the longest line. All brackets in any one group are typed at the
same scale point.

6 Type the following on A5 landscape paper. (a) Use the same linespacing as in the exercise. (b) Margins:
   12 pitch 22–82, 10 pitch 12–72. (c) Leave five spaces between the columns. (d) Replace the handwritten
   bracket with round brackets.

```
SPACING BEFORE AND AFTER PUNCTUATION

Full stop               Two spaces at end of sentence.

Comma      )
Semicolon  }            No space before, one space after.
Colon      )

Dash                    One space before and one space after.

Hyphen                  No space before and no space after.

Exclamation sign)       No space before, 2 spaces after at end
Question mark    )       of sentence.
```

NB: It is permissible to type the single-line text against any of the 3 lines to which it refers

---

4 Type the following on A5 landscape paper. (a) Read the passage through before starting to type. (b) From the top edge of the paper turn up seven single spaces. (c) Margins: 12 pitch 22–82, 10 pitch 12–72. (d) Double spacing. (e) Keep to the lines as in the copy.

THE OFFICE

Types of Departments

Sales Department requests the Stores Department to pack and label the goods ordered by the customer. They arrange for an invoice to be issued and advise the Finance Department of the amount the customer has to pay.

Stores Department packs and labels the goods to be sent to the customer and arranges with the Despatch Department for delivery to the customer.

Production target—8 minutes

5 Please follow the instructions in 4 above, but use A5 portrait paper and margins of 12 pitch 13–63, 10 pitch 6–56.

CARE OF THE TYPEWRITER

It is important that you look after your typewriter carefully as it is an expensive piece of equipment.

CLEANING

Dust and dirt particles can cause your typewriter to develop faults. Therefore, you should keep it as clean as possible, and carefully brush any dust away with a long-handled, soft-bristled brush. Take care not to spill any correction fluid on to your typewriter. Apart from looking unsightly, it may cause faults, particularly if any drops on to the type bars or daisywheel.

COVER

Keep your typewriter covered at all times when not in use.

Superscripts (Superior or raised characters)

A superscript is a character that is typed half a space above the line of typing. To type a superscript, turn the paper down half a space and type the character(s) to be raised; then return to the original typing line. If your machine does not have half spacing, use the interliner. In the exercise below, notice the degree sign. On its own it is typed immediately after the figure, but when followed by C (Centigrade/Celsius) or F (Fahrenheit), there is a space between the figures and the degree sign but no space between the degree sign and the letter C or F. Use lower case o for the degree sign, unless your keyboard has a degree sign on it, eg, 10 °C. Superscripts are used for typing degrees and mathematical formulae, eg, $a^2 - b^2$.

Subscripts (Inferior or lowered characters)

A subscript is a character that is typed half a space below the line of typing. To type a subscript, turn the paper up half a space and type the character(s) to be lowered; then return to the original typing line. If your machine does not have half spacing, use the interliner, eg, H_2O, $C_{12}H_{22}O_{11}$. Subscripts are used for typing chemical formulae.

2   Type the following lines three times each. (a) A5 landscape paper. (b) Double spacing. (c) Margins: 12 pitch 22–82, 10 pitch 12–72.

    Subscripts are used in typing H_2SO_4, $CaCO_3$, N_2O and CO_2.

    Superscripts are used for typing the degree sign 4 °C.

    A right angle equals 90°; 1° equals 60', and 1' equals 60".

    At 10 am the temperature was 4 °C; at 2 pm it was 20 °C.

    $ax + b^2 = a^2 - bx.$ $a^2 (a - x) + abx = b^2 (a - b).$ $x^2 - a^2.$

Accents

When a typewriter is used for a great deal of foreign correspondence, the keys are usually fitted with the necessary accents. However, when accents are used only occasionally, the following are put in by hand in the same coloured ink as the ribbon.

           acúte   gràve   circûmflex   tĩlde

Usually typed as special characters are:

diaeresis and umlaut = quotation marks typed over letter, eg, Düsseldorf
cedilla = letter c, backspace and comma, eg, Alençon

3   Type the following on A5 landscape paper. (a) Double spacing. (b) Margins: 12 pitch 20–85, 10 pitch 11–76. (c) Take one carbon copy. (d) Insert the accents on the top and carbon copy.

  Franz Nüsslein, 18 Münchnerstrasse, Düsseldorf, West Germany.

  André Brésilien, 25 av Gallieni, Alençon, France.

  Señor Juan Garcia, Edificio Phoenix del Mar, Alicante, Spain.

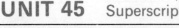 Some word processors and word processing software have special symbols, such as accent marks, that can be inserted during typing.

SKILL BUILDING

Follow instructions given at top of page 42. Margins: 12 pitch 22–82, 10 pitch 12–72. Single spacing, with double between exercises.

A Review alphabet keys

1 The fox came quietly into the open, and enjoyed walking over the field which was bathed in hazy sunshine.

B Improve control of hyphen key

2 day-to-day, up-to-date, self-made, 1901-1972, three-quarters
3 air-to-air, take-off, re-create, re-elected, bird's-eye view
4 Two-thirds of the citizens had up-to-the-minute information.
5 Mr Evans-Gray said he would call at the do-it-yourself shop.

C Improve control of figures

6 1234 5678 9012 3456 7890 0102 9394 8586 7654 8902 1092 34878
7 My office telephone number is 0203 465234 and my home number is 0321 479857. Note the dates 1914-1918; 1939-1945. These numbers were in your notebook: 01-467 7302, and 01-234 3668.

D Improve control of adjacent keys

8 oi toil boil soil foil join voice noise coins choice adjoins
9 rt tart part dart cart sort forts sport mirth berths sported
10 The many voices joined in cheering the sporting darts teams.

E Spelling skill Correct the one misspelt word in each line. (See page 182 for answer)

11 relying useless dismissed benifited acknowledge manufacturer
12 minutes cursory Wedesday dependent approximate appointments
13 We should benefit from the manufacture's sale on Wednesday.

Skill measurement 27 wpm 1½ minutes Not more than 2 errors

SM20 At the moment, there is no guide to help us to judge how far   12
we are from the roadside or from the car in front of us. We   24
know that a device is being made that will help us gauge how   36
far away we may be. **(SI 1.22)**   40

1 | 2 | 3 | 4 | 5 | 6 | 7 | 8 | 9 | 10 | 11 | 12 |

Record your progress 1½ minutes

R15 Have you ever been to a large airport just to watch the end-   12
less movement of people and planes? You can see hundreds of   24
folk getting on and off these exciting jets, and it makes me   36
wonder how such unique planes zoom so gently into the air or   48
land without skidding. **(SI 1.27)**   52

1 | 2 | 3 | 4 | 5 | 6 | 7 | 8 | 9 | 10 | 11 | 12 |

Special signs, symbols and marks

A variety of words (sign, symbol, mark) is used when referring to the characters on this page. One speaks of punctuation marks, the brace symbol and the £ sign. The word symbol is employed mainly for mathematical and scientific formulae and in computer terminology.

Degree	Small o, raised half a space.	6°
Feet	Apostrophe typed after the figure(s).	8'
Inches	Double quotation marks typed immediately after figure(s).	7"
Minus	To show subtraction — hyphen with space either side.	6 – 4 = 2
Minutes	Apostrophe typed immediately after figure(s).	10'
Multiplication	Small x with a space either side.	4 × 5
Seconds	Double quotation marks typed immediately after figure(s).	9"
To	Hyphen	21–25

Constructing special signs, symbols and marks

Some characters, not provided on the keyboard, can be typed by combining two characters, ie, by typing one character, backspacing and then typing the second character, or by typing one character and then the second immediately afterwards. In a few cases the interliner must be used to allow the characters to be raised or lowered.

Asterisk	Small x and hyphen.	x
Brace	Continuous brackets typed one underneath the other. (See exercise on page 116.)	( ) ( ) ( )
Cent	Small c, backspace and type oblique (slash).	¢
Dagger	Capital I, backspace and type hyphen.	Ɨ
Division	Hyphen, backspace and type colon.	÷
Dollar	Capital S, backspace and type oblique.	$
Double Dagger	Capital I raised half a space, backspace and type another capital I slightly below; or capital I and equation sign.	Ɨ
Equation	Two hyphens — one slightly above the other.	=
Exclamation	Apostrophe, backspace and type full stop.	!
Plus	Hyphen and lowered apostrophe.	+
Square brackets	Oblique and underscore — see explanation below	[ ]

On modern typewriters many of the above characters are provided. On others it is difficult to type the division or plus as combined characters. Where this is the case, it would be wise to insert these in matching-colour ink.

When the **asterisk** has to be typed in the body of the text (exercise 4 on page 116), it is typed as a superscript (raised character). Before typing the combination asterisk, turn the cylinder one half space towards you, type small x, backspace and type hyphen; then turn back to normal typing line. Where the asterisk is already fitted, DO NOT lower the paper before typing, as the sign on the type face is already raised.

To type a **square bracket** take the following steps:

Left bracket:
(a) Type oblique sign.
(b) Backspace one and type underscore.
(c) Turn cylinder back one full linespace and type underscore.
(d) Turn cylinder up one full linespace, backspace once and continue with typing up to the right bracket.

Right bracket:
(a) Type oblique sign.
(b) Backspace two and type underscore.
(c) Turn cylinder back one full linespace and type underscore.
(d) Turn cylinder up one single space, tap space bar once, and continue typing.

1 Type each of the following lines three times. (a) Double spacing. (b) Margins: 12 pitch 22–82, 10 pitch 12–72.

$\underline{/756 \div 12 = 63/} \quad \underline{/12 \times 5 = 60/} \quad \underline{/200 \div 2 = 100/} \quad \underline{/10 + 15 = 25/}$

$\underline{/20 + 6 \div 2 = 13/} \quad \underline{/200 \times 2 \div 4 + 30 = 130/} \quad \underline{/40 + 6 \div 2 = 23/}$

Typing measurements

When typing measurements note the following:
(a) The letter 'x' (lower case) is used for the word 'by',
     eg, 210 mm × 297 mm (space before and after the 'x').
(b) ONE space is left after the numbers and before the unit of measurement,
     eg, 210 (space) mm; 2 (space) ft 6 (space) in.
(c) Groups of figures should not be separated at line ends.
(d) Most abbreviations do not take an 's' in the plural,
     eg, 6 in; 6 lb; 2 mm; 4 kg.
(e) When using OPEN PUNCTUATION there is no full stop after any abbreviation, unless at the end of a
     sentence.

1 Type each of the following lines three times on A5 landscape paper. (a) Margins: 12 pitch
   22–82, 10 pitch 12–72. (b) Pay particular attention to the spacing in the measurements.

```
One rug measures 82 cm × 76 cm; and the other, 65 cm × 44 cm.

The carpets were all 6 ft 6 in × 5 ft 7 in or 16 ft × 15 ft.

Send me 5 lb of potatoes, 2 oz of pepper, and 500 g of sugar.
```

Use of words and figures

(a) Use words instead of figures for number one on its own and for numbers at the beginning of a
     sentence. But if number one is part of a list of figures, it should be typed as a figure, eg, 'Follow the
     instructions 1, 2 and 3'.
(b) Use figures in all other cases.

2 Type the following exercise on A5 landscape paper. (a) Margins: 12 pitch 22–82, 10 pitch
   12–72. (b) Turn up seven single spaces from the top of the paper. (c) Double spacing.
   (d) Read the passage through before starting to type. (e) Follow the line-endings given in
   the exercise. (f) Note the use of words and figures.

THE POST OFFICE UNDERGROUND RAILWAY

This railway links 6 sorting offices with Paddington and
Liverpool Street and runs under the streets of London, so
avoiding traffic jams. Forty thousand mail bags are carried
every day, and the trains run through 6½ miles of tunnels
and 8 stations. There are 20 trains which run at a speed of
35 miles per hour.

It was opened in December 1927 and is operated by remote
control with no drivers, guards or passengers.

Follow instructions given at top of page 42. Margins: 12 pitch 22–82, 10 pitch 12–72. Single spacing, with double between exercises.

A Review alphabet keys

1 The size of the paper requested by the teacher was important
   as it made a difference to the vertical and horizontal spacing of the exercises, but the marking was adjusted.

B Improve control of figure keys

2 wet 235 let 934 get 535 his 682 did 383 lid 983 jar 714 1468
3 pat 015 out 975 are 143 sir 284 how 692 you 697 has 612 2579
4 Orders Nos 2981/88 and 2995/88 were sent on 3 November 1988.
5 Cheque No 021048 is for £536.97 and No 021069 for £5,634.78.

C Improve control of punctuation and symbol keys

6 61* 2" 3% 4 @ £5 6 & 7 '8' (9 - 0) "No" "Yes" 3/8 - 1/8 & Co
7 She said, "No, I will not call and see Brady & Co tomorrow."
8 My cheque for £5.29 has been cancelled. Here is another for
   £55.29. The final total (£2,876.54) should read £22,876.54.

D Build accuracy on suffix drill

9 -able payable suitable reliable dutiable desirable available
10 -ible legible sensible terrible feasible divisible indelible
11 It is feasible that the available news is not very reliable.

E Spelling skill Correct the one misspelt word in each line. (See page 182 for answer)

12 ensueing pitiful debited totally conceit pagination aggregate
13 ceiling forfeit eigths leisure precede repetition aggravate
14 Jack's conceit and arogance were really pitiful to witness.

Skill measurement 30 wpm 2 minutes Not more than 2 errors

SM32 Some large offices have a pool of typists who share the work   12
      to be done, but we do not know whether or not this is a good   24
      plan. It is a matter upon which each firm should make a de-   36
      cision based on the pressure of work and the number of staff   48
      employed as typists. You may prefer a job in a typing pool.   60
                                                          (SI 1.22)

      1 | 2 | 3 | 4 | 5 | 6 | 7 | 8 | 9 | 10 | 11 | 12 |

Record your progress 2 minutes

R23   In September 1985, 9,000 people were killed in an earthquake   12
      in Mexico City. Also, in June 1986 slight damage was caused   24
      by a weak tremor which recorded as 5.4 on the Richter scale.   36
      In March 1986, an earthquake struck southern Turkey and some   48
      14 people were injured in 4 villages as houses fell. We are   60
      lucky in Great Britain as there are only one or 2 zones that   72
      have slight earth tremors. **(SI 1.32)**   77

      1 | 2 | 3 | 4 | 5 | 6 | 7 | 8 | 9 | 10 | 11 | 12 |

Some examples of longhand abbreviations

In a rough draft certain longhand words may have been abbreviated, but these must be typed in full and spelt correctly. Some of these abbreviations are given below.

Abbreviation	Word in full	Abbreviation	Word in full	Abbreviation	Word in full
accom	accommodation	dept(s)	department(s)	resp	responsible
a/c(s)	account(s)	exp	experience	sh	shall
advert(s)	advertisement(s)	ffly	faithfully	shd	should
amt(s)	amount(s)	gntee(s)	guarantee(s)	sec(s)	secretary(ies)
approx	approximately	mfr(s)	manufacturer(s)	togr	together
appt(s)	appointment(s)	necy	necessary	thru/thro'	through
bn	been	opp(s)	opportunity(ies)	w	with
co(s)	company(ies)	rec(s)	receipt(s)	wd	would
cttee(s)	committee(s)	recd	received	wh	which
dr	dear	recom	recommend	wl	will
def	definite(ly)	ref(s)	references	yr(s)	your(s) year(s)

Days of the week and months of the year — The usual longhand abbreviations are used, eg, Mon, Wed, Thurs, Jan, Feb, Sept, Dec.

NOTE: (a) & (ampersand), Co, and Ltd, are only abbreviated in the names of companies.

(b) In the Royal Society of Arts Stage I typing examinations, abbreviated words to be typed in full are followed by a full stop. The words should be typed in full, and the full stop must not be typed.

3 After studying the above abbreviations, read the following passage to see that you understand it; then type a copy on A5 landscape paper. (a) All abbreviations to be typed in full. (b) Margins: 12 pitch 22–82, 10 pitch 12–72. (c) Single spacing. (d) Follow the line-endings in the copy.

```
NATIONAL GIROBANK

The advert for the Girobank states that it is now the
sixth largest bank in the country in terms of accounts.   The
number of current accounts recd have more than doubled
in the last 7 yrs.

The National Girobank is resp for nearly 8 million
transactions each week, & has approx 2 million
customers.

Shd you bank with National Girobank you wd find that
it has over 100 automatic cash dispensers, insurance
services, & VISA credit card services.
```

4 Type the following exercise on A5 landscape paper. (a) Margins: 12 pitch 22–82, 10 pitch 12–72. (b) Single spacing. (c) Follow the line-endings.

ADVERTISING

In order to attract possible customers, mfrs. usually find it necy. to advertise. A good advert. shd increase sales.

Some professions are not allowed to advertise & many firms th. cd. advertise, choose not to do so directly. I do recom. television & radio for consumer products where the advert. does not need to contain a great deal of information — particularly accom. to let.

(TYPIST — A carbon copy of this memo, please)

URGENT

FROM   Fred Holborough

TO   Mrs Irene Horne, A/cs. Dept.

DATE

CURRENT PRICE-LISTS

As you know it is a matter of some urgency that we complete the preparation of the current price-lists. Because of the increase in the prices of many of our raw materials, there are considerable amendments to be made.

Wd. you, therefore, please check the enclosed lists very carefully & return them to me by Thurs, 24 Nov, at the latest.

FH/ (Your initials)

(TYPIST — A5 paper)

H ——— + G —— B —— S ——

BOOK THE DATE BEFORE IT'S TOO LATE

SATURDAY, 17 DEC 1988

S T A F F   C H R I S T M A S   D I S C O

Sam Silvers & the Swingers

* * * * *

Bring yr family and friends

Lots of food & good fun

TICKETS: ONLY £5

VENUE: Staff Canteen

Follow instructions given at top of page 42. Margins: 12 pitch 22–82, 10 pitch 12–72. Single spacing, with double between exercises.

A Review alphabet keys

```
1  The male patient lay back quietly in the oxygen tent dozing,
   just after his operation for a broken hip was over.
```

B Build speed on word family drill

```
2  nip lip hip gip rip tip dip sip van can ban ran pan fan man.
3  bold cold fold hold gold sold told full dull hull bull pull.
4  The man told us that he ran to stop the van as it moved off.
5  He sold a full can of ice-cold orange to that happy old man.
```

C Improve control of symbols and punctuation marks

```
6  "2" 3 is/was 4 @ £5 6 & 7 '8' 9 (9 - 8) Mr & Mrs one's £1023
7  They asked, 'Will you both come to Jim's party on 14 March?'
8  Mr & Mrs J Burgess (address below) paid £34 for the antique.
9  He/she requires 20 only @ £5 each, and 18 only @ £5.50 each.
```

D Improve control of adjacent reaches

```
10  po port spot pole pond pose upon sport spoil oppose suppose.
11  we west sweet sweep Crewe tower power fewer between western.
12  Many porters at Crewe Station were very popular with people.
```

E Spelling skill Correct the one misspelt word in each line. (See page 182 for answer)

```
13  woollen sherriffs difference catalogues references compliment
14  usually achieved receivable absorption committees gauranteed
15  The comittees require references for all recent applicants.
```

Skill measurement 27 wpm 2 minutes Not more than 2 errors

```
SM21  He said that if you want a garden then you will have to do a   12
      great deal of work, but in these days you can buy many tools  24
      which will be helpful for the heavy work, and thus save time  36
      and effort.  You would not need to employ hired help, and so  48
      you could then save some money.  (SI 1.13)                    54
```

      1 | 2 | 3 | 4 | 5 | 6 | 7 | 8 | 9 | 10 | 11 | 12 |

Record your progress 2 minutes

```
R16  She exhaled deeply as they crossed the frozen lake and moved   12
     swiftly past the hole lined with jagged ice.  The sleds were   24
     light and the 6 dogs well rested; consequently, there was no   36
     need to think about a stop until we were in the next hamlet.   48
     Then a sudden squall brought more snow and the track's mark-   60
     ings were lost.  (SI 1.22)                                     63
```

     1 | 2 | 3 | 4 | 5 | 6 | 7 | 8 | 9 | 10 | 11 | 12 |

HOLBOROUGH & GREEN BUILDING SERVICES

VACANCY IN OFFICE SERVICES

TYPIST: A4 paper, double spacing
& a carbon copy please.
Correct the circled words

MAIN DUTIES

Normal secretarial duties to include —

(handeling) the post

maintaining filing systems

dealing with correspondence.

OTHER DUTIES

As we are a small, growing company the opportunity may (arose) for the
(sucessful) candidate to travel and attend conferences and exhibitions.

QUALIFICATIONS

Reasonable GCE 'O' levels

GCE 'A' levels or higher (prefered)

Accurate spelling and typing skills

Shorthand an advantage

A knowledge of word processing

A current driving licence

GENERAL

Single Spacing {

The company employs only non-smokers. The successful applicant should be
well spoken, good at communicating, and capable of exercising a large measure
of common sense.

FH/Vac/88/HP

Word processor operator: Key in Document 3 (filename VACNY) for 12–pitch print-out.
Embolden shoulder headings. When complete, turn to page 181 and follow instructions for text
editing.

Securing an acceptable right margin

Up to this stage in the book, you have always returned the carriage/carrier at the same point as the line-ends in the exercise from which you have been copying. This is not usually possible, of course, and in a great many exercises you will have to decide on your own line-endings and also see that you do not have an untidy right margin. If you are using a manual or electric typewriter, a bell will ring to warn you that you are nearing the right margin.

Most electronic keyboards have normal carrier return, justified right margin and automatic return. This automatic return is referred to as automatic word wraparound. Some have devices which indicate that you are approaching the right margin and some do not. Consult the handbook that accompanies your machine.

Before you can practise making your own line-endings, it is necessary for you to become accustomed to listening for an audible signal (margin bell, etc) that warns you that you are nearing the end of the typing line. On your own typewriter, find out how many spaces there are after you hear the margin bell or warning device before you reach the set right margin. If you are using an electronic keyboard, we suggest that you do not utilize the automatic carrier return for the time being. Find out how the normal return works and what audible signal, if any, there is.

1 Type the following on A5 landscape paper and note the instructions in the text. (a) Use single spacing. (b) Margins: 12 pitch 22–82, 10 pitch 12–72. (c) Listen for the audible signal, but follow the copy line for line.

```
RIGHT MARGIN AUDIBLE-WARNING DEVICE

Five to 10 spaces from the right margin a bell or other sig-
nal on your machine will warn you that you are almost at the
end of the writing line.  It is necessary to train yourself
to listen for this signal, and to react as follows:

If the bell/device signals at the beginning of a new word of
more than 5-10 letters, divide the word at the first avail-
able point.

If the bell/device signals at the end of a word, do not type
a further word on that line unless it has less than 5-10
characters (or 2 words such as 'for it' or 'I am', etc) or
unless the new word can be divided at an appropriate point.

It is not obligatory to divide a word; we do it to avoid
having an unsightly right margin.
```

Margin-release key

If at the right margin you cannot complete a word, the carriage/carrier can be unlocked by pressing the margin-release key (usually found at the top right or left of the keyboard). The word can then be completed. The margin-release key will release the left margin as well as the right one.

2 Type each of the following sentences exactly as it appears, using the margin-release key when necessary. (a) Use A5 landscape paper. (b) Double spacing. (c) Margins: 12 pitch 22–82, 10 pitch 12–72.

```
Hard copy is the name given to the text when it is printed out on paper.

Soft copy is the name applied to the data displayed on the VDU screen.

Text-editing is making changes to text after it has been keyed in.
```

TYPIST — Carbon copy & envelope, please

FH/Vac/88/HP

Insert date + name + address of addressee

Dear Sir

SECRETARIAL VACANCY

Thank you for sending us yr. Prospectus. We are a small   l.c.
building firm & have just advertised the enclosed vacancy
for a sec. We wd. appreciate it if you cld. recom. any
of yr. students who may be interested in applying for
the post, & who wl. finish training at Christmas.

I understand that the students wl. not be able to take
up appts. until Jan., but we wish to complete our
interviews over the next 2 weeks.

The following are important:

1 Accurate spelling & typing skills.
2 Common sense + a sense of humour.
3 The ability to work on their own initiative.
4 Willingness to work overtime at certain
   times of the yr.

We wd. appreciate a reply within the next few days.

Yrs ffly

Fred Holborough
Managing Director

Guide for dividing words at line-ends

In order to avoid having a wide gap (without any typing) on any one line at the right margin, you may feel it desirable to divide a long word. Always type the hyphen at the end of the line before typing the remaining part of the word on the next line. Here are a few hints to help you when you feel you have to decide on where to divide a word:

Divide

(a) According to the pronunciation
prop-erty, not pro-perty
chil-dren not child-ren
(b) According to syllables
per-fect, under-stand
(c) After a prefix, or before a suffix
com-bine, wait-ing
(d) Between double consonants
excel-lent, neces-sary
(e) Words already hyphenated at the hyphen
pre-eminent, self-taught

Do not divide

(a) Words of one syllable or their plurals
niece, nieces, case, cases
(b) At a point which would bring two letters only to the second line
waited not wait-ed
(c) After an initial one letter syllable
again, not a-gain
(d) Sums of money or figures
£10,500, 1,250,850
(e) On more than three consecutive lines
(f) Proper names unless absolutely essential

3 Copy each of the following lines once for practice and then once for accuracy. (a) Use A5 landscape paper. (b) Margins: 12 pitch 22–82, 10 pitch 12–72. (c) Single spacing. (d) Note where the word is divided and where division is not possible.

```
sten-cil, pad-lock, mur-mur, pen-cil, prac-tise, elec-trical
com-ply, con-sent, dis-agree, sec-tion, trust-ing, pay-ments
cab-bage, stut-ter, neces-sity, suf-fix, sup-pose, sup-plied
self-support, re-entrance, dinner-time, chil-dren, prob-lems
case, cases, box, boxes, dose, doses; quickly, wrecked, deed
unit, await, adore, eject, ideal, obey; Adams, London, Paris
```

4 Type the following paragraphs. If you feel that the right-hand margin will be unsightly, then divide words at the line-ends. (b) Margins: 12 pitch 22–82, 10 pitch 12–72. (c) Double spacing.

```
ELECTRONIC COMMUNICATIONS


Electronic mail stores and delivers messages from one place to

another.  Equipment can communicate by means of telecommunication

lines, such as telephone and telegraph lines, and satellites.

The information passed between machines communicating with one

another is not a copy on paper but in the form of electronic

signals, and data is printed after transmission and when

received.


One benefit is the speed with which large amounts of information

are transmitted by one organization to another; however, speed

is expensive, but it is becoming cheaper each year.
```

Typist — A4 paper please

HOLBOROUGH & GREEN BUILDING SERVICES

UNITS 5 & 6 MINSTER INDUSTRIAL PARK
Friars Avenue London NW6 3QH

Telephone: 01 624 7402

P R I C E   L I S T

	Plain	Coloured
	£	£
SMOOTH PAVING SLABS		
2' x 2' x 1½"	1.40	1.60
2' x 1' x 1½"	1.00	1.20
1' x 1' x 1½"	0.60	0.75
RIVERN PAVING SLABS		
2' x 2' x 1½"	1.60	1.80
2' x 1' x 1½"	1.20	1.40
1' x 1' x 1½"	0.80	0.95
DOUBLE-SIDED WALL BLOCKS	1.10	1.25
COPING TO MATCH	0.90	1.00

FAST DELIVERY SERVICE

FH/PrL/88
November 1988

 Word processor operator: Key in Document 1 (filename SLABS) for 12–pitch print-out. Embolden underlined words but do not underline. When complete, turn to page 181 and follow instructions for text editing.

SKILL BUILDING

Follow instructions given at the top of page 42. Margins: 12 pitch 22–82, 10 pitch 12–72.
Single spacing, with double between exercises.

A Review alphabet keys

1 Mike was so full of zeal for the project but exaggerated his
   abilities very much, and they were not quite up to the task.

B Practise line-end division

2 able, mail-able, read-able, suit-able, sens-ible, flex-ible.
3 so-cial, par-tial, ini-tial, finan-cial, spe-cial, pala-tial
4 pro-mote, pro-vided, per-mit, per-fume, pur-suit, pur-suant.
5 dis-may, dis-miss, dis-patch, dis-place, dis-grace, des-pair

C Speed up carriage/carrier return

6 I will.
   I will go.
   They may go today.
   Ask them to go with you.

D Improve control of consecutive strokes

7 my enemy mammy myriad myself mystery gloomy clammy mystique.
8 ft lift soft loft left cleft bereft drifter crofter swiftly.
9 There was mystique, and mystery, around the crofter's house.

E Spelling skill Correct the one misspelt word in each line. (See page 182 for answer)

10 movable pastime synonym justify through inconveneince eighth
11 arguing believe pitiful proceed receipt unecessarily ascent
12 The unnecessary inconvenience was hard to beleive or justify.

Skill measurement 28 wpm One minute Not more than one error

SM22 Each year there are some new typewriters for you to use, and   12
      you must know about them so that you are up to date when you   24
      wish to change jobs. (SI 1.11)   28

SM23 A computer is now being made that will store voice patterns.   12
      It will know your voice when you speak to it, and it will be   24
      able to reply to you. (SI 1.21)   28

      1 | 2 | 3 | 4 | 5 | 6 | 7 | 8 | 9 | 10 | 11 | 12 |

Record your progress One minute

R17 From our magazine you will see that we have spent many years   12
     fitting all kinds of carpets - all our staff are specialists   24
     and quietly complete their jobs. In truth, they are experts   36
     who have spent their lives in this trade. (SI 1.25)   44

     1 | 2 | 3 | 4 | 5 | 6 | 7 | 8 | 9 | 10 | 11 | 12 |

HOLBOROUGH & GREEN
BUILDING SERVICES

TYPING POOL – REQUEST FORM

Typist's log sheet

Originator **FRED HOLBOROUGH Managing Director**   Department —   Date **17 Nov 88**   Ext No **1**

 Typists operating a word processor, or electronic typewriter with appropriate function keys, should apply the following automatic facilities: top margin; carrier return; line-end hyphenation; underline OR bold print (embolden); error correction; centring; any other relevant applications.

Remember to (a) complete the details required at the bottom of the form; (b) enter typing time per document in appropriate column; and (c) before submitting this Log sheet and your completed work, enter TOTAL TYPING TIME in last column so that the typist's time may be charged to the originator.

Docu-ment No	Type of document and instructions	Copies – Original plus	Input form¶	Typing time per document	Total typing time ⅏
1	Price list	1 original	T		
2	Letter & envelope – Mr A St John Colwell BA Principal Colwell Secretarial College Cambridge House Aspen Gardens LONDON NW6 2AW	1 original + 1 carbon	MS		
3	Advertisement for Secretarial vacancy	1 original + 1 carbon	AT		
*4	An urgent memo	1 original + 1 carbon	MS		
5	Advertisement for Christmas disco	1 original	MS		
				TOTAL TYPING TIME	

TYPIST – please complete:

Typist's name: Date received: Date completed:
                          Time received: Time completed:

If the typed documents cannot be returned within 24 hours, typing pool supervisor should inform the originator. Any item that is urgent should be marked with an asterisk (*).

¶ T = Typescript   AT = Amended Typescript   MS = Manuscript   SD = Shorthand Dictation   AD = Audio Dictation
⅏ To be charged to the originator's department.

UNIT 44   Integrated production typing project—No 2   **108**

Variable linespacer

The variable linespacer is found on the left or right platen knob. By pressing this in, the platen roller can be moved to any position desired. Its purpose is to ensure that you have proper alignment of the details to be typed on dotted lines, ruled lines or when inserting details in a form letter or memo.

Memoranda (memorandums)

A message from one person to another in the same firm, or from the Head Office to a Branch Office, or to an agent, is often in the form of a memorandum — usually referred to as a 'memo'. Memoranda (the plural 'memorandums' is now widely accepted) may be typed on any of the usual sizes of paper. The layout of headings may vary from organization to organization.

Important points to remember when typing memos on headed forms:

(a) Margins: 12 pitch 13–90, 10 pitch 11–75. These margins may vary depending on the size of the form and the length of the message to be typed.

(b) After the words in the printed headings leave two clear character spaces before typing the insertions, and use the variable linespacer to ensure their alignment.

(c) Date: correct order — day, month, year. The month is not usually typed in figures.

(d) Some memos have a subject heading which gives the reader information about the contents of the memo. The heading is typed two single spaces below the last line of the printed headings, ie, turn up two single spaces.

(e) If there is no subject heading, start the body of the memo two single spaces after the last line of the printed headings.

(f) The body of the memo is usually typed in single spacing, with double between paragraphs.

(g) After the last line of the body, turn up two single spaces and type the reference. This is usually the dictator's and typist's initials which identify the department or person dictating the memo.

(h) If an enclosure is mentioned in the body of the memo, this must be indicated by typing Enc (or Encs if more than one enclosure) at the left margin. After the reference turn up at least two single spaces before typing Enc or Encs.

NOTE: A memo with printed heading is given in the *Handbook and Solutions Manual* and may be copied.

1 Type the following memo on a printed A5 memo form. (a) Follow the instructions given above. (b) Margins: 12 pitch 13–90, 10 pitch 11–75. (c) If you are using 10 pitch, you will have to make your own line-endings.

MEMORANDUM

From   Adam Dark   General Manager

To   Alexis Millar   Typing Pool Supervisor

Date   20 July 1988
           ↓   *Turn up 2 single spaces*
HOUSE STYLE FOR LETTERS
           ↓   *Turn up 2 single spaces*
It has now been decided that all departments should use the blocked format for letters. Please, therefore, give instructions to all typists to adopt this house style in future. For their guidance, a copy of the enclosed blocked letter should be given to each of them.

↓   *Turn up 2 single spaces*
AD/HS
↓   *Turn up 2 single spaces*
Enc

Column display in fully-blocked letters

When the matter is to be displayed in columns, three spaces should be left between the longest line of one column and the start of the next. The first column starts at the left margin and tab stops are set for each of the other columns as explained on page 80 (d–h).

6   Type the following letter from Eastways Developments (UK) Ltd, on A4 letterhead paper. (a) Margins: 12 pitch 22–82, 10 pitch 12–72. (b) Take a carbon copy. (c) Type a C6 envelope. (d) Mark the letter and envelope PERSONAL. (e) Insert a subject heading WORD PROCESSING TRAINING COURSES.

```
PV/TY

9 May 1988

Mrs Janet Gray
26 Jessop Road
SWANSEA
West Glamorgan   SA8 2PQ

Dear Mrs Gray

I am pleased to hear that you wish to accept the vacancy offered to you for
the post of secretary to our General Manager, Mr P Slade. As stated in my
previous letter, it will be necessary for you to attend the following word
processing courses, on the dates given, before taking up your appointment.

WPC1    Room G04, 6th floor    1 day    Wednesday, 18 May
WPC2    Room G04, 6th floor    1 day    Wednesday, 25 May
WPC3    Room G02, 6th floor    1 day    Wednesday, 1 June

The courses will be held at the local Technical College in Clarendon Street.
If you are unable to attend on any of these dates, I should be glad if you
would let me know immediately.

Yours sincerely



PAULINE VERITY
Personnel Department
```

7   Type the following letter from Eastways Developments (UK) Ltd, on A5 letterhead paper. (a) Margins: 12 pitch 13–63, 10 pitch 5–56. (b) Take one carbon copy. (c) Type a C6 envelope. (d) Date: 10 May 1988. (e) The details as far as the subject heading are exactly as those given in the letter above.

> I refer to my letter of 9 May.
> Unfortunately the word processing course on 25 May
> has been cancelled. I should be glad, therefore, if
> you would attend the course detailed below.
> WORDTECH Training School   24 May   0900–1630
> I am enclosing a map which gives the location
> of the Training School.

(f) The complimentary close, etc, is the same as in the letter above.

2 Type the following memo on a printed A5 memo form. (a) Margins: 12 pitch 13–90, 10 pitch 11–75. (b) If you are using 10 pitch, you will have to make your own line-endings.

MEMORANDUM

From   Alexis Millar

To   All Typists

Date   21 July 1988

HOUSE STYLE FOR LETTERS

Management has decided that, as from today, all letters will be typed in blocked format. For your guidance, I am giving you a sample which you should place in your TYPISTS' MANUAL before page 23. If you have queries, please do not hesitate to discuss these with me.

AM/PM

Enc

3 Type the following memo on a printed A5 memo form. (a) Margins: 12 pitch 13–90, 10 pitch 11–75.

MEMORANDUM

From   Jean Alcott-Brown   Purchasing Director

To   John Dawson   Chief Buyer

Date   22 July 1988

GRAPHICS

I notice in the Press that computer manufacturers are now offering machines with graphics facilities. I feel certain that if this resource were available to us, we could create, prepare and print our own data sheets (including charts and graphs), overhead transparencies, manuals, newsletters, contracts, etc, at less cost than our present production bills.

Please obtain quotations and all relevant details.

JA–B/JM

4 Type the following memo on a printed A5 memo form. (a) Margins: 12 pitch 13–90, 10 pitch 11–75. (b) Make your own line-endings.

From Company Secretary

To All Directors

Date 23 July 1988

A meeting of the Board of Directors will be held in the Board Room on Monday, 28 July, at 1430 hours.

The main item for discussion is the International Business Exposition at the National Exhibition Centre (NEC) Birmingham.

PB/AC

Simple display in fully-blocked letters

Emphasis may be given to important facts in a letter by displaying these so that they catch the eye of the reader. In fully-blocked style, this display starts at the left margin, one clear space being left above and below, as in the specimen letter that follows.

5 Type the following letter from Eastways Developments (UK) Ltd on A4 letterhead paper.
(a) Margins: 12 pitch 22–82, 10 pitch 12–72. (b) Take one carbon copy. (c) Type a DL envelope.

```
Our Ref  JOPM/PT/480                              25 June 1988


M S Padbury Esq
6 The Hollow                    NOTE: The date has been typed on the same line as
Redhill                         the reference and ends level with the right margin.
HEREFORD                        To do this, from the right margin backspace once for
HR2 7HG                         every character and space in the date. A number of
                                organizations prefer to have the date typed in this
                                position. Follow house style or layout of input from
Dear Mr Padbury                 which you are copying.

ESTIMATE FOR PATHS AND LAWN

Thank you for inviting me to estimate for replacing the con-
crete paths in your garden, re-laying the turf, etc.  The
estimate is as follows:-
                                              Turn up 2 single spaces

18" × 18" York paving slabs - £200.00
Turf for re-laying the lawn - £430.50
                                              Turn up 2 single spaces
The total cost, with VAT and labour, will be £985.00, but
if the present lawn was patched instead of being replaced
completely, this would result in a saving of £100.


I am enclosing a leaflet showing the various styles and
colours of paving slabs, and I look forward to receiving
your further instructions.


Yours sincerely
```

Standard margins

In the next (page 108) and subsequent **Integrated production typing projects**, very few instructions will be given about margins and layout of documents. You should decide and use what you consider to be the most suitable margins for the length of document and type of display. One important point to remember is that the right margin is **never** wider than the left margin unless you are given special instructions.

In this book, to make the typing look balanced and attractive, we have nearly always chosen the same length of typing line for both 12 and 10 pitch (one exception were the memoranda); thus margins of 12 pitch 22–82, 10 pitch 12–72, means that you have a 60–space typing line, and if you are using A5 portrait paper with margins of 12 pitch 13–63, 10 pitch 6–56, you are typing with a 50–space line.

If no margin settings are given for an exercise, the following suggestions will be helpful:

A5 portrait	Typing line 50 spaces	12 pitch 13–63	10 pitch 6–56
A4 and A5 landscape	Typing line 60 spaces	12 pitch 22–82	10 pitch 12–72
	Typing line 70 spaces	12 pitch 18–88	10 pitch — not suitable
Memoranda		12 pitch 13–90	10 pitch 11–75

If you are given specific measurements (millimetres/inches) for margins — say, one inch on the left and half an inch on the right — then it is better to measure and mark the paper, in pencil, before inserting it into the machine and setting the margins. Please see exercise on page 121 for further information about margins.

SKILL BUILDING

Follow instructions given at top of page 42. Margins: 12 pitch 22–82, 10 pitch 12–72. Single spacing, with double between exercises.

A Review alphabet keys

1 The azure blue sky was quite a breathtaking event for Trixie to see, but it lasted just a few moments as the storm clouds blew up and covered the sun.

B Improve control of vowel keys

2 locate unusual receiving suggestion examination distribution
3 assume anxious financial sufficient explanation requirements
4 Your suggestion has been received and we are anxious to have an explanation of your quite unusual financial requirements.

C Build accuracy on common prefix drill

5 pro- procure profess process protect promote prolong profile
6 con- contain confirm condemn conceal confess consist content
7 Promise that you will not prolong the process. Also confirm that Connie will not conceal the contents of that container.

D Improve control of consecutive strokes

8 ny any many rainy nylon canny granny anyhow anybody anything
9 gr ogre great grown agree angry grade hungry grumble vagrant
10 It was agreed that we should try to grow a good grade grape.

E Spelling skill Correct the one misspelt word in each line. (*See page 182 for answer*)

11 forceful privilege admissable manufacturer immediately local
12 withold perceived absorption uncontrolled opportunity aloud
13 It was admissible for us to withhold the check until today.

Skill measurement 28 wpm 2 minutes Not more than 2 errors

SM24 When you eat your Brazil nuts at Christmas do you ever think 12
of the men who pick them and of the risks they run to do so? 24
One of the risks is the falling of nuts from the trees which 36
grow to a very great height. What we usually call nuts are, 48
in fact, really the seeds from the tree. **(SI 1.20)** 56

1 | 2 | 3 | 4 | 5 | 6 | 7 | 8 | 9 | 10 | 11 | 12 |

Record your progress 2 minutes

R18 Different kinds of wild plants do not grow in the same place 12
because they need the soil and conditions to suit them, just 24
as you have your likes and dislikes. If you acquire a plant 36
which excels in a warm, dry place, it is prone to die if you 48
move it to a zone which is cold and damp. It is possible to 60
alter its habits over a period of time. **(SI 1.20)** 68

1 | 2 | 3 | 4 | 5 | 6 | 7 | 8 | 9 | 10 | 11 | 12 |

3 Type the following letter from Eastways Developments (UK) Ltd, on A4 letterhead paper.
(a) Margins: 12 pitch 22–82, 10 pitch 12–72. (b) Take a carbon copy. (c) Type a DL
envelope. (d) Mark the letter and envelope URGENT.

Ref TRH/OP

8 June 1988

S F Palmer & Co Ltd
8 Crosslands Road
USK
Gwent   NP5 1XA

Dear Sirs

NOTE: The postcode may be typed on the same line as the last item in the address. Leave 2 to 6 character spaces before typing the postcode.

LANDSCAPING OF FACTORY GROUNDS

Our proposed plan for the landscaped area around yr factory is enclosed, together w a detailed estimate.

The Section Manager of our Design Dept, Mr H Rashid, is personally dealing w yr plan & estimate, & I shd be grateful y you wd ask to speak to him on extension 315.

Our pricing policy enables us to offer the best possible value to our customers, & our estimate shd be fully competitive w any other you may be considering.

Yrs ffly
EASTWAYS DEVELOPMENTS (UK) LTD

Trevor R Hambridge
Sales Manager

4 Type the following letter from Eastways Developments (UK) Ltd, on A5 letterhead paper.
(a) Margins: 12 pitch 13–63, 10 pitch 6–56. (b) Take a carbon copy. (c) Type a C6
envelope. (d) Mark the letter FOR THE ATTENTION OF MR P DANBY.

16 June 1988
Messrs Danby & Johnson Garden Suppliers 6 Marylebone Rd LONDON NW1 5JX
Dear Sirs
GARDEN FURNITURE
I enclose our usual leaflets & ask you to note 3 points —
(Inset 5 spaces)   (1) Eastways' quality is the same as ever.
(2) Our range remains unchanged.
(3) Our prices also remain unchanged.

This stability has bn achieved by good management. May I also remind you that continuity of supply is guaranteed through until next Nov, & that every order receives our most careful attention.

Yours ffly   F R ORE (MRS)   Director   Encs

Tabulation

Arrangement of items in columns

You may be required to arrange items in column form in such a way that they are horizontally centred on the page, with equal spaces between the columns and with equal margins. This can be done easily by means of the backspacing method you have already used in display work.

Tabulator key

All typewriters have three tabulator controls which you should locate on your machine as their positions vary on the different makes.
(a) A tab set key to fix the tab stops.
(b) A tab clear key to clear the tab stops.
(c) A tab bar or key to move the carriage/carrier to wherever a tab stop is set.

Preliminary steps for arranging items in columns

(a) Move margin stops to extreme left and right.
(b) Clear all previous tab stops that may be already set. On most machines this can be done by pressing the clear key while returning the carriage/carrier. On other machines there are special devices for this purpose.
(c) Insert paper seeing that the left edge is at 0.
(d) Set the left margin and tab stops at the points given.
(e) Test your tab stop settings by returning the carriage/carrier and then depressing the tab bar or key.

Typing the table

(a) Type the main heading at the left margin.
(b) Turn up two single (one double) spaces.
(c) At left margin type first item in first column.
(d) Tabulate to the second column and type first item; then tabulate to each of the remaining columns and type the first item.
(e) Continue in the same way with the rest of the table.

NOTE: It is essential that you complete each horizontal line before starting the next line.

1   Carrying out the instructions given above, type the following table on A5 landscape paper. (a) Start the heading on the 14th single space from the top of the paper. (b) Set the left margin at the point given; the figures in brackets are for 10 pitch. (c) Set the tab stops as shown. (d) Double spacing.

SOME SERVICES OF THE POST OFFICE

Left margin:
25 (16)

1st tab: 39 (30)
2nd tab: 59 (50)

Swiftair	Datapost	Admail
Intelpost	Special Delivery	Driving Licences
Expresspost	Recorded Delivery	Passports
TV Licences	Pensions	Postage Stamps

Carbon copies

All business firms keep an exact copy of letters, invoices, and other documents they send out. For this purpose the typist may use carbon paper. To take a carbon copy—

(a) Place face downwards on a flat surface the sheet on which typing is to be done.

(b) On top of this, with coated (shiny) surface upwards, place a sheet of carbon paper.

(c) Place on top of these the sheet of paper on which the carbon copy is to be made. This is usually a sheet of bank (flimsy) paper, as compared with the top sheet which is usually bond (better quality) paper. If additional copies are required, repeat steps (b) and (c).

(d) Pick up all sheets together and insert into machine with coated surface of carbon paper facing cylinder.

(e) Make sure that feed rolls grip all sheets at the same time.

Carbon paper has a dull side and a glossy side. The glossy side does the work. It is put against the paper on which the copy is to be made. You always have one more sheet of typing paper than of carbon paper.

Straighten sides and top of pack carefully before inserting it in your machine.

Hold pack by fingers of left and right hands and place behind cylinder, with glossy side of carbon facing cylinder.

Hold pack with left hand; turn cylinder smoothly with right hand.

Check to see that glossy side of carbon is facing page on which copy is to appear. Align top edge of pack with alignment scale and turn up seven single spaces.

Erasing on carbon copies   Do not handle the carbon paper more than is absolutely necessary, as you may transfer marks to both top and carbon copies if your fingers are dirty.

(a) *Correction Paper/Lift-off Tape*   Before inserting the correction paper for the top copy in front of the printing point, or using the lift-off tape, insert the special correction paper prepared for carbon copies between the shiny side of your carbon paper and the carbon copy. Then place the correction paper for the top copy in front of the printing point and type the incorrect letter through all sheets. *Remove the strips of paper* and type the correct letter(s).

(b) *Correction Fluid*   Apply the appropriate fluid to the error on the carbon copy. It is imperative that the fluid should be quite dry before any attempt is made to type in the correction.

(c) *Rubber*   Before erasing, insert a strip of thickish paper between the shiny side of your carbon paper and the carbon copy. Then erase on the top copy. Remove the strip of paper and erase on the carbon copy. If you are taking more than one carbon copy, insert strips of paper behind the shiny surface of each sheet of carbon paper. Erase on the carbon copy/copies. *Remove the strips* and then return the carriage/carrier to the typing point and type the correct letter(s).

Photocopying

Most companies now use a copier and you may be asked to 'photocopy' or 'photostat' an original document, instead of taking a carbon copy. There are many different makes and models but the machines are simple to operate, and you will soon learn how to use the particular model in your office.

2 Following the instructions given on page 79, type this table on A5 landscape paper. (a) Start the heading on the 14th single space from the top of the page. (b) Set the margin and tab stops at the points given; the figures in brackets are for 10 pitch. (c) Double spacing.

```
           MEETINGS - TERMS USED
```
Left margin: 1st tab: 43 (34)
29 (20)   Adjournment   Casting vote   Poll   2nd tab: 58 (49)

           Ballot   Ex officio   Unanimous

           Ad hoc   Quorum   Show of hands

           Convenor   Proxy   Resolution
```

## Horizontal centring—Steps to determine starting point for each column

(a) Backspace once for every two characters and spaces in the longest item of each column, saying them to yourself in pairs. If there is an odd letter left over in any column, carry this on to the next column.

(b) Add together the total number of spaces to be left between all the columns plus any odd character (if there is one) from the last column and divide by two - backspace this number (ignore fractions).

(c) Set left margin stop at the point thus reached.

(d) Starting from the left margin, tap space bar once for each character and space in the longest line of the first column and once for each blank space between first and second column. Set first tab stop at this point for the start of the second column and make a note of this figure.

(e) Starting from this first tab stop, again tap space bar once for each character and space in the longest item of the second column and for each blank space between second and third columns.

(f) Set second tab stop at this point for the start of the third column and make a note of this figure.

(g) Continue in the same way for any additional columns.

(h) Return carriage/carrier and test tab stop settings.

3 Carrying out the instructions given above, type the following table on A5 landscape paper. (a) Type the heading on the 14th single space from the top edge of the paper. (b) Leave three spaces between columns. (c) Double spacing.

```
    COMPUTER TERMS

    Cursor   Control Keys   Format

    Visual Display Unit   Numeric Keypad   Terminal

    Hard Copy   Graphics   Status Line

    Floppy Disk   Update   Input
```
```

Addressing envelopes

Approximately one-third in from left edge

First line half way down ────────────────→ Mr R Maybury MA BSc
                                          'The Shrubbery'   Each item on
                                          Holly Road   a separate

Post town in capitals ───────────────→ TEWKESBURY   line
                                          Glos

One space between the two halves of code ──→ GL2O 5AA

C6 envelope — 162 × 114 mm (6⅜″ × 4½″)

```
URGENT

Dr J Bhattay
8 Leigh Drive
Byfleet
WEYBRIDGE
Surrey
KT14 7RD
```

2   Type the following addresses on DL envelopes. Mark the first envelope PERSONAL and the second FOR THE ATTENTION OF MR F PORTER.

C R Maunder Esq 2 North Terrace Fenit TRALEE Co Kerry Irish Republic
Messrs F Porter & Co 16 High Street ASHBOURNE Derbyshire DE6 1BZ
G M Morris & Co Ltd 11 Main Road LLANDEILO Dyfed SA19 6EP
Mr F Ratanji 8 Oak Road BANBURY Oxon OX15 6DB
Mr P McCready PhD JP 32 Manley Avenue Fetterangus PETERHEAD Aberdeenshire AB4 8HJ
Messrs Tinsley & Sons 6 Fore Street TIVERTON Devon EX16 8HP
Rev I L Yoxall Holly Tree House Butterton LEEK Staffs ST13 7SY
The Tyson Engineering Co FREEPOST Belgrave Road Highgate BIRMINGHAM B5 2JD
McCluskey Bros 10 Waterford Road LARNE Co Antrim

Freepost

An organization wishing to receive a reply (or response to an advertisement) from customers, without them having to pay postage, may (by obtaining a licence from the Post Office) tell the customers to use the word FREEPOST on the envelope. The word is usually typed in capitals on a line by itself after the name of the organization.

Memo

It is sometimes necessary to type an envelope for a memo, especially if it is marked PRIVATE or CONFIDENTIAL. When addressing the envelope, do not type the word 'To', which appears on the memo form, but just the name and designation, if there is one, of the addressee. If the memo is marked PRIVATE, URGENT, CONFIDENTIAL, etc, then this special mark must also be typed, preferably before the name of the addressee. If you are given the address of the addressee, then obviously this must also be typed on the envelope.

Vertical centring

The proper vertical arrangement of columns will add greatly to the effectiveness of your display. Use the same method for vertical centring as explained on page 45.

4 Type the following table on A5 landscape paper. (a) Centre vertically and horizontally. (b) Leave three spaces between columns. (c) Double spacing.

OXFORD COLLEGES

All Souls	Pembroke	St Hilda's	The Queen's
Somerville	Hertford	Christ Church	Corpus Christi
Lincoln	Balliol	Exeter	Magdalen
St Hugh's	St John's	Trinity	Wadham
Worcester	St Peter's	Merton	New College

The calculations for the vertical centring in the above exercise are given below:

(a) Number of vertical linespaces on A5 land-scape paper = 35

(b) Number of vertical lines and spaces in table = 11

(c) Difference to be divided between top and bottom margins $35 - 11 = 24$

(d) Divide by 2 = 12

(e) Begin typing heading on 13th line, so leaving 12 clear

5 Type the following table on A5 landscape paper. (a) Centre vertically and horizontally. (b) Leave three spaces between columns. (c) Single spacing.

VEGETABLE SAMOOSA

Ingredients

Potatoes	Ginger	Turmeric Powder
Cauliflower	Onion	Garam Masala
Peas	Garlic	Salt
Coriander Leaves	Chilli Powder	Pepper

6 Type the following table on A5 portrait paper. (a) Centre vertically and horizontally. (b) Leave three spaces between columns. (c) Double spacing.

MAILROOM EQUIPMENT

Letter opener	Guillotine
Folding machine	Envelope sealing machine
Collator	Addressing machine
Franking machine	Flap sorters

Envelopes

There are numerous sizes of envelopes, but the size will be used that best fits the letter and enclosures. The three most commonly used sizes are:

C5 — 229 × 162 mm (9″ × 6⅜″) takes A5 paper unfolded and A4 folded once
C6 — 162 × 114 mm (6⅜″ × 4½″) takes A4 folded twice and A5 folded once
DL — 220 × 110 mm (8⅝″ × 4¼″) takes A4 equally folded into three and A5 folded once.

1 Type the following on A4 paper. (a) Margins: 12 pitch 20–85, 10 pitch 11–76. (b) Single spacing, with double between each numbered item. (c) Inset the numbered items six spaces from the left margin.

GUIDE FOR TYPING ENVELOPES

The Post Office prefer addresses on envelopes to be displayed in accordance with the following guidelines.

1 The name and address should always be parallel to the longer side of the envelope.

2 On most envelopes the address should be started about one-third in from the left edge.

3 Do not leave less than 38 mm (1½″) from the top edge of the envelope before typing the first line; preferably start about half-way down so that the address is not obliterated by the postmark.

4 Each line of the address should occupy a separate line.

5 Single spacing is preferable on smaller envelopes - double spacing on larger envelopes.

6 The post town should be typed in CLOSED CAPITALS.

7 The postcode is the last line in the address and should have a line to itself. The code is always typed in BLOCK CAPITALS. Do not use full stops or any punctuation marks between or after the characters in the code. Leave one clear space between the 2 halves of the code.

8 Special instructions such as PERSONAL, CONFIDENTIAL, PRIVATE or FOR THE ATTENTION OF, which appear on the document to be enclosed in the envelope, should be typed 2 spaces above the name and address.

Always type the envelope for each letter immediately after typing the letter.

Forms of address — Open punctuation

DEGREES AND QUALIFICATIONS — no punctuation. No spaces between the letters representing a degree or qualification, but one clear space between each group of letters, eg, Mrs (space) A (space) Sinclair (space) MA (space) PhD
Mrs A Sinclair MA PhD

COURTESY TITLES
(a) Must always be used with a person's name, eg, Miss P T Allsop   F Garni Esq   Mr B D Hayden   Mrs G Jahn
Ms E H Kershaw
(b) Use either Mr or Esq when addressing a man, never both
(c) Rev replaces Mr or Esq, eg, Rev H I Livingstone
(d) Partnerships — the word Messrs is sometimes used before the name of a partnership, eg, Messrs Ling & Sons
Messrs Naughton & Co   Messrs Mynett & Shaw
(e) Courtesy titles are not used in the following cases:
  (i) before the name of a limited company, eg, K Shuker & Co Ltd   L Hocking & Sons Ltd   Tehan & Watts PLC
  (ii) with impersonal names, eg, The British Non-ferrous Metal Co
  (iii) when a title is included in a name, eg, Sir Brian Warrender & Co   Sir Christopher Derricott-Browne

Typing column headings—Blocked style

In addition to the main heading of a table, each column may have a heading. The length of the column heading must be taken into account when deciding which is the longest line in each column. When there are headings above columns, proceed as follows:

(a) Find longest line in each column. It could be the heading or a column item.

(b) Backspace as usual to find left margin, remembering to take into account the spacing between columns, and set left margin and tab stops, and make a note of these figures. Column headings and column items start at left margin and at the tab stops set for the longest line of each column/heading.

(c) Turn up two single (one double) after the main headings.

(d) Turn up two single (one double) after the column headings.

7 Following the above instructions, type this exercise on A5 landscape paper. (a) Centre the whole table vertically and horizontally. (b) Leave three spaces between columns. (c) Double spacing.

ABBREVIATED WORDS

Turn up one double

Abbreviation	Word in Full	Abbreviation	Word in Full
ack	acknowledge	suff	sufficient
incon	inconvenience	misc	miscellaneous
govs	governments	temp	temporary
sig	signature	exs	exercises

Turn up one double

8 Type the following exercise on A5 landscape paper. (a) Centre the table vertically and horizontally. (b) Leave three spaces between columns. (c) Double spacing.

MAPPINGTON SOCIAL STUDIES CENTRE

Meetings arranged for June 1988

Date	Topic	Speaker
2 June	Housing Benefit	Michael F Levy
9 June	Social Services and the Community	John Rhoden
16 June	Healthy Eating	Pamela Ore
23 June	Welfare not Warfare	Jeremy Seager

9 Type the following exercise on A5 portrait paper. (a) Centre the table vertically and horizontally. (b) Leave three spaces between columns. (c) Double spacing.

SOURCES OF REFERENCE

General	Specialized
Pears Cyclopaedia	Hansard
Whitaker's Almanack	Post Office Guide
Stock Exchange Year Book	Telex Directory

Follow instructions given at top of page 42. Margins: 12 pitch 22–82, 10 pitch 12–72. Single spacing, with double between exercises.

A Review alphabet keys

1 The dozens of climbers were frequently exhausted when trying to complete the fantastic job of climbing the very high rock mountain.

B Improve accuracy on use of shift key

2 Vale Kay Union Ruth Gwen Edna Lily Adam Nora Zena John Terry
3 York Coxon Olive Frank Henry Devon Innes Queen Wilson Barrie
4 Ask Miss Edna Trim to see Mr P St John Barrington on Monday.
5 Adam, Olive, Frank, Lily and Ruth left Devon for York today.

C Improve accuracy on word-building drill

6 tend attend attends attended attending attendance attendants
7 be belie belief believe believes believed believing believer
8 We believe their attendance has tended to be poor this term.
9 The attendants believe that the attendance will now improve.

D Improve control of both hands

10 loaf pure knife lived judge upper ounces populate minimized.
11 jive nine house begin carol dream evenly imported detection.
12 I lived in the upper regions where people were hard to find.

E Spelling skill Correct the one misspelt word in each line. (See page 182 for answer)

13 forcible salaried arguements underrate courageous emphasized.
14 modelled steadily inhabited posseses especially vaccinated.
15 He emphasized that he did not underate all their arguments.

Skill measurement 30 wpm 1½ minutes Not more than 2 errors

SM30 You will be pleased to learn that we have made more machines   12
this year than we did last year, and that we are also making   24
all vital spare parts. Over the next 2 months we shall take   36
orders only for the new models we are producing. **(SI 1.22)**   45

SM31 There is nothing that annoys a business man more than clerks   12
who forget to do jobs given to them. A very good idea is to   24
have a pad on your desk, so that you can write down straight   36
away anything that you may be required to do. **(SI 1.27)**   45

     1 | 2 | 3 | 4 | 5 | 6 | 7 | 8 | 9 | 10 | 11 | 12 |

Record your progress 1½ minutes

R22 Dear Ms Knight, Since July 1987 we have had your name on our   12
mailing lists, and although we have, from time to time, sent   24
you details of many exclusive properties, you have not tele-   36
phoned as you said you would. We are now anxious to know if   48
you have any queries and still wish to buy a desirable resi-   60
dence at an amazingly low price. **(SI 1.33)**   66

     1 | 2 | 3 | 4 | 5 | 6 | 7 | 8 | 9 | 10 | 11 | 12 |

From this point onwards there are four Integrated production typing projects, and each project is preceded by a Typist's log sheet (copy in the *Handbook and Solutions Manual*). Refer to the Log sheet for instructions and relevant details before and during the typing of the documents.

When we look at a typewritten document, we notice immediately if it is well or badly displayed. We do not know, and do not care about, the speed at which it was typed. When we read it, any errors in typing are immediately noticed. Therefore, good display and accuracy are of first importance. But your employer, unlike the reader, is concerned about the time you take to produce a document.

Production target time

Reading the manuscript or typescript through to see that you understand the contents (which is of paramount importance), deciding on linespacing and margins, reading and following instructions, are all essential typing techniques that require immediate decisions and must be carried out speedily and accurately. In addition, we have set a Production target for each document and you should keep a record of the times in your Typist's log sheet. At first you will reach the target time only after concentrated practice. Keep typed documents in a folder marked **for signature**, and the folder (with the tasks in document number order) together with the Log sheet should be handed to your teacher when you are sure that all the documents (in any one project) are MAILABLE and ready for approval and signature where appropriate. Also, keep a separate folder for the project documents that have been approved/signed — file the documents under the project number and in document number order.

Errors

If you make an error, correct it immediately; however, after you finish typing, and BEFORE removing the paper from the machine, read through the complete document and correct any errors you may have missed while typing. Diligent proofreading is crucial.

Mailable

This means the contents must make sense; no omissions (you could have a serious omission and the document may still make sense); no uncorrected errors (misspellings, incorrect punctuation, typing errors, etc); no careless corrections (if part of the wrong letter(s) is showing, the correction is not acceptable); no smudges; no creases. Consistency in spelling, in format, in typing sums of money, etc, is vital. Occasionally, your teacher may return a document marked C&M (correct and mail). This means that there is an error that will not be difficult to correct neatly, and after correction the document may be mailed.

Typist's log sheet

The information in the Typist's log sheet will follow a pattern: name of employer will be the first item at the top; the name of the originator and the department (where appropriate) will be handwritten; the date may or may not be given, but letters and memos must have a date unless there are instructions to the contrary. If you have access to a word processor, a text-editing electronic typewriter, or a correction only electronic typewriter, follow the general instructions given on the Log sheet against the symbol. More specific instructions for the word processor and text-editing electronic typewriter will be given in projects 2, 3 and 4. As soon as you receive your Log sheet and input data (information prepared by the originator/author) enter your name plus date and time received near the bottom of the sheet. When all the documents have been completed and are ready for approval/signature, calculate and enter the 'Total typing time' at the bottom of the last column, and also record the date and time of completion.

Urgent

Notice that any input marked with an asterisk (*) is urgent and should be dealt with first. Type the word URGENT at the top of the document, and see that it is ready for approval/signature by the teacher, within 30 minutes of your starting to type the project.

Each project will be a little more complex than the previous one; also, less and less advice will be given about margins, paper to use, spaces to leave, etc.

Project number 1

In this first project, you are employed by **Kenkott Scotia PLC** and attend classes where you are pursuing four modules of a Secretarial Studies Unit. As you are making good progress with your typing, you have been asked to work in the typing pool where Ms Alexis Millar is supervisor.

If you were a qualified typist, the supervisor would hand you, with little or no comment, the input data so that you could convert the amended typescript or handwritten drafts into a typewritten document. However, as you are still training, Ms Millar will list much more detail than is usually supplied, and she will circle any word errors to be corrected.

Insetting matter from left margin

Matter may be inset from the left margin to give a certain part of the work greater emphasis. This matter may or may not consist of numbered items. You must follow any instructions given to you as to how many spaces to indent. There is always one clear linespace before and after inset matter.

When insetting matter you may either:
(a) Set a tab stop at the point where each of the lines in the inset portion will commence; or
(b) re-set the left margin. When using this method, it is most important to remember to go back to the original margin when you have finished typing the inset portion. It is wise to make a reminder mark on the copy at the point where you need to revert to the original margin again.

Some electronic machines allow for a second temporary margin to be set while retaining the original margin.

3   Type the following on A4 paper. (a) Use single spacing, with double between the paragraphs and the numbered items. (b) Margins: 12 pitch 22–82, 10 pitch 12–72.

```
TRAVELLERS' CHEQUES

Travellers' cheques are accepted around the world in hotels, restaurants,
and shops, and can be cashed at banks for a small charge.  Sterling
travellers' cheques are available in values of £10, £20, £50 and £100.

There are 2 precautions you should take to safeguard your travellers'
cheques.
```

Inset 5 spaces
```
              1  Never countersign your cheques in advance.

              2  Keep a record of the number and values of cheques in quite a
                 different place from the cheques themselves.
```

```
When travelling abroad it is also wise to take some foreign currency,
between £20 and £30, to cover the first few days' expenses.
```

4   Type the following on A5 portrait paper. (a) Single spacing. (b) Margins: pitch 13–63, 10 pitch 6–56.

SHIRTS

Repairing cuffs

The method of repairing worn shirt cuffs varies according to whether the cuff is a single or double one.

Inset 5 spaces

(a) SINGLE CUFF
     Tuck the frayed edge inside itself and sew a new hem.

(b) DOUBLE CUFF
     Remove the whole cuff, turn it over w. the frayed edge inside & re-attach it to the sleeve.

I recom. th. you def. use a thread wh. wl. exactly match the fabric colour of the shirt. You wl. also need a pair of small, sharp scissors, pins, a sewing machine, & an iron.

KENKOTT SCOTIA PLC

TYPING POOL – REQUEST FORM

Typist's log sheet

Originator *S McDonald* Department *Sales*　　Date *18 Oct. 88*　Ext No *2134*

> Typists operating a word processor, or electronic typewriter with appropriate function keys, should apply the following automatic facilities: top margin; carrier return; line-end hyphenation; underline OR bold print (embolden); error correction; centring; any other relevant applications.

Remember to (a) complete the details required at the bottom of the form; (b) enter typing time per document in appropriate column; and (c) before submitting this Log sheet and your completed work, enter TOTAL TYPING TIME in last column so that the typist's time may be charged to the originator.

Docu-ment No	Type of document and instructions	Copies – Original plus	Input form¶	Typing time per document	Total typing time ¥
* 1	Menu (to be typed for the Social Club Sec). Use A5 plain paper.	1 Orig.	AT		
2	Personal letter. Use A5 portrait paper.	1 ..	AT		
3	Notice (the Social Club Sec wd like this typed again). Use A5 plain landscape paper.	1 ..	AT		
4	Letter to Mr Singh on letterhead A4 paper.	1 ..	AT		
5	Notice (Social Club). Use plain A5 landscape paper.	1 ..	AT		
6	Notice to Heads of Depts.	1 ..	AT		
7	Memo to Pat Johnson. Make corrections indicated. Use headed memo paper.	1 ..	AT	TOTAL TYPING TIME	

TYPIST – please complete:

Typist's name:　　　　　Date received:　　　　　Date completed:
　　　　　　　　　　　Time received:　　　　　Time completed:

> If the typed documents cannot be returned within 24 hours, typing pool supervisor should inform the originator. Any item that is urgent should be marked with an asterisk (*).

¶ T = Typescript　AT = Amended Typescript　MS = Manuscript　SD = Shorthand Dictation　AD = Audio Dictation
¥ To be charged to the originator's department.

Enumerated items

Paragraphs and items are sometimes numbered or lettered as follows. The numbers or letters may stand on their own or be enclosed in brackets. Always leave one clear linespace between enumerated items. Two character spaces follow the last figure, letter or bracket. There is always one clear linespace before and after enumerated items.   eg

1^2 Address	$(1)^2$ Address	A^2 Address	$(a)^2$ Address
2 Telephone Number	(2) Telephone Number	B Telephone Number	(b) Telephone Number

1 Type the following on A4 paper. (a) Use single spacing if an item goes on to more than one line, but double spacing between each item. (b) Margins: 12 pitch 22–82, 10 pitch 12–72. (c) Leave two character spaces after the item number. (d) Top margin: 51 mm (2 inches), ie, turn up 13 single spaces from the top edge of paper.

POSTCODES

Post Office Guidelines

The following points should be borne in mind when typing, or writing, postcodes.

Turn up 2 single

1   Block capitals must be used.

NOTE: With OPEN punctuation there is no full stop after the figure or letter that lists the items

Turn up 2 single

2   No punctuation.

Turn up 2 single

3   Never underline.

Turn up 2 single

4   The postcode is always the last item, preferably on a line by itself. If it is necessary to type it on the same line as the previous item, leave 2 to 6 character spaces before typing the postcode.

Turn up 2 single

5   Leave one clear space between the 2 parts of the code.

2 Type the following on A5 portrait paper. (a) Use single spacing, with double between each item. (b) Margins: 12 pitch 13–63, 10 pitch 6–56. (c) Leave two character spaces after the bracketed letters.

HISTORIC HOUSES OF BRITAIN

Britain's historic houses are very famous for their architecture, their treasures as well as their history. Three of these houses are briefly described below.

(A) PENSHURST PLACE, KENT   Built about 1341, Penshurst is a fascinating house with a splendid great hall.

(B) BLAIR CASTLE, PERTHSHIRE   Since 1269 this Scottish Highland castle has had a very eventful history. It has some very fine furnishings & decorations.

(C) PENRHYN CASTLE, GWYNEDD   George Pennant inherited the castle & a great fortune fr. his uncle in 1808. The money came fr. Jamaican sugar plantations & Welsh slate quarries.

Leave 25mm (1inch) clear at the top of the page. Centre the longest line and set left margin - start all lines
                         at this point. The date to
                              replace "8 January 1988"
                                 is 2̶6̶ 25 October
                                      1988

```
M E N U

KENKOTT SOCIAL CLUB
ANNUAL DINNER - 8̶ ̶J̶A̶N̶U̶A̶R̶Y̶ ̶1̶9̶8̶8̶


Cheese and Walnut Dip
French Bread and Butter

Glazed Baked Gammon
Pressed Tongue
Cold Roast Sirloin

SALMON CUTLETS IN ASPIC WITH MAYONNAISE

Green Salad
Tomato and Onion Salad

Pineapple Chiffon Flan
```

Mr McDonald typed this letter himself. He is not pleased with the result! Please type it for him.   *Margins: 12 pitch 13-63*
                                              10   "   6-56

```
32 Lanark Road
Govan
GLASGOW
G51 3UR
```

←——— *Insert date*

```
Mr L McKenna
Manager
Scotia Building Society
40 Argyle Street
GLASGOW
G2 1AA

Dear Mr McKenna
```
                    in full
```
Further to our (tel) conversation of this
morning, my wife and I will be (plaesed) to call
on you next Monday at 10.30 am to arrange a
mortgage for the house we hope to buy in Paisley.

Yours (sincereleyy)
```

SKILL BUILDING

Follow instructions given at top of page 42. Margins: 12 pitch 22–82, 10 pitch 12–72. Single spacing, with double between exercises.

A   Review alphabet keys

1   The executive was next in line for the position of Editor on the Gazette as the skills required for the job were just the ones possessed by him.

B   Build accuracy on one-hand words

2   dresses nylon extra jolly great knoll agree pylon gave on my
3   opinion trade union aware only safe upon area joy car him at
4   In our opinion, you were aware of the trade union wage rate.
5   I agree the extra trade in nylon dresses gave him great joy.

C   Build accuracy on double-letter words

6   programmes possible running supply arrive proof agree added.
7   difficult football baggage accept excess rubber attend carry
8   Is it possible to supply a proof of the football programmes?
9   We agree that it was difficult to accept the excess baggage.

D   Improve control of both hands

10 swim frail action stroll punter nominate fraction impressed.
11 just dwell brains pooled number populate immodest kilowatts.
12 It would seem right to take action and nominate Joan Howlet.

E   Spelling skill   Correct the one misspelt word in each line. (*See page 182 for answer*)

13 potato ocasion exercise hardware guardian reducing familiar
14 wholly separate definite feasible expenses gaurdian pleasant
15 On this occasion I was quite familar with the charges made.

Skill measurement   30 wpm   One minute   Not more than one error

SM28 The weather is likely to remain mild in the south, with some   12
      light rain, but in the north there may be ground frost which   24
      could cause ice on some roads.   **(SI 1.10)**   30

SM29 Road conditions have been quite difficult for some time, but   12
      we are sure they will improve. We share your view, and know   24
      we must be patient and careful.   **(SI 1.23)**   30

      1 | 2 | 3 | 4 | 5 | 6 | 7 | 8 | 9 | 10 | 11 | 12 |

Record your progress   One minute

R21   If you are asked to compile a business letter, you must: (a)   12
      use short words if they express clearly what you want to say   24
      and (b) also keep your sentences short. Tackle the job with   36
      zeal, acquire a good style, and avoid vague statements.   47
                                                        (SI 1.25)

      1 | 2 | 3 | 4 | 5 | 6 | 7 | 8 | 9 | 10 | 11 | 12 |

Margins: 12 pitch 25 - 85
            10 "   12 - 72   *Use double spacing*

HOLIDAYS - PLANNING AHEAD

For those of you going on the Kenkott Social Club touring
holiday next year, would you please note the following
points:

— *2 clear spaces*

(MEDICLE) TREATMENT ✓ If, as part of a course of medical
treatment, you need to take medicine whilst you are on
holiday, please remember to pack this in your HAND luggage.

— *2 clear spaces*

ELECTRICITY SUPPLIES ✓ The same supply voltage as in the
United Kingdom - 220/240 Volts AC - is used throughout most
of Europe, so all you need is an earthed 2-pin plug to run
any applicances you are taking.

*Mr McDonald had this letter typed some time ago
and, for a variety of reasons, it was not
mailed. However, Mr Singh has written again
and we would like the following
letter sent. Margins:* 12 pitch 25 - 85
            10 "   12 - 72

Our Ref   SMcD/

*Type your initials
after the oblique*

18 October
~~23 August~~ 1988

Mr Dhami Singh
213 Northgate Avenue
Anniesland
GLASGOW
G13 1HD

Dear Mr Singh

                                14 October
Thank you for your letter dated ~~21 August~~ asking for credit
terms.

Would you please be kind enough to complete the enclosed
form and return it to me.

All our prices are wholesale, and for order's over £1,000 we
allow 2½% discount if the full amount is paid within 30 days
of date of invoice.

As soon as we receive your completed form, we will be pleased
to make an (apointment) and welcome you to our warehouse.

Yours sincerely

Sinclair McDonald
SALES DIRECTOR

Enc

Credit notes

(a) Usually printed and typed in red.
(b) Used to cancel an incorrect invoice.
(c) Used for crediting goods or packing cases returned.

(d) A supplier who credits a customer for goods/services relating to taxable supplies, must issue a VAT credit note, which should give: VAT registration number, amount credited for each item, rate and amount of VAT credited, etc.

4 Type the following credit note on a suitable form. Please see *Handbook and Solutions Manual* for a printed form.

CREDIT NOTE   NO 1368

CASA DE EUROPA PLC
269 Britannia Way
RICHMOND   Surrey   TW9 1JA

Telephone 01-447 9229   Telex 56980

VAT registration No 992 3872 78   Date 15 July 1988

P K Jackson & Son Ltd
47 Ludlow Road
REDDITCH
Worcs
B98 8J·Z

Original tax invoice No 4561
Date of invoice 05.07.88

Reason for credit	Quantity	Description	Total	
			£	
Damaged in transit	1	Dresden Figurine	100	00
		Total Credit	100	00
		Plus VAT	15	00
		TOTAL	£115	00
E & OE				

VAT SUMMARY

Code	%	Goods	Tax
1	15	£100.00	£15.00

Margins: 12 pitch 25-85
        10 ..   12-72

Social Club Notice Board

CITY OF GLASGOW SYMPHONY ORCHESTRA

Extra Concert Discount

Subscribers to the Tuesday and Thursday Series can enjoy the concert on 29 October at 20% discount.

Returned Ticket Service

If it is not possible for you to attend a concert in your subscription series, let the Box Office have your tickets back for resale.

Centre this table vertically and horizontally on A5 landscape paper.   Leave 3 clear spaces between the columns.

HEADS OF DEPARTMENTS

Jean Alcott-Brown	Marketing Director
Frances Goldsmith	Financial Director
Terry Luxon	Production Director
Sinclair McDonald	Sales Director
Alex Scott	Administrative Director

The following memo is not mailable and will have to be typed again — a memo must have a date

Margins: 12 pitch 13-90
        10 ..   11-75

From   Sinclair McDonald

To   ←Patricia Johnson

Date

ACTION FOR JOBS

I enclose a copy of this booklet which gives information about employment, training and enterprise programmes suggested by the Department of Employment and Manpower Services Commission.

12
Would you please order 2 copies and see that the 9 Heads of Department have copies. I feel we should look closely at the Open Tech Programmes.

SMcD/ *Your initials here*

Enc

Invoices — Value Added Tax (VAT)

A trader, registered for VAT, who supplies taxable goods to another taxable person, must issue a VAT invoice giving the VAT registration number, tax point, type of supply, etc.

3 Type the following invoice on a suitable form. Please see *Handbook and Solutions Manual* for printed form. Because of the small amount of space available, notice the use of figures for the date after 'Tax point'.

INVOICE

	NO 4561

CASA DE EUROPA PLC
269 Britannia Way
RICHMOND   Surrey   TW9 1JA

Telephone 01-447 9229   Telex 56980

VAT registration No 992 3872 78   Date 5 July 1988

```
P K Jackson & Son Ltd
47 Ludlow Road
REDDITCH
Worcs
B98 8JZ
```

Tax point 05.07.88
Type of supply Sale

Your order No   PUR 1996/88   Account No   J/2085   Advice note No   35949

Quantity	Description	Unit cost	Total cost
		£	£
6	Edinburgh Crystal Tumblers	30.00	180.00
2	Dresden Figurines	100.00	200.00
2	Aynsley Portland Vases	60.00	120.00

VAT SUMMARY

Code	%	Goods	Tax
1	15	£500.00	£75.00

Total goods	500.00
Discount	0.00
Total VAT	75.00
TOTAL	£575.00

Subject to our conditions of sale. Copy on request.
E & OE

SKILL BUILDING

Follow instructions given at top of page 42. Margins: 12 pitch 22–82, 10 pitch 12–72. Single spacing, with double between exercises.

A Review alphabet keys

1 With maximum efficiency vivacious Eliza completed the formal
tests, was judged to be the best candidate, and acquired the
highest marks.

B Improve control of figure keys

2 wee 233 our 974 try 546 ere 343 wit 285 ire 843 too 599 6789
3 330 339 338 337 336 992 993 994 995 123 456 789 101 293 2345
4 Final 7%, payable 3 November, making 12½%. Profit £455,980.
5 Flight 417 leaves at 1350, while Flight 148B leaves at 1619.

C Build accuracy on suffix drill

6 using ending asking making turning morning replying advising
7 comment shipment equipment settlement adjustment arrangement
8 We will not comment about the shipments of equipment to you.
9 In the morning we shall be asking him what car he is taking.

D Practise alternate hand drill

10 jam hale curl lake make foam roam turn forms provide profits
11 pay burn work hale worm paid kept spar usual turkeys handles
12 My visual aid showed the profits we make on the new handles.

E Spelling skill   Correct the one misspelt word in each line. (See page 182 for answer)

13 valuable marriage function paralel secretary advertisements
14 exercise envelope physical planning colleague miscelaneous.
15 My Secretary's function was to exercise complete discresion.

Skill measurement   29 wpm   One minute   Not more than one error

SM25 We hear that you plan to buy new desks, chairs and files, so   12
we are sending you a copy of our price-lists which will give   24
you a wide range of choice. **(SI 1.07)**   29

SM26 Against the clear blue morning sky, the white sails of their   12
graceful yachts made an ever-changing pattern as they danced   24
and swayed in the breeze. **(SI 1.21)**   29

   1 | 2 | 3 | 4 | 5 | 6 | 7 | 8 | 9 | 10 | 11 | 12 |

Record your progress   One minute

R19 It may be next June before I can be certain of the number of   12
folk who may be present at the Market Square for this year's   24
Fair. Four years ago our efforts added up to zero, but I am   36
sure we have already sold more tickets than in 1987. **(SI 1.22)** 46

   1 | 2 | 3 | 4 | 5 | 6 | 7 | 8 | 9 | 10 | 11 | 12 |

PRODUCTION DEVELOPMENT

INVOICE 2981

MATLOCK FURNITURE SUPPLIES   Telephone
North Bakewell Road   0629 074485
MATLOCK
Derbyshire   DE4 3AP

NOTE: After the second horizontal line, turn up two spaces and type the £ sign in the appropriate columns. Then turn up another two spaces before starting the items.

Figures — units must always be typed under units, tens under tens, etc. Follow the text layout carefully when typing the total column.

10 August 1988

Mr & Mrs T Brookes
32 Buxton Road
MATLOCK
Derbyshire   DE4 1AA

Where possible, leave two clear spaces after the vertical lines before typing the items — with the exception of the money columns where decimal points must fall underneath one another.

QUANTITY	DESCRIPTION	PRICE	TOTAL
		£	£
1	Resin Patio Table	90.00	90.00
4	Resin Leisure Chairs	25.50	102.00
1	Patio Parasol	40.00	40.00
1	Rocking Deck Chair	30.75	30.75
			262.75
	Delivery charge		12.00
			£274.75
	Prices include VAT		
	E & OE		

Invoices

An invoice is the document sent by the seller to the purchaser and shows full details of the goods sold. The layout of invoices varies from organization to organization according to the data to be recorded. Invoices are printed with the seller's name, address and other useful information.

1   There is a skeleton invoice form in the *Handbook and Solutions Manual* and copies may be duplicated. Insert a copy into your typewriter and set left margin and tab stops for the beginning of each column. Then type the information exactly at it appears.

2   On another invoice form display the following:

Invoice No: 3001   Supplier: same as above   Date: 12 August 1988
Purchaser: L D Williamson & Co   48 York Road   Matlock   Derbyshire   DE4 1AP

3 Build-in Barbecues	23.50	70.50
3 Pairs Turning Tongs	3.75	11.25
3 'Triple' Fish Holders	4.50	13.50
		95.25

Delivery charge   4.75

Typist
Prices include VAT   Please calculate and   £ _____
E & OE   type in total

Typing sums of money in columns

Refer to the instructions given on page 41 with regard to the typing of decimals. Then note the following: The £ sign is typed over the first figure in the £'s column. Example £
Units, tens, hundreds, etc, fall under one another.

```
£
230.16
 12.10
  0.24
147.00
```

1 Type the following on A5 portrait paper, taking care to type the decimal points, units, tens and hundreds figures under one another. (a) Centre the exercise vertically and horizontally. (b) Leave three spaces between the columns. (c) Double spacing.

```
   £          £          £

245.46     247.14     105.89

199.95     236.01     214.78

 10.44      19.64      66.99

  3.45       6.78       6.38
```

Interliner lever

The interliner lever may be found on the right or left side of the typewriter. Locate this on your machine. The interliner lever frees the platen from the ratchet control, so that the platen may be turned freely forward or backward as required. When the lever is returned to its normal position, your machine will automatically return to the original spacing.

Double underscoring of totals

If you have to type double lines underneath the totals, use the interliner. When typing totals, proceed as follows:

(a) Type the underscore for the first lines above the totals. (Do not turn up before typing the first lines). These lines extend from the first to the last figure of the longest item in each column including total.

(b) Turn up twice and type the totals.

(c) Turn up once, and then type the lines below the totals.

(d) Turn the cylinder up slightly by using the interliner lever and type the second lines. Then return the interliner lever to its normal position.

2 Display the following exercise on A5 landscape paper. (a) Single spacing for the main part. (b) Leave three spaces between columns. (c) Follow the instructions for the total figures. (d) Decimal points must fall under one another.

```
£            £            £            £
  228.90       12.34       212.34       109.87
  404.75      566.78        33.44       654.57
  323.25       90.12       105.62     1,010.85
1,234.56       35.45     1,212.05       354.25
  789.00    1,237.95       343.18     1,213.65
  654.32      220.16       331.26       434.12  ←— Do not turn up
                                                ←— Turn up 2 spaces
3,634.78     2,162.80     2,237.89     3,777.31
                                                ←— Turn up 1 space
                                                ←— use interliner
```

 If you are using an electronic keyboard, you may wish to use the appropriate keys for the decimal tab and for the double underscoring.

Follow instructions given at top of page 42. Margins: 12 pitch 22–82, 10 pitch 12–72. Single spacing, with double between exercises.

A   Review alphabet keys

1   Flexible working is generally favoured and requested by most employees as they can just avoid the crazy traffic.

B   Build speed on word family drill

2   look took hook book nook cook best pest rest jest west nest.
3   call hall fall pall wall tall will pill bill hill fill mill.
4   He took a look at the book and said that he would call soon.
5   The birds will nest in a nook of the west wall of that mill.

C   Build speed on fluency drill

6   right both they land wish held firm hand sign paid when form
7   busy lane fork pays dial make rich maps with half fuel road.
8   They wish both firms to sign the forms and pay for the land.
9   It is a busy lane to the right of a fork road by the chapel.

D   Practise alternate hand drill

10   she jay hale kale pale lame flame handy signal disown dispel
11   fox ape gown town worn torn quake rigid theory thrown formal
12   He was formal and rigid, and his excuses were pale and lame.

E   Spelling skill   Correct the one misspelt word in each line. (See page 182 for answer)

13   courtesy received decision knowlege competent disagreeable.
14   forcible sentence transfer companies signature inaccessable.
15   She was uncompetent and disagreeable when making a decision.

Skill measurement   29 wpm   2 minutes   Not more than 2 errors

SM27   One of the great problems of today is the pressure of noise: 12
noise in the streets, in the home, by day, and sometimes far   24
into the night. Are buses and lorries the chief cause? No.   36
As we hear these all day, we get used to them. So it is the   48
infrequent sounds, such as those made by jet planes. **(SI 1.16)**   58

   1 | 2 | 3 | 4 | 5 | 6 | 7 | 8 | 9 | 10 | 11 | 12 |

Record your progress   2 minutes

R20   Many people who pay rent are entitled to a rent allowance or   12
rebate - an allowance if a private tenant or a rebate if you   24
are a council tenant.   28

You should write to your local council. Then they will need   40
to know your income, and the larger your family the more you   52
are justified in seizing the chance of getting help, and the   64
more quickly you may expect help. **(SI 1.36)**   70

   1 | 2 | 3 | 4 | 5 | 6 | 7 | 8 | 9 | 10 | 11 | 12 |

3 There is a skeleton of the form below in the *Handbook and Solutions Manual* and copies may be duplicated. Insert the form into your typewriter and then type in the handwritten words, following layout as in the textbook.

PERSONNEL RECORD CARD (PRC/1/88)

Previous employer

R P Mitchell Ltd
3 Hawthorn Way
Doncaster
South Yorkshire DN1 1AA

From *3 February 1986*   To *27 March 1987*

Last position held

Shorthand Typist

Last school attended

Foster Comprehensive
Castle Hill
Doncaster
South Yorkshire DN1 1AA

From *August 1980*   To *June 1985*

Further education

Course *Private Secretary's Certificate*   Day/Full-time *Day*

Books £ *47.00*   Fees £ *129.00*

Dates *August 1985 – June 1986*   Result *Pass*

Starting position *Shorthand Typist*   Date *1 April 1987*

Changes   From   To

Assistant Secretary   *18 December 1987*

SURNAME *NEWTON*   OTHER NAMES *Ruth Margaret*

Forms

Business organizations have a great variety of forms which have been printed, or duplicated, with guide headings, boxes, columns, etc, and the typist has to type in additional information. When the insertion is typed on the same line as the printed heading, there are two clear spaces before the start of the insertion. Where the insertion comes below a printed heading, it is typed on the next line. However, if the column is deep and the information to be inserted is short, it will look better with a clear space between the printed heading and the inserted matter.

Information typed in opposite headings should be on the same line as the base of the printed heading and, therefore, it is important to know how close your typewriter prints to its aligning scale. Type a sentence and study exactly the space between the typing and the scale so that, when you insert a form and wish to align your typing with the bottom of the printed words, you will know how much to adjust the paper with the variable linespacer. When typing over ruled or dotted lines, no character should touch the ruled or dotted line. Therefore, with the variable linespacer adjust the typing line so that, when typed, the descending characters y, p, g, etc, are very slightly above the dotted line or underline.

6 Using another copy of the printed form letter (on the previous page), insert the following information:

Your Ref MAP/RES **Our Ref** AT/your initials **Date** 18 July 1988
Addressee J Ellis and Co Ltd 17 Hanover Road STRANRAER Wigtonshire DG9 7SA
Order Number 513/22 **dated** 15 July **for** 4 PERFECT COLOUR Copiers 6 Word Processor Acoustic Covers.
The second **despatched on** 20 July **but the** first **until** 25 July.

Deletions

It is often necessary to delete letters or words in a form, form letter or a circular letter. For instance, in the exercises below you are writing to EITHER a man or a woman, so that either **Sir** or **Madam** will have to be deleted. To delete previously typed characters, use an x aligned precisely with the characters previously typed.

7 Using a copy of the printed form letter from the *Handbook and Solutions Manual*, type the handwritten details from the following exercise.

W M ELECTRONICS

Deerpark BELFAST BT1 1AA
Telephone 0232 644223 Telex 99783

Your Ref ML/AB
Our Ref JCH/ID

1 August 1988
Miss J Bannerman
R Bannerman Ltd
Gaigneuk
Airdrie
Lanarkshire ML6 6AA

Dear Sir/Madam

Thank you for your cheque number 045612 dated 27 July   for £3,200.

You mention that you have deducted 2½% for prompt payment, but the invoices, numbered 12361 and 12418   , have been outstanding for more than 30 days and, therefore, you are not entitled to the discount.

We are sorry that we cannot allow this discount, and regret that the sum of £80.00 will be included in your statement for July.

Yours faithfully

Joyce C Hall (Ms)
Chief Cashier

8 Using another copy of the printed form letter, insert the following details:

Your Ref EA/AS **Our Ref** JCH/ID **date** 1 August 1988 **Addressee** Mr Richard Peterson Barclay & Co Ltd 90 Waterloo Road BALLYMENA Co Antrim BT43 6AA
Dear Sir **cheque number** 004534 **dated** 28 July **for** £4,300 **deducted** 2½%
numbered 77829 and 82245 **more than** 30 days **sum of** £107.50 **statement for** July

4 There is a skeleton of the form below in the *Handbook and Solutions Manual* and copies may be duplicated. Insert the form into your typewriter and then type in the handwritten words.

APPLICATION FOR EMPLOYMENT WITH

AP/87/MAC

Kenkott Scotia PLC   Byrnes Terrace   Langside   GLASGOW   G41 3DI

Position applied for *Shorthand Typist*

Surname (in capitals) *NEWTON*   Forenames *Ruth Margaret*

Address *42 Forest Road   Doncaster   South Yorkshire   DN5 0AT*

Telephone number *0302 466223*   Nationality *British*

Date of birth *3 May 1968*   Place of birth *Doncaster*   Age *19*

Married/single *Single*   Mrs/Miss/Ms/Mr *Ms*

Last school and further education

	From	To
Foster Comprehensive	*August 1980*	*June 1985*
Doncaster College of F E	*August 1985*	*June 1986*

Qualifications (please list your highest grade only in any one subject)

Subject	Level	Result
Maths	*'O'*	*A*
Geography and History	*'O'*	*B*
English	*'A'*	*A*
Private Secretary's Certificate		*Pass*

Previous employers

(1)   Name *R P Mitchell Ltd*

Address *3 Hawthorn Way   Doncaster   South Yorkshire   DN1 1AA*

From *3 February 1986*   To *24 March 1987*

Position held *Shorthand Typist*   Salary *£5,570*

(2)   Name ....

Address ....

From ....   To ....

Position held ....   Salary ....

Form letter

Many documents that businesses use will contain similar information and wording and, in order to save time, form or skeleton letters, containing the constant (unchanging) information, are prepared and are duplicated or printed and only the variable items (name and address, etc) are inserted by the typist in the blank spaces which have been purposely left to accommodate these items.

The electronic keyboard and the VDU have made production of repetitive text very much easier and time-saving. The skeleton letter, containing the constant information, is keyed in and stored on a disk. When required, it can be retrieved by pressing a function key, and any insertion can be made quickly and easily (there is no difficulty with alignment when you have a VDU) and the complete letter printed out, so that it looks like an original—as distinct from a duplicated or printed document with the variables added.

Filling in form letters

The following steps should be taken when you fill in a form letter:

(a) Insert the form letter into the machine so that the first line of the body of the letter is just above the alignment scale.

(b) By means of the paper release adjust the paper so that the base of an entire line is in alignment with the top of the alignment scale (this position may vary with certain makes of machines) and so that an 'i' or 'l' lines up exactly with one of the guides on the alignment scale.

(c) Set margin stops and paper guide. The margin stops should be set to correspond to the margins already used in the duplicated letter.

(d) Turn the platen back two single spaces (four notches for machines with half-spacing) and, if not already typed, insert salutation at the left margin.

(e) Turn the platen back a sufficient number of spaces and type the reference.

(f) Turn up two single spaces and type the date.

(g) Turn up two single spaces and type the name and address of addressee.

(h) Insert any details required in the body of the letter. Remember to leave one clear space after the last character before starting to type the 'fill in'.

(i) Check carefully.

5 Following the instructions given above and using a copy of the printed form from the *Handbook and Solutions Manual*, type in the handwritten details.

W M ELECTRONICS

Deerpark BELFAST BT1 1AA
Telephone 0232 644223   Telex 99783

Your Ref *MAR/J*
Our Ref *AT/BG*

14th July 1988
John R Gaunt Ltd
Bridge Street
LIMERICK
Co Limerick

Dear Sirs

We thank you for your order numbered *48/242* dated *12th July* for

3 LSR Microfilm Readers/Printers
3 LSR2 Microfilm Cameras

The *first* item will be despatched on *18 July* but the *second* item will not be sent until *22 July*.

We regret this delay.

Yours faithfully
W M ELECTRONICS